THE SCIENTIFIC METHOD
IN FORENSIC SCIENCE

THE SCIENTIFIC METHOD IN FORENSIC SCIENCE

A Canadian Handbook

Mike Illes, PhD, and Paul Wilson, PhD

CANADIAN
SCHOLARS
Toronto | Vancouver

The Scientific Method in Forensic Science: A Canadian Handbook
Mike Illes and Paul Wilson

First published in 2020 by
Canadian Scholars, an imprint of CSP Books Inc.
425 Adelaide Street West, Suite 200
Toronto, Ontario
M5V 3C1

www.canadianscholars.ca

Library and Archives Canada Cataloguing in Publication

Title: The scientific method in forensic science : a Canadian handbook / Mike Illes
    and Paul Wilson.
Names: Illes, Mike, 1962- author. | Wilson, Paul, 1968- author.
Description: Includes bibliographical references and index.
Identifiers: Canadiana (print) 2020018833X | Canadiana (ebook) 20200188348 |
    ISBN 9781773381633 (softcover) | ISBN 9781773381640 (PDF) | ISBN
    9781773381657 (EPUB)
Subjects: LCSH: Forensic sciences—Canada—Textbooks. | LCSH: Forensic
    sciences—Textbooks. | LCGFT: Textbooks.
Classification: LCC HV8073 .I45 2020 | DDC 363.250971—dc23

In chapter 4, "Investigation of a Model for Stain Selection in Bloodstain Pattern Analysis" (2011) by Mike Illes and Michelle Boué, originally published in *Canadian Society of Forensic Science*, *44*(1), 1–12, is reprinted with permission.

Cover design by Rafael Chimicatti
Cover image by Daniele Levis Pelusi on Unsplash
Page layout by S4Carlisle Publishing Services

Printed and bound in Ontario, Canada

CONTENTS

FOREWORD

Key events have forced us to critically evaluate our past practices, shaping the manner in which forensic science experts conduct analyses, write their reports, and give expert testimony. Such events in Canada have included the Kaufman Commission and the Goudge report, building on miscarriages of justice to improve best practices. The US National Academy of Sciences (NAS) report, targeting 14 forensic disciplines, brought the larger forensic science community together. What became clear was that previously anecdotal or experience-based determinations had to make way for evidence-based practice. This was to be achieved, in part, through education and research that embraced the scientific method.

The Scientific Method in Forensic Science: A Canadian Handbook describes pivotal events and the resulting recommendations, which have helped shape forensic science in Canada. While we recognize the importance of the scientific method, do we truly understand its substance? The book steers you through this practice, from formulating hypotheses, conducting experiments, and searching for facts all the way to the fundamentals of critical thinking and evaluating published journal articles.

It is now recognized that students and experts should work together to conduct research, as each possesses unique skills. Students contribute to academic style research design and statistical knowledge—however, importantly, the research design benefits from the mentorship and world view of the experienced practitioner. This partnership serves to create a more robust research design. Building on the necessity for collaborative research, *The Scientific Method in Forensic Science: A Canadian Handbook* highlights critical steps in research design and effective reporting of findings, geared to both students and practitioners.

The Scientific Method in Forensic Science: A Canadian Handbook is perfect for those beginning their education and research career in forensic science as well as offering a wonderful resource for those practising in the field. A book such as this one is fundamental to the educating of a new generation of forensic scientists.

Hélène N. LeBlanc, MSc, PhD, M–ABFE
Associate Professor
Board Certified Forensic Entomologist

PREFACE

This book has been written for the Canadian forensic science student and professional practitioner. It provides an experience-based learning opportunity for understanding the scientific method and evidence-based analysis as they relate to forensic science in Canada. In 2015, I was assigned by my Forensic Science Department chair to teach a course on the scientific method for second-year forensic science students. I immediately reviewed the previous year's course syllabus and a copy of the textbook that had been in use. To my disappointment, the textbook was on research design for a criminology course and contained very little forensic content. My search began for a text that would support forensic science students and practitioners in Canada. Specifically, I was hoping to find a textbook that would provide the theory combined with forensic case studies and other experience-based examples. The search was unsuccessful, and in fact there were very few forensic science books available with Canadian content. This presented the opportunity to completely redevelop this course. I redesigned the course with teachings on the scientific method in forensic science; how to read a journal article; and how to write a forensic science report, with assigned readings from peer-reviewed forensic and scientific journals. I taught the course for several years and was still not satisfied with the content, because the diversity of readings for each topic was overwhelming for one course.

That was the motivation for writing this book. The chapters to follow summarize the literature for each research topic. They relate to forensic science in Canada and abroad. The scope of the book covers not only science and its connection to forensic science but, more importantly, how real-life forensic case experiences relate to the science. This book is also part of my PhD, researching forensic epistemology. Each chapter will contain a short introduction, a glossary, discussion questions, further readings, and additional instructional pop outs. What follows is a summary of each chapter.

CHAPTER 1—INTRODUCTION: THE PARADIGM SHIFT IN FORENSIC SCIENCE

This chapter introduces the reports that have significantly changed forensic science in Canada and internationally. We review these reports from a high-level perspective while exploring why there has been a paradigm shift within forensic science, and we discuss why it is critical for those interested in forensic science to understand the scientific method and evidence-based analysis. Throughout the chapters, we provide examples of how forensic science has roots in science (e.g., chemistry, biology, anthropology) and policing (e.g., fingerprints, footwear comparison), as well as the variation in the scientific underpinnings among the numerous disciplines.

CHAPTER 2—CONCEPTS OF SCIENCE AND THE SCIENTIFIC METHOD

Chapter 2 explores how science and scientific reasoning fit within forensic science and the evolution of various forensic science disciplines. Knowledge, information, scientific explanations, and common sense will be defined and discussed. The reader will gain an appreciation for the role of scientific reasoning and how approaches such as falsification and hypothesis testing are essential to forensic applications. This will provide a foundation for using evidence-based practice, a central theme throughout the book.

These chapters lead into a discussion on further skill sets and knowledge, such as critical thinking, problem solving, and ethics—skills vital to forensic professionals.

CHAPTER 3—CRITICAL THINKING IN FORENSIC SCIENCE

Critical thinking underpins most university curricula. We will explore the research that defines and supports critical thinking—including notions of rationality, honesty, open-mindedness, discipline, judgment—and how these fit within forensic investigations.

Problem solving is a concept that is closely connected to critical thinking. Because of this, we explore how to respect and incorporate multiple perspectives, how to monitor our beliefs and knowledge, how to plan ahead, evidence-based justification and argumentation, and how to reconcile conflicts.

CHAPTER 4—HOW TO CRITICALLY REVIEW A PUBLISHED JOURNAL ARTICLE

Chapter 4 examines how to critically review a journal article. The initial appraisal will look at authorship, date of publication, additions or revisions, publisher, and the title of the journal. We will discuss the purpose of each component of a scientific journal article, including the abstract, introduction, methods, results/discussion, and conclusion. We critically review each component so that readers can develop the required skill sets for doing comprehensive article reviews.

CHAPTER 5—WHAT THE LITERATURE SAYS: FROM STUDENT TO EXPERT

A literature review is just like a criminal investigation. As a forensic scientist or investigator, you will be required to collect evidence prior to a charge being laid and any attempt at prosecution in court. The same applies to a research question or to an expert witness who has the responsibility of providing the courts with objective, impartial, and independent evidence that has been researched. In this chapter, we explore the appropriate use of high- and low-level publication sources, some basic search strategies, accessing the evidence base, types of literature reviews, and the role of the literature review within research and for the forensic practitioner.

CHAPTER 6—THE USE, MISUSE, AND ABSENCE OF STATISTICS IN FORENSIC SCIENCE CASEWORK

This chapter explores case examples that used statistics or probability theory in court. We provide an "exercise pop out" on the statistical methods that are discussed, for those who may not be familiar with these concepts. We consider the use of mathematics in several case studies, such as in the applications of wildlife DNA in Canada and human DNA court cases and also in the 1999 murder trial and conviction of Sally Clark in the United Kingdom. The reader will learn the benefits and risks of applying statistics and probability from a practitioner's view, with critical scientific discussion surrounding each case.

CHAPTER 7—RESEARCH DESIGN FOR THE FORENSIC SCIENCE STUDENT AND PRACTITIONER

Here we review the basic concepts of research design and provide forensic research examples for a correlational study and experimental design. Concepts include quantitative, qualitative, and mixed-method approaches; the stages of research design; and basic scientific concepts, such as applied versus pure research. There will be an emphasis on core research practices like planning the experiment, conducting a literature review, and formulating hypotheses and questions.

CHAPTER 8—THE IMPORTANCE OF ETHICS AND IMPARTIALITY IN FORENSIC SCIENCE

Forensic science has an array of professional guidelines from multiple sources, such as the Canadian Society of Forensic Science—the list of organizations is very long. With this in mind, we wanted to include a basic outline of ethics in Canadian forensic science and research, to define ethics, and to discuss case study examples. The reader will learn about the university research ethics board system and the Canadian Tri-Council Policy Statement on Ethical Conduct for Research Involving Humans.

This chapter will also cover examples of bias in forensic science and suggest possible solutions. It will stress the role of the scientific method and evidence-based analysis in helping to reduce or control bias.

CHAPTER 9—THE KEY TO EFFECTIVE COMMUNICATION IN FORENSIC SCIENCE

This will synthesize the information provided in all previous chapters, creating a path of scientific research to support evidence-based reporting and presentation. The reader will note how the book has reinforced the development of report writing and a court presentation style that parallels the scientific method, academic journal articles, theses, and dissertations. This chapter will also emphasize writing and oral structure, advocating for the truth, owning your expertise, and the importance of peer review. There is a notable difference between presentations in academia and in legal settings. Therefore, we emphasize a balance between scientific integrity and readability/understandability when an expert is presenting within a legal context.

This book blends scientific concepts and forensic science case examples in each chapter, making it a fundamental text for any forensic science student or professional. Chapter 1 speaks to the importance of this, as forensic scientists and practitioners are increasingly required to use more science in forensic science. It discusses the need for such things as research, validation, repeatability, oversight, peer review, accountability, transparency, report structure, statistics, and impartiality. The rest of the book provides a foundation for the use of methods to help with these issues from a Canadian and global perspective.

Mike Illes, PhD

CHAPTER 1

Introduction: The Paradigm Shift in Forensic Science

Marking of an Exhibit

Photo credit: Mike Illes

Reason, observation, and experience; the holy trinity of science.
—*Robert Green Ingersoll (1924)*

The autumn of 2008 was the beginning of change for the **forensic science** community in Canada. The report of the Inquiry into Pediatric Forensic Pathology in Ontario was released by Justice Stephen T. Goudge, followed a year later by the US National Academy of Sciences (NAS) report called *Strengthening Forensic Science in the United States: A Path Forward* (Goudge, 2008; NAS, 2009). These reports highlighted, on a global stage, issues of insufficiency in scholarly peer-reviewed research, scientific training, scientific underpinnings for some forensic disciplines, and governance in forensic science. In 2012, the Hart House report, or its more formal name of *Forensic Science in Canada: A Report of Multidisciplinary Discussion* (Pollanen et al., 2013), was released, containing a Canadian perspective on some of the issues described in the NAS report. The Honourable Susan E. Lang produced the *Report of the Motherisk Hair Analysis Independent Review* (Lang, 2015), which caused concern about the forensic analysis that was being conducted within the Motherisk Drug Testing Laboratory in Ontario. In 2016, the US president at the time, Barack Obama, requested that the President's Council of Advisors on Science and Technology (PCAST) advise him on how the United States could ensure the scientific validity of feature-comparison methods in forensic science (PCAST, 2016). In addition, two earlier reports were significant in highlighting forensic science issues in Canada: the *Report of the Kaufman Commission on Proceedings involving Guy Paul Morin* and the *Bernardo Investigation Review* of Justice Archie Campbell.

Instructional Pop Out

Check out chapter 9 on the role of expert evidence in Canada within the report *The Path to Justice: Preventing Wrongful Convictions*: www.ppsc-sppc.gc.ca/eng/pub/ptj-spj/ptj-spj-eng.pdf

THE PARADIGM SHIFT IN FORENSIC SCIENCE

Facts do not cease to exist because they are ignored.
—*Aldous Huxley,* Complete Essays 2, *1926–1929*

A skeptical scientific thinker will wonder why the **scientific method** has become so important in forensic science and why it was not inherent to the discipline as in other fields. The following explains the **paradigm shift** and why it is happening in the forensic science community. Thomas Kuhn (1962) was a scientific philosopher who introduced the term "paradigm shift." Kuhn suggests that science evolves through periodic shifts and is not a linear or continuous process. He also describes a paradigm shift as the scientific community establishing a problem to be solved. This is happening in the forensic sciences and began in the early aughts, when people started to recognize the shortfalls—such as problems with the core assumptions used in individualization or the possibility of **contextual bias**—within casework. Questions have arisen about bias within forensic casework, with research intensifying on how contextual information, such as suspect identity and investigation details, can impact the forensic scientist (Dror, 2013, 2014). In the past, individualizing a person by fingerprints has been considered the norm but the scientific validity of this practice has now been questioned (Saks & Koehler, 2005).

In addition, there have been publicized errors causing a lack of societal confidence in forensic science. One example would be the unlawful arrest of an American, Brandon Mayfield, in May 2004 by the Federal Bureau of Investigation (FBI) for the bombing attack of a commuter train in Madrid, Spain. This arrest was based solely on mistaken fingerprint identification. The fingerprint impression was found on a bag of detonators associated with the attack in Madrid and was eventually identified by the Spanish National Police Corps as belonging to an Algerian man (Office of the Inspector General, 2006; Tangen, 2013). Brandon Mayfield

wrongfully Convicted
(Ru whats wrong)

spent two weeks in jail. The root causes of the misidentification were bias and unscientific approaches to the fingerprint comparison.

The following sections have been written to summarize the main forensic science issues within the Kaufman, Campbell, Goudge, NAS, Hart House, PCAST, and Motherisk Hair Analysis reports or directive, and these should be used in conjunction with the corresponding full documents (Campbell, 1996; Goudge, 2008; Kaufman, 1998; Lang, 2015; NAS, 2009; Pollanen et al., 2013).

The Kaufman Commission on Proceedings Involving Guy Paul Morin *(learned last semester)*

Christine Jessop was murdered in 1984 at the age of nine and her next-door neighbour, Guy Paul Morin, was charged with the murder. In 1986, he was acquitted of the murder; however, a new trial was ordered by the Ontario Court of Appeal and

Instructional Pop Out

See Kaufman report (1998): www .attorneygeneral.jus.gov.on.ca/ english/about/pubs/morin/ morin_esumm.html

he was found guilty of first-degree murder. In 1995, he appealed his conviction based on new **deoxyribonucleic acid (DNA)** evidence and was ultimately acquitted of the charge. The evolving details of the case raised questions about the administration of justice in Ontario and an inquiry into the conduct of the investigation and the Ontario **Centre of Forensic Sciences (CFS)** was commissioned. In 1998, the Honourable Fred Kaufman, a former judge of the Quebec Court of Appeals, completed a report on the proceedings involving Morin (Kaufman, 1998).

The report consisted of several chapters: the scope and nature of the inquiry, forensic evidence and the CFS, the use of jailhouse informant information, the investigation by the York Regional Police, the investigation by Durham Regional Police, and Morin's prosecution. In the end, there were 119 recommendations, including direction on police and forensic laboratory procedures, the use of the scientific method, and scientific language and trial procedures. The Kaufman report changed processes for the CFS and made suggestions on improving forensic science more generally, and many items have been rearticulated in more recent reviews, such as the NAS report (Kaufman, 1998; NAS, 2009).

The CFS is the principal laboratory that processes forensic casework for criminal investigations in Ontario. Forensic scientists from the CFS examined hair, fibres, and blood in the Jessop homicide investigation. Hair from Jessop's body and Morin's car was analyzed. Justice Kaufman found that the hair comparison evidence had little or no probative value in proving Morin's guilt and that the scientists failed to provide adequate and accurate communications on the limitations of a hair comparison that was not based on quantitative data or statistical analysis (see chapter 6). The scientists also provided preliminary opinions to the police prior to the completion or peer review of a formal forensic analysis report (see chapter 9) (Kaufman, 1998).

Fibres were collected from Jessop's clothing and Morin's car and residence. The forensic scientists examined thousands of fibres in this case. Justice Kaufman noted that the fibre evidence had been contaminated at the CFS prior to examination and that the origin of that contamination could not be found. He also indicated that knowledge of this contamination was withheld by the CFS scientists from the police, the prosecutors, the defence, and the court at the first trial. In fact, it was found that the existence of in-house contamination was generally known to occur within the biology section of the CFS. For Morin's second trial, further examination was completed on the contaminated fibres and this examination yielded potential exculpatory findings. However, this information was not communicated to the prosecution or the defence. The disclosure of laboratory notes, reports, and draft reports, including statistical data analysis results, are legal requirements in today's Canadian court system (*R. v. Natsis*, 2018). Beyond this, the limitations of fibre evidence were not adequately or accurately conveyed to the police, prosecutors, or court. Justice Kaufman was also concerned that the original fibre evidence had been lost by the CFS between the first and second trials (Kaufman, 1998).

CFS expert-opinion evidence was provided on microscopic indications of blood in Morin's vehicle. These tests were presumptive, suggesting there was a possibility of blood in the vehicle. The CFS serologist accurately articulated the limitations of these findings.

In summary, the commission indicated that CFS scientists must perform their duties in an objective, independent, and accurate manner. Justice Kaufman described the failings within this investigation as rooted in systemic problems—not just within the CFS, but as noted in cases worldwide. Of the 119 recommendations, the commission provided 33 recommendations for the forensic science evidence in this case (Kaufman, 1998).

Although this report was published in 1998, you will read about similar problems and recommendations within the following reports and directive. Links to the misuse of terms and scientific processes can also be established between recent cases such as *R. v. France* and *R. v. Millard*. See chapters 2, 4, and 5 to understand the importance of the scientific method, peer review, and literature review.

The Bernardo Investigation Review: Report of Mr. Justice Archie Campbell

Paul Bernardo sexually assaulted and murdered many women in Scarborough, Peel, and Niagara regions in southern Ontario between 1987 and 1992. The report released in 1996 by Justice Campbell on the Bernardo investigation provided insight into the systemic failure of investigating

Instructional Pop Out

See Campbell report (1996): www .attorneygeneral.jus.gov.on.ca/ inquiries/cornwall/en/hearings/ exhibits/Wendy_Leaver/pdf/10_ Campbell_Summary.pdf

this serial killer. Justice Campbell was asked to review the roles of the police, the CFS, the coroner's office, and the provincial government during the Bernardo investigation; the report summarized 27 recommendations that discussed laboratory and police procedures within the proceedings. The core issues were as follows: (1) the province of Ontario needed to develop a **major case management (MCM)** system; (2) the CFS required better turnaround on DNA testing and better coordination of work between forensic scientists and police investigators; (3) better training for those who investigate sexual assaults; (4) a province-wide coordinated response to serial predators; (5) standardized training on and use of technology, such as a computerized case-management system; and (6) the funding to support these objectives (Campbell, 1996).

Major Case Management

The main recommendation from the Campbell report was to improve communication between criminal justice stakeholders; this led to the development of a system of case management for major and inter-jurisdictional investigations. Subsequently, Ontario's Ministry of Community Safety and Correctional Services developed the MCM in 2004 (MCMM, 2004). This system raised the standards of major case investigations in Ontario, as requested by Justice Campbell in his recommendations: a major case–management system was required for major and inter-jurisdictional serial predator investigations, and a commitment for change was required from the police and law enforcement communities, the Ontario government, and the community at large (MCMM, 2004).

These recommendations highlighted the need for better communication among the police, forensic scientists, and others who worked within the Ontario justice system in the early 1990s. Within the *Ontario Major Case Management Manual* (MCMM), the following criteria of offences are deemed to be major cases:

a.   homicides as defined in subsection 222 (4), *Criminal Code of Canada*, and attempts

b.   sexual assaults, and all attempts (for the purpose of this standard, is deemed to include sexual interference, sexual exploitation and invitation to sexual touching)

c.   occurrences involving non-familial abductions and attempts

d.   missing person occurrences, where circumstances indicate a strong possibility of foul play

    e. occurrences suspected to be homicides involving found human remains

    f. criminal harassment cases in which the offender is not known to the victim

    g. any other case designated as a major case by the Major Case Management Executive Board. (MCMM, 2004, p. 7)

Any of these offences occurring in Ontario would initiate the MCM system and within that system a command triangle would form, in which a major case manager will oversee the investigation, assigning a primary investigator and a file coordinator. This set-up provides for appropriate communications, the engagement of experts, the application of technology and systems, and oversight.

Forensic Science in MCM

The *MCM Manual* does not have a section that is specific to forensic science; however, the following are the requirements of an Ontario **forensic identification officer** (or **crime scene investigator [CSI]**, in other countries):

    1. In every major case, a forensic identification officer shall be selected and assigned by the forensic identification supervisor to undertake the following forensic identification functions and duties:

        a. report directly to the primary investigator or designate

        b. work in close cooperation with the scene investigator and liaise with the primary investigator

        c. photograph and videotape all homicide scenes

        d. consider photographing and videotaping other major case crime scene(s) depending on the complexity of the case and the nature of the scene

        e. observe and/or photograph/video tape exhibits

        f. identify and sort the exhibits and photographs

        g. make observations and notes which relate the position of the exhibit to the focal point of the scene

h. take measurements, where necessary, suitable for a plan drawing

i. record time, date, location, description, and number for each exhibit

j. coordinate the marking of the exhibit, container, etc. with initials, number and date, accompanied by the notes of the scene investigator

k. secure and preserve all exhibits against loss, contamination, deterioration, theft, or other detriment

l. contact the Centre of Forensic Sciences or other forensic testing facilities regarding the status of exhibits submitted by the forensic identification officer(s) at least every 30 days and report the results of the contacts to the Command Triangle

m. when forensic testing results are obtained in writing, compare the results against requested examinations

n. in consultation with the scene investigator, issue clear, concise directions in matters relating to search patterns and protection from health hazards

o. when delegating duties, provide adequate instruction and ensure compliance with appropriate standards and practices

2. A **scenes of crime officer** may undertake the duties of a forensic identification officer in any major case other than homicide, when the primary investigator, in consultation with the forensic identification officer, determines that the scenes of crime officer is qualified to conduct the required tasks.

3. A scenes of crime officer shall have successfully completed the required training or have equivalent qualifications and skills as approved by the ministry.

4. The officer, who performs a forensic identification function, shall have successfully completed the required training or have equivalent qualifications and skills as approved by the ministry. (MCMM, 2004, pp. 21–22)

The required training for the forensic identification function as approved by the ministry is a forensic identification course provided by the Ontario Police College or the Canadian Police College. These courses provide basic training in how to process crime scenes and how to present this evidence in court (CPC, 2018).

In addition to stipulating how crime scene forensics needed to be managed, Justice Campbell provided insight into new policy for the CFS. The main issue within the investigation was that while the CFS had Paul Bernardo's DNA as of December 13, 1990, the results were not obtained until February 1, 1993. The lack of communication between the Metro Toronto Police—the chief investigating agency for the earlier sexual assaults in Scarborough—and the CFS led to concerns regarding the system, and Justice Campbell viewed this as a systemic failure. He included the following recommendations:

- A reasonable turnaround time for DNA testing is required, in the range of 30 days.
- A continuing commitment of resources is required to achieve and maintain this turnaround time in face of technological change and rising workload.
- A system is required to better co-ordinate the work of forensic scientists and police investigators. (Campbell, 1996)

Although not part of the *MCM Manual*, the CFS developed their own internal policy to help manage these risk issues.

Cause of death
by corpse examination

The Goudge Report

The Inquiry into Pediatric Forensic Pathology in Ontario was initiated after a review by the Chief Coroner found flaws in the work of celebrated forensic pathologist Dr. Charles Smith, who had

Chief
Coroner

Instructional Pop Out

See Goudge report (2008): www
.attorneygeneral.jus.gov.on.ca/
inquiries/goudge/report/v1_en_
pdf/Vol_1_Eng.pdf

provided reports and expert testimony throughout the province. The review was conducted by five highly respected forensic pathologists, who reported the following:

- In all but one of the 45 cases examined, the reviewers agreed that Dr. Smith had conducted the important examinations that were indicated.
- In nine of the 45 cases, the reviewers did not agree with significant facts that appeared in either Dr. Smith's report or his testimony.
- In 20 of the 45 cases, the reviewers took issue with Dr. Smith's opinion in either his report or his testimony, or both. In 12 of those 20 cases, there had been findings of guilt by the courts. (Goudge, 2008)

Justice Goudge stated the following within the executive summary of his report:

This Inquiry was given two tasks. The first is to determine what went so badly wrong in the practice and oversight of pediatric forensic pathology in Ontario, especially as it relates to the criminal justice system. [...] My second task is to make recommendations to restore and enhance the public confidence in pediatric forensic pathology. (Goudge, 2008)

*Science in general ← Kaufman
+
Pathology only ← Goudge
Similar*

There were 169 recommendations made in this report. When read alongside the NAS and PCAST reports, we can see how the following recommendations from the Goudge inquiry represent national and likely global concerns for the forensic science disciplines:

- require education, training, and certification in Canada
- recruit and retain qualified experts
- provide adequate, sustainable funding to grow the disciplines
- require best practices
- a forensic pathologist should relay the truth
- independence is detrimental; connect with other experts

- work should be independently reviewable and transparent
- reports must be understandable to those in the justice system
- teamwork is beneficial
- commit to providing quality work
- provide reliable expert scientific evidence for the justice system
- provide evidence-based, not experience-based, analysis and testimony
- commit to system-based oversight (Goudge, 2008)

Instructional Pop Out

The Case of William Mullins-Johnson

Innocence Canada was involved in the exoneration of William Mullins-Johnson, who was convicted of sexual assault and murder due to inaccurate forensic pathology evidence. Sarah Harland-Logan (2016) wrote an extensive chronology of Mullins-Johnson's path of conviction, appeals, and eventual release. The following is a summary of the major events, with a focus on the forensic evidence.

On June 26, 1993, Mullins-Johnson was babysitting his sister's three children, one of whom was four-year-old Valin. Valin had gone to bed with a fever and Mullins-Johnson checked on her once in the evening. The next morning Valin's mother entered her room and found Valin dead in her bed. An investigation ensued, with three physicians completing post-mortem examinations. The doctors provided evidence that Valin's cause of death was strangulation that happened on the evening of June 26. They also indicated that Valin had been subject to chronic sexual abuse. Mullins-Johnson was eventually charged and a conviction for first-degree murder was registered in 1994. Unsuccessful appeals were launched in the Ontario Court of Appeal and the Supreme Court of Canada.

In 2004, Dr. Michael Pollanen re-examined the forensic pathology evidence and found that the conclusions provided should be rejected and that Valin had died of natural causes. The evidence of sexual assault was a mistake in interpreting post-mortem changes and the after-effect of the autopsy process. In 2007, William's conviction was rescinded and he was acquitted of the crimes.

Show's how proper training is needed for proper accusation.

This is one example of several similar cases, debated in the Goudge report, where forensic evidence was wrongly interpreted and **evidence-based analysis** not employed.

The NAS Report

In November 2005, the US Congress authorized the National Research Council of the National Academy of Sciences to study the status of forensic science within the United States. The NAS report was published in February 2009, specifically naming the forensic disciplines and providing a general scientific analysis of each. The authors of the report then focused on the universal scientific and US-specific problems within forensic science. They outlined why issues had occurred, what to do about these problems, and how to fix the fragmented US system, and listed recommendations with a focal point on both the universal scientific and US-specific issues. The publishing of this report has inspired many individuals to provide suggestions on how to put more science into forensic science (Bono, 2011; Gertner, 2011; Harris, 2012; Laub, 2011; Margot, 2011; Mnookin et al., 2011; Page, Taylor, & Blenkin, 2011a, 2011b, 2011c; Saks, 2010). Readers are encouraged to search out and review each reference.

Instructional Pop Out

See NAS report (2009):

https://www.ncjrs.gov/
pdffiles1/nij/grants/
228091.pdf

The NAS report scrutinized 14 disciplines, including areas of the comparison disciplines (friction ridge, crime scene footwear impression analysis, hair and fibre, questioned document examination, etc.), biological evidence, analysis of controlled substances, analysis of paint and coatings, analysis of explosives and fire debris, forensic odontology, bloodstain pattern analysis, crime scene analysis, and digital analysis. The main problems that seemed to pervade all disciplines were as noted:

- "disparities in the forensic science community," including those regarding "funding, access to analytical instrumentation, the availability of skilled and well-trained personnel, certification, accreditation, and oversight";

- a "lack of mandatory standardization, certification, and accreditation";
- "the broad range of forensic science disciplines";
- issues "relating to the interpretation of forensic evidence";
- a "need for research to establish limits and measures of performance";
- "the admission of forensic science evidence in litigation"; and
- US-based "political realities," such as the difference of regulations between state and federal governments. (NAS, 2009)

The authors of the NAS report gave 13 central recommendations to enhance forensic science within the United States. Some of these do not specifically apply to the Canadian or global forensic systems—for example, the development of a nationwide fingerprint data system. However, we should strive for this type of interoperability on an international level and explore universal scientific issues within forensic science. The following recommendations were included:

- "...establish standard terminology to be used in reporting on and testifying about the results of forensic science investigations."
- "Research is needed to address issues of accuracy, reliability, and validity in the forensic science disciplines."
- "...encourage research programs on human observer bias and sources of human error in forensic examinations."
- "...develop tools for advancing measurement, validation, reliability, information sharing, and proficiency testing in forensic science and to establish protocols for forensic examinations, methods, and practices."
- "The National Institute of Forensic Science (NIFS), in consultation with its advisory board, should establish a national code of ethics for all forensic science disciplines and encourage individual societies to incorporate this national code as part of their professional code of ethics."
- "...attract students in the physical and life sciences to pursue graduate studies in multidisciplinary fields critical to forensic science practice, Congress should authorize and appropriate

funds to the National Institute of Forensic Science (NIFS) to work with appropriate organizations and educational institutions to improve and develop graduate education programs..."

• "...improve medicolegal death investigation..." (NAS, 2009)

The Hart House Report

In 2012, the Hart House report, or its more formal name, *Forensic Science in Canada: A Report of Multidisciplinary Discussion* (Pollanen et al., 2013), was released, containing a Canadian perspective on some of the issues described in the NAS report. This Canadian report explored nine disciplines within forensic science: forensic pathology; forensic anthropology; forensic odontology; forensic nursing; forensic entomology; forensic physical sciences; forensic toxicology; forensic biology; and forensic psychiatry. The report provided a summary, disciplinary overview, services, education, research, and professional organizations for each of the nine disciplines. Its main objectives were to describe the current state of forensic science in Canada, summarize the challenges and opportunities in forensic science, and provide recommendations to strengthen forensic science across the country.

> **Instructional Pop Out**
>
> See *Forensic Science in Canada: A Report of Multidisciplinary Discussion*: www.crime-scene-investigator.net/forensic-science-in-canada.pdf

The report concludes that the forensic science system in Canada is a "patchwork of contributions" that lacks national grant funding, and this contributes to the non-existence of a research culture in Canada. The country's geography has contributed to a scattering of forensic scientists and academics, making it difficult to interact and coordinate effectively. Expert credentialing in forensic science is also absent or disjointed among the different disciplines (Pollanen et al., 2013).

The authors recommend that a research culture be established in Canada and that forensic science be recognized as a discipline by granting agencies. An increase in training for police, scientists, lawyers, and judges is essential, particularly using online components. The report indicates the need to develop master's- and doctoral-level research-based programs, along with adopting best practices such as international guidelines, standards, professional certification, accreditation, and ethics criteria. Other recommendations included developing memoranda of understandings for fee-for-service forensic providers, peer review and quality assurance systems, and career paths for forensic identification officers (Pollanen et al., 2013).

Unlike the NAS report, the Hart House report did not discuss the scientific foundations of the various forensic science disciplines and regrettably did not have the same impact on forensic science at a national or global level. However, it did summarize the state of Canadian forensics and should be a central read for any forensic science practitioner and student wishing to work in Canada.

NAS= Better as they got to the root of the problem + fixed it.

The PCAST Report

Following the release of the NAS report, the US Department of Justice formed the Attorney General's National Commission on Forensic Science (NCFS), which expired in April 2017. The commission's mandate was to "enhance the practice and improve the reliability of forensic science" (NCFS, 2018). The Organization of Scientific Area Committees (OSAC) for Forensic Science was also formed to help the United States strengthen the use of forensic science by developing better standards. Around the same time, the President's Council of Advisors on Science and Technology (PCAST) had been working on a report entitled *Forensic Science in Criminal Courts: Ensuring Scientific Validity of Feature-Comparison Methods*. This report was released in September 2016 and, like the NAS report, garnered significant attention in the global forensic community.

This report, like the Goudge and NAS reports, reviewed the disciplines and their scientific shortcomings and provided possible solutions. The PCAST specifically looked at the feature-comparison disciplines, including DNA analysis of single-source and simple-mixture samples, DNA analysis of complex-mixture samples, bitemarks, latent

Table 1.1. PCAST Summary of Recommendations for the Comparison Disciplines

Discipline	PCAST Recommendation
DNA analysis of single-source and simple-mixture samples	Scientifically robust
DNA analysis of complex-mixture samples	Substantially more evidence is needed to establish foundational validity across broader settings
Bitemarks	PCAST considers the prospects of developing bitemark analysis into a scientifically valid method to be low. They advised against devoting significant resources to such efforts
Latent fingerprints	PCAST finds that latent fingerprint analysis is a foundationally valid subjective methodology
Firearms identification	Fingerprints and firearms require further validation of the subjective method and need to move to an objective methodology
Footwear analysis	Footwear—no appropriate black box study—not scientifically valid
Hair analysis	Microscopic hair comparisons alone cannot lead to personal identification

Source: PCAST, 2016

fingerprints, firearms identification, and footwear and hair analyses. Table 1.1 is a summary of the PCAST recommendations for each discipline.

PCAST also provided the following four overarching recommendations to the Office of Science and Technology Policy (OSTP) and National Institute of Standards and Technology (NIST). The recommendations were: improving assessment of foundational validity; developing objective methods for DNA analysis of complex-mixture

Instructional Pop Out

Read the following for contrasting views of the PCAST report:

www.fbi.gov/file-repository/
fbi-pcast-response.pdf/
view (see PCAST, 2016)

www.ncbi.nlm.nih.gov/
pubmed/28688344
(see Evett et al., 2017)

samples, latent fingerprint analysis, and firearms analysis; improving the organizational structure for scientific area committees; and developing a research and design strategy for forensic science (PCAST, 2016).

Report of the Motherisk Hair Analysis Independent Review

The Honourable Susan E. Lang was asked to review the hair-strand drug and alcohol testing used by the Motherisk Drug Testing Laboratory (MDTL) between 2005 and 2015. The MDTL was located in the Hospital for Sick Children in Toronto, and it was considered to be the leader in the field of hair testing for drug abuse from the late 1990s to

Instructional Pop Out

See Report of the Motherisk Hair Analysis Independent Review (2015):

www.attorneygeneral.jus. gov.on.ca/english/ about/pubs/lang/

April 2015. The laboratory tested 1,600 individuals at the request of Ontario child protection agencies between 2005 and 2015. The laboratory provided evidence of drug exposure in developing fetuses and infants, and laboratory personnel provided expert opinions that were used when making decisions that involved issues of child protection. The laboratory's expertise was used in criminal cases (Lang, 2015).

It was found in the report of the Motherisk hair analysis that the hair test results and opinions were not adequate or reliable. The turning point was in 2014, when the Ontario Court of Appeal allowed Tamara Broomfield to appeal her criminal convictions for charges that she had administered cocaine to her young child. The convictions were based on evidence that was provided by a scientist from the laboratory. New evidence was tendered from the chief toxicologists in the Office of the Chief Medical Examiner of Alberta, criticizing the hair testing methods and interpretation. The court concluded that there was controversy about the science and methods based on the new evidence from the examiner in Alberta, quashing the two drug-related convictions. This resulted in the Ontario government establishing the independent review.

The independent review was mandated to report on the following:

- the adequacy and reliability of the hair-strand drug and alcohol testing methodology utilized by MDTL between 2005 and 2015 for use as evidence in child protection and criminal proceedings
- the extent to which the operation of the MDTL laboratory between 2005 and 2015 was consistent with internationally recognized forensic standards
- whether the use of evidence derived from MDTL's hair-strand drug and alcohol testing in criminal and child protection proceedings has implications warranting an additional review or process with respect to specific cases or classes of cases and, if so, the nature and extent of any such review or process (Lang, 2015)

Like many of the other reports that we have examined, the Motherisk independent review indicates that the forensic experts lacked training and experience in forensic science; the laboratory used unconfirmed results and had no standard operating procedures; the methods used were not used in forensic toxicology; they did not keep records of the testing; and there was no oversight of the laboratory technicians (Lang, 2015).

SUMMARY

The overall recommendation of the NAS and other reports is the need for more science within forensic science. There are also several consistent themes among the evaluations, including asking for appropriate education for and oversight of practitioners; using evidence-based and not experience-based analysis and testimony; and enabling further research.

This book details the scientific method as well as research that emphasizes the application of an evidence-based approach to forensic science. This chapter outlined what caused the paradigm shift in forensics and how critical it is for the reader to understand how to work scientific concepts into their chosen discipline.

Brian Yamashita

Personal Profile

Brian Yamashita was born and raised in Winnipeg, Manitoba, the fifth of nine children born to Japanese-Canadian parents who had been displaced from the west coast during World War II. He attended the University of Manitoba, graduating with a BSc (Hons) degree in chemistry. Armed with a National Research Council scholar-

ship, he then went on to do graduate studies at the University of Western Ontario in London, Ontario. After receiving his PhD for research in laser spectroscopy, Brian travelled to Dalhousie University in Halifax, Nova Scotia, to do further work in spectroscopy as a Killam post-doctoral fellow.

Brian's Path to Forensic Science

It was in Halifax that he first met forensic identification officers with the Royal Canadian Mounted Police (RCMP), when they came to his lab to request that he use the argon ion laser to examine chemically treated pieces of evidence. Although as an undergraduate Brian knew some chemistry grad students who had joined the RCMP to work with trace evidence in the forensic lab, it was not an area he had considered for himself. The RCMP members urged him to apply for a new position being created in Ottawa, but Brian had already accepted a position as an instructor at the University of Victoria. During his three years in Victoria, Brian maintained contact with the RCMP officers in Ottawa and was notified when other positions became available. After a year as a research associate with Atomic Energy of Canada, Brian finally joined the RCMP as a civilian member in 1989.

Brian's Role as a Forensic Scientist

The position in Ottawa was a unique, one-of-a-kind job—it was not in the forensic laboratory, but in support of the RCMP's forensic identification members. The RCMP had the wisdom to realize that while crime scene investigation techniques were getting more complex, identification members often did not have academic scientific backgrounds and could benefit from the assistance of a trained scientist. Although Brian's background in spectroscopy provided a natural connection to use forensic light sources and fluorescent techniques to visualize fingerprints and other evidence, he was also asked to familiarize himself with other disciplines, like anthropology or bloodstain pattern analysis, with the goal of being able to help police officers understand some of the science involved. Laser spectroscopy led him to criss-cross the country to teach RCMP and non-RCMP officers how to use lasers and other light sources, in combination with chemical treatments, to make forensic evidence more visible. In addition to publishing papers on fingerprint development and forensic light sources, he has also lectured or published papers on forensic entomology, health and safety, photography, barefoot impression comparison, DNA, casting, forensic anthropology, the scientific method, bloodstain pattern analysis, and vacuum metal deposition.

Another important aspect of Brian's position was to provide advice and assistance to forensic identification members across the country, both RCMP and non-RCMP, when questions arose as to best practices. Besides lecturing in courses or at workshops, this involved responding to scene of crime inquiries by phone or email. His suggestions of chemicals or techniques to try in specific situations has resulted in more evidence being uncovered or connections to other specialists with the required expertise.

In recent years, Brian's interest has expanded from trying to improve methods used to develop latent fingerprints into considering the fingerprint comparison procedure itself. Positive identification no longer rests on a minimum number of corresponding characteristics but requires a more objective defence of conclusions to be presented in court.

After almost 28 years of service, Brian retired from the RCMP in 2017.

QUESTIONS TO PONDER

1. Based on the information in this chapter, what are your thoughts about forensic science in Canada and globally?
2. List three recommendations that are common to the NAS, Goudge, and PCAST reports. Why do you think they are common between the reports?
3. Why do you think that there is a lack of science in forensic science?
4. How many groups are within the OSAC and what is their function? See www.nist.gov/topics/organization-scientific-area-committees-forensic-science
5. What creates a scientific paradigm shift and who is Thomas Kuhn?
6. How does MCM work in Ontario?
7. What does the PCAST report indicate about bitemark analysis? Why do you think this area of forensic science is so controversial?
8. How would you fix some of the problems discussed in this chapter?
9. Do you think the people exonerated of an offence, like those in the Goudge report and Motherisk hair analysis review, deserve compensation from the government?

GLOSSARY

Centre of Forensic Sciences (CFS): the principal laboratory that completes forensic examinations for criminal investigations in Ontario (CFS, 2018).

contextual bias: a bias that occurs when contextual information from a case or scene has influenced an analysis or opinion (Quigley-McBride & Wells, 2018).

crime scene investigator (CSI): a person who collects evidence at a crime scene. This term is used extensively in the United States and other countries (MP, 2018; OSAC, 2018).

deoxyribonucleic acid (DNA): a molecule that contains the instructions an organism needs to develop, live, and reproduce (Rettner, 2017).

evidence-based analysis: the use of the best and most current evidence to provide a forensic opinion (Hansen, 2014).

forensic identification officer: a specialist who is responsible for collecting and preserving the physical evidence at a scene, processing them in the laboratory, and presenting findings in court. In Canada, a forensic identification officer must be certified by completing a forensic identification course (CIS, 2018; CPC, 2018).

forensic science: the application of scientific methods and techniques to matters under investigation by a court of law (Oxford English Dictionary, 2018).

Innocence Canada: a Canadian non-profit organization dedicated to identifying, advocating for, and exonerating individuals convicted of a crime that they did not commit (Innocence Canada, 2018).

major case management (MCM): a model used to approach complex crime such as multi-jurisdictional occurrences and to help solve major crime (MCMM, 2004).

paradigm shift: a fundamental change in an approach (Kuhn, 1962).

scenes of crime officer (SOCO): in Canada, a scenes of crime officer examines less complex crime scenes. They receive less training than a forensic identification officer (TPS, 2018).

scientific method: a procedure of inquiry generally consisting of observations, experimentation, and formulating and testing hypotheses (Andersen & Hepburn, 2016).

FURTHER READINGS

Campbell, A. (1996). *Bernardo Investigation Review*. Toronto.

Evett, I. W., Berger, C. E. H., Buckleton, J. S., Champod, C., & Jackson, G. (2017). Finding the Way Forward for Forensic Science in the US—A Commentary on the PCAST Report. *Forensic Science International, 278,* 16–23. doi:10.1016/j.forsciint.2017.06.018

Federal/Provincial/Territorial Heads of Prosecutions Subcommittee on the Prevention of Wrongful Convictions. (2011). *The Path to*

Justice: Preventing Wrongful Convictions. Ottawa: Public Prosecution Service of Canada.

Goudge, S. T. (2008). *Inquiry into Pediatric Forensic Pathology in Ontario* (Ontario Ed.). Toronto. Retrieved from www.attorneygeneral.jus.gov.on.ca/inquiries/goudge/report/v1_en_pdf/Vol_1_Eng.pdf

Howes, L. M., Martire, K. A., & Kelty, S. F. (2014). Response to Recommendation 2 of the 2009 NAS Report—Standards for Formatting and Reporting Expert Evaluative Opinions: Where Do We Stand? *Forensic Science Policy and Management: An International Journal,* 5(1–2), 1–14. doi:10.1080/19409044.2014.880973

Innocence Canada. (2018). Innocence Canada. Retrieved from http://www.innocencecanada.com/

Innocence Project. (2018). About the Innocence Project. Retrieved from https://www.innocenceproject.org/about/

International Association for Identification. (2016). Response to PCAST Report. September. Retrieved from https://theiai.org/docs/8.IAI_PCAST_Response.pdf

Kaufman, F. (1998). *Report of the Kaufman Commission on Proceedings Involving Guy Paul Morin.* Retrieved from https://www.attorneygeneral.jus.gov.on.ca/english/about/pubs/morin/morin_esumm.html#top

Lang, S. E. (2015). *Report of the Motherisk Hair Analysis Independent Review.* Toronto.

MCMM. (2004). *Ontario Major Case Management Manual.* Toronto: Ministry of Community Safety and Correctional Services.

Mnookin, J. L. (2010). The Courts, The NAS, and the Future. *Brooklyn Law Review, 75*(4), 1–67.

Morrison, G. S., Kaye, D. H., Balding, D. J., Taylor, D., Dawid, P., Aitken, C. G., ... Willis, S. (2017). A Comment on the PCAST Report: Skip the "Match"/"Non-match" Stage. *Forensic Science International, 272,* e7–e9.

NAS. (2009). *Strengthening Forensic Science in the United States: A Path Forward* (T. N. A. Press Ed.). Washington: National Academy of Sciences.

PCAST. (2016). *Report to the President Forensic Science in Criminal Courts: Ensuring Scientific Validity of Feature Comparison Methods* (Executive

Summary). President's Council of Advisors on Science and Technology, United States.

Pollanen, M. S., Bowes, M. J., VanLaerhoven, S. L., & Wallace, J. (2013). *Forensic Science in Canada: A Report of Multidisciplinary Discussion.* Toronto: Centre for Forensic Science and Medicine, University of Toronto.

Sanger, R. M. (2016). The New PCAST Report to the President of the United States on Forensic Science. *Santa Barbara Lawyers Magazine, 530,* 24–27.

REFERENCES

Andersen, H., & Hepburn, B. (2016). Scientific Method. In E. N. Zalta (Ed.), *Stanford Encyclopedia of Philosophy.* Retrieved from https://plato.stanford.edu/entries/scientific-method/

Bono, J. P. (2011). Commentary on the Need for a Research Culture in the Forensic Sciences. *UCLA Law Review, 58,* 781–787.

Campbell, A. (1996). *Bernardo Investigation Review.* Toronto.

CFS. (2018). Centre of Forensic Sciences—Introduction. Retrieved from https://www.mcscs.jus.gov.on.ca/english/centre_forensic/CFS_intro.html

CIS. (2018). Canadian Identification Society—Training. Retrieved from http://www.cis-sci.ca/training

CPC. (2018). Canadian Police College—Forensic Identification Course. Retrieved from http://www.cpc-ccp.gc.ca/programs-programmes/forensic-ident-judiciaire/fic-cij-eng.htm

Dror, I. (2013). The Ambition to be Scientific: Human Expert Performance and Objectivity. *Science and Justice, 53*(2), 81–82. doi:10.1016/j.scijus.2013.03.002

Dror, I. (2014). Practical Solutions to Cognitive and Human Factor Challenges in Forensic Science. *Forensic Science Policy and Management: An International Journal, 4*(3–4), 105–113. doi:10.1080/19409044.2014.901437

Evett, I. W., Berger, C. E. H., Buckleton, J. S., Champod, C., & Jackson, G. (2017). Finding the Way Forward for Forensic Science in the US—A

Commentary on the PCAST Report. *Forensic Science International, 278*, 16–23. doi:10.1016/j.forsciint.2017.06.018

Gertner, N. (2011). Commentary on the Need for a Research Culture in the Forensic Sciences. *UCLA Law Review, 58*, 789–793.

Goudge, S. T. (2008). *Inquiry into Pediatric Forensic Pathology in Ontario.* Toronto. Retrieved from www.attorneygeneral.jus.gov.on.ca/inquiries/goudge/report/v1_en_pdf/Vol_1_Eng.pdf

Hansen, H. F. (2014). Organisation of Evidence-Based Knowledge Production: Evidence Hierarchies and Evidence Typologies. *Scandinavian Journal of Public Health, 42*(13 Suppl), 11–17. doi:10.1177/1403494813516715

Harland-Logan, S. (2016). William Mullins-Johnson. Retrieved from https://innocencecanada.com/exonerations/william-mullins-johnson/

Harris, D. A. (2012). *Failed Evidence: Why Law Enforcement Resists Science.* New York: New York University Press.

Innocence Canada. (2018). Innocence Canada. Retrieved from http://www.innocencecanada.com/

Kaufman, F. (1998). *Report of the Kaufman Commission on Proceedings Involving Guy Paul Morin.* Ministry of the Attorney General. Retrieved from https://www.attorneygeneral.jus.gov.on.ca/english/about/pubs/morin/morin_esumm.html#top

Kuhn, T. S. (1962). The Structure of Scientific Revolutions. In O. Neurath and T. Kuhn (Eds.), *International Encyclopedia of Unified Science* (FUS II–2). Chicago: University of Chicago Press.

Lang, S. E. (2015). *Report of the Motherisk Hair Analysis Independent Review.* Ministry of the Attorney General.

Laub, J. H. (2011). *The National Institute of Justice Response to the Report of the National Research Council: Strengthening the National Institute of Justice.* US Department of Justice. Retrieved from https://www.ncjrs.gov/pdffiles1/nij/234630.pdf

Margot, P. (2011). Commentary on the Need for a Research Culture in the Forensic Sciences. *UCLA Law Review, 58*, 795–801.

MCMM. (2004). *Ontario Major Case Management Manual.* Toronto: Ministry of Community Safety and Correctional Services.

Mnookin, J. L., Cole, S. A., Dror, I. E., Fisher, B. A. J., Houck, M. M., Inman, K., … Stoney, D. A. (2011). The Need for a Research Culture in the Forensic Sciences. *UCLA Law Review, 58*(3), 725–779.

MP. (2018). Metropolitan Police, UK—Scenes of Crime Officers. Retrieved from https://metropolitanpoliceservice.weebly.com/scenes-of-crime-officers-soco.html

NAS. (2009). *Strengthening Forensic Science in the United States: A Path Forward* (T. N. A. Press Ed.). Washington: National Academy of Sciences.

NCFS. (2018). National Commission on Forensic Science. Department of Justice Archives. Retrieved from https://www.justice.gov/archives/ncfs

NIST. (2019). Crime Scene Investigation Subcommittee. Retrieved from https://www.nist.gov/topics/forensic-science/crime-scene-investigation-subcommittee

Office of the Inspector General. (2006). *A Review of the FBI's Handling of the Brandon Mayfield Case: Unclassified Executive Summary.* US Department of Justice.

OSAC. (2018). The Organization of Scientific Area Committees for Forensic Science—Crime Scene Investigation Subcommittee. Retrieved from https://www.nist.gov/topics/forensic-science/crime-scene-investigation-subcommittee

Oxford English Dictionary. (2018). Forensic Science. Retrieved from https://en.oxforddictionaries.com/

Page, M., Taylor, J., & Blenkin, M. (2011a). Uniqueness in the Forensic Identification Sciences—Fact or Fiction? *Forensic Science International, 206*(1–3), 12–18. doi:10.1016/j.forsciint.2010.08.004

Page, M., Taylor, J., & Blenkin, M. (2011b). Forensic Identification Science Evidence Since Daubert: Part I—A Quantitative Analysis of the Exclusion of Forensic Identification Science Evidence. *Journal of Forensic Sciences, 56*(5), 1180–1184. doi:10.1111/j.1556-4029.2011.01777.x

Page, M., Taylor, J., & Blenkin, M. (2011c). Forensic Identification Science Evidence since Daubert: Part II—Judicial Reasoning in Decisions to Exclude Forensic Identification Evidence on Grounds of Reliability. *Journal of Forensic Science, 56*(4), 913–917. doi:10.1111/j.1556-4029.2011.01776.x

PCAST. (2016). *Report to the President Forensic Science in Criminal Courts: Ensuring Scientific Validity of Feature–Comparison Methods* (Executive Summary). President's Council of Advisors on Science and Technology, United States.

Pollanen, M. S., Bowes, M. J., VanLaerhoven, S. L., & Wallace, J. (2013). *Forensic Science in Canada: A Report of Multidisciplinary Discussion.* Toronto: Centre for Forensic Science and Medicine, University of Toronto.

Quigley-McBride, A., & Wells, G. L. (2018). Fillers can Help Control for Contextual Bias in Forensic Comparison Tasks. *Law and Human Behavior, 42*(4), 295–305. doi:10.1037/lhb0000295

R. v. France. (2017). *Her Majesty the Queen v. Joel France.* ONSC 2040, CR-17-10000034-0000.

R. v. Millard. (2018). *Regina v. Dellen Millard.* ONSC 4410, CR-16-50000176-0000.

R. v. Natsis. (2018). *Her Majesty the Queen v. Christy Natsis.* ONCA 425, C61328.

Rettner, R. (2017). DNA: Definition, Structure & Discovery, Live Science. Retrieved from https://www.livescience.com/37247-dna.html

Saks, M. J. (2010). Forensic Identification: From a Faith-Based "Science" to a Scientific Science. *Forensic Science International, 201*(1–3), 14–17. doi:10.1016/j.forsciint.2010.03.014

Saks, M. J., & Koehler, J. J. (2005). The Coming Paradigm Shift in Forensic Identification Science. *Science, 309*(5736), 892–895.

Tangen, J. M. (2013). Identification Personified. *Australian Journal of Forensic Sciences, 45*(3), 315–322. doi:10.1080/00450618.2013.782339

TPS. (2018). Toronto Police Service. Forensic Identification Services— Training. Retrieved from http://www.torontopolice.on.ca/forensics/training.php

CHAPTER 2

Concepts of Science and the Scientific Method

Forensic Science in the Classroom

Photo credit: Mike Illes

I fully agree with you about the significance and educational value of methodology as well as history and philosophy of science. So many people today—and even professional scientists—seem to me like somebody who has seen thousands of trees but has never seen a forest. A knowledge of the historic and philosophical background gives that kind of independence from prejudices of his generation from which most scientists are suffering. This independence created by philosophical insight is—in my opinion—the mark of distinction between a mere artisan or specialist and a real seeker after truth.

—*Albert Einstein, correspondence to Robert Thorton in 1944*[1]

This chapter explores some basic concepts of science, including scientific explanations, evidence-based practice, theories and laws, paradigm shifts, forensic evidence analysis, and why scientific research is required in forensics. We also examine how science and scientific reasoning fit within forensic science. We will define *knowledge* and *information* and investigate how scientific explanations differ from common sense. The reader will gain an appreciation for the role of scientific reasoning and how ideas like falsification and hypothesis testing are essential to forensic applications. This will provide a foundation for using evidence-based practice, a central theme throughout the book.

SCIENTIFIC EXPLANATIONS

Scientific explanations differ from intuitive, or common-sense, explanations. Though both start with an observation, a scientific explanation is based on rigorous research inquiry. Conversely, common-sense explanations are based on our experience or our own sense of the world (Bordens & Abbott, 2011). Knowing how we think plays a role in our everyday and scientific decision making. We generally use intuition in everyday decision making—it is a rapid appraisal, and E. M. Evans (2018) refers to it as System 1, or fast thinking. System 2, or slow thinking, is the reasoning power that we use when analyzing more complex scientific issues. J. S. B. Evans (2010) provides a great example of these systems: when someone is learning to drive a car, they use System 2 thinking until they become accustomed to driving. After learning the routine driving tasks, System 1 can be used until a novel problem occurs, like icy roads, then System 2 is initiated, analyzing the problem to react appropriately.

Think of a time when you have been studying for an exam or reading/concentrating on reviewing complex journal articles. After a period, you become tired and need a break even though you haven't moved around much. If we used slow thinking all the time, we would be drained of our energy very quickly. Therefore, in most of our everyday thinking we can depend on our System 1 or fast thinking. However, when considering complex issues, like a crime scene examination or conducting scientific research, it is imperative to use more intricate reasoning strategies.

Scientific explanations are said to be empirical, rational, testable, parsimonious, general, tentative, and rigorously evaluated (Bordens & Abbott, 2011). Empirical explanations are based on observation or experience. Rationality indicates that the explanation is based on logic, and parsimony provides a path of economy or the use of the simplest explanation. There are several schools of thought on explanatory methodologies that can be followed to accomplish the above list of requirements. Table 2.1 provides some general concepts.

> ## Instructional Pop Out
>
> View the video "Brain Tricks—This Is How Your Brain Works" by AsapSCIENCE (2019) to help understand how the human brain functions and the different types of thinking. We will concentrate on "slow thinking," as slow thinking is scientific thinking: www.youtube.com/watch?v=JiTz2i4VHFw

A scientific explanation is based on the application of accepted scientific methods. The path to evidence-based analysis in forensic science requires a process that follows currently accepted scientific procedures. Mnookin (2010) has suggested that "forensic scientists have regularly testified in court to matters that are, quite honestly, both less proven and less certain than they are claimed to be. They have overstated their degree of knowledge, underreported the chances of error, and suggested greater certainty than is warranted. More generally, many kinds of forensic science are not entirely based on the methods and approaches that we usually associate with validated research science."

An evidence-based system founded on scientific research will provide the transparency and legitimacy that is required (Edmond, Thompson, & Tangen, 2013; Koehler, 2018; Mnookin, 2010; *R. v. Millard*, 2018; *R. v. Natsis*, 2018; Sjerps & Berger, 2012). The first steps to finding sound evidence are (1) understanding science, (2) having the ability to properly review a journal article (see chapter 4), and (3) completing an extensive literature search on the topic (chapter 5).

Table 2.1. Methods of Inquiry Used by Scientists and Forensic Science Practitioners

Method of Inquiry	Knowledge
Method of authority	• Relates to an expert source, such as a non–peer-reviewed book or directly from a person. • It does not provide evidence supporting claims. • The information is based on authority alone and does not always provide valid answers. • This type of knowledge cannot be trusted and may not be truly authoritative. • Authority is usually biased by a point of view.
Rational method	• Depends on logical reasoning rather than on authority. It was developed by René Descartes.
Scientific method	• A combination of authoritative sources, deductive reasoning, and other features, such as falsification. • It forms the basis of the most powerful approach to knowledge yet developed.

Source: Bordens & Abbott, 2011

Instructional Pop Out

Be sure to read the Supreme Court of British Columbia decision *R. v. Bornyk*, 2017 BCSC 849 (CanLII): http://canlii.ca/t/h3w87

This case provides a great example of the importance of understanding how scientific evidence and expert opinions can be considered in the Canadian court system. It is a case on friction ridge/fingerprint analysis, which is a forensic discipline based in the policing environment. In the original trial, a lower-court judge questioned the scientific reliability and expert opinion of a police officer, ruling the evidence inadmissible. In the end the Supreme Court of British Columbia ruled in support of the use of fingerprint evidence in the Canadian court system.

The court heard expert-opinion testimony from Dr. Della Wilkinson (crown witness) and Dr. Simon Cole (defence witness), who had similar viewpoints on the research—and lack thereof—supporting the scientific underpinning of the friction ridge discipline. The witnesses referenced the NAS report, the **ACE-V** process (see following instructional pop out), quality of the fingerprints, the lack of statistical analysis, best practices, and the fact that zero-error rates (used in friction ridge analysis) are not scientifically plausible. The defence argued that the process used by the friction ridge analyst was flawed and contained contextual bias (*R. v. Bornyk*, 2017). This case illustrates the importance of research and how it supports scientific conclusions and evidence-based testimony.

The take-home message from this court decision and the appeal decision is that the judge in the first trial erred by conducting his own analysis of the fingerprints, absent the assistance of the expert witness (*R. v. Bornyk*, 2015). The discipline of fingerprint comparison has a scientific underpinning, and it was accepted by the court as being "highly individualized" and that "no evidence was laid in front of me that there is a person with identical fingerprints to another, not even identical twins" (*R. v. Bornyk*, 2017).

KNOWLEDGE AND INFORMATION

The distinction between *knowledge* and *information* is important to forensic science because the division of tasks depends on the experience and education of the practitioner. *Knowledge* is defined as skills and experience gained through education, whereas *information* is the facts that have been provided in a situation (Williams, 2015). If a forensic identification practitioner finds evidence (e.g., a fingerprint impression) at a crime scene, they would retrieve this evidence and it would be information. This fingerprint would be analyzed by a friction ridge expert, who would apply their knowledge, gained from education/training, regarding the impression and provide an opinion based on their analysis, comparison, and evaluation of the fingerprint. The expert should possess **domain knowledge** together with formal reasoning skills that include abstract thinking and using the scientific method.

As a student, you may have wondered why there is so much rote learning of domain knowledge, specifically in your first and second years of college or university. This occurs because domain knowledge of a specific area of study is required before a person can develop critical thinking and problem-solving skills in that discipline. The development of knowledge in forensic science is complex because it deals with multiple scientific disciplines that are used in the judicial system. Additionally, the thresholds of these systems are different; courts make decisions based on circumstantial evidence and reasonable doubt, while science is grounded in robust validated research.

Instructional Pop Out

ACE-V—a Forensic Debate on Scientific Method

ACE-V is an acronym for "analyze, compare, evaluate, and verify," which is a process used within several of the comparison disciplines. ACE-V was originally developed within a forensic laboratory for the examination of questioned documents (Tierney, 2013). It was also adopted by the policing community for friction ridge skin analysis, but this application was not thoroughly researched until recently (Langenburg, 2012; Pacheco, Cerchiai, & Stoiloff, 2014). ACE-V is considered to be an appropriate model for friction ridge comparison and is used extensively within several countries. However, it is not the only method used to compare friction ridges. Several authors have attempted to compare ACE-V to the scientific method, while others suggest that it is a protocol, not a method (Champod et al., 2004; Triplett & Cooney, 2006; Wertheim, 2000). ACE-V is one area of friction ridge analysis that requires critical thought. It is vital that anyone completing friction ridge comparisons be aware of the different models and able to support their use of a specific model and its limitations.

It has been suggested by the NAS report that "ACE-V does not guard against bias, is too broad to ensure repeatability and transparency, and does not guarantee that two analysts following it will obtain the same results. For these reasons, merely following the steps of ACE-V does not imply that one is proceeding in a scientific manner or producing reliable results" (NAS, 2009). This has been supported by Langenburg: "Presently, there are few studies in the literature directly pertaining to the testing and validation of fingerprint comparison methodology" (Langenburg, 2011).

Taylor and colleagues (2012) published *Application of Spatial Statistics to Latent Print Identifications: Towards Improving Forensic Science Methodologies* and suggest that ACE-V is a suitable model; however, the authors have also provided validation that random match probabilities should be used for friction ridge comparisons. This research on the use of randomly matched probabilities could be considered a paradigm shift within the friction ridge comparison discipline.

EVIDENCE-BASED PRACTICE

Evidence-based practice is a way to use knowledge from research in forensic science. This practice, which engages scientific method concepts, is not an isolated function within a discipline. For the forensic practitioner it will involve lifelong, self-directed learning and be applied at every stage, from crime scene to court. The literature also suggests that evidence-based reporting will assist in learning evidence-based practice, useful in applying reasoning to crime scene processing (Doak & Assimakopoulos, 2007; Karson & Nadkarni, 2013; Leake, 2007).

This practice follows a set of guidelines that parallel scientific discovery. Therefore, forensic analysis and reports should be completed in a style that is similar to a scientific journal article (Found & Edmond, 2012). We will discuss the required report content in chapter 9; however, a general approach to evidence-based reporting presented by Leake (2007) includes:

1. defining and describing the problem
2. searching for the evidence

3. selecting only the best evidence
4. presenting and writing up your findings under headings

Evidence-based practice has been used in several different fields of study; however, we believe an excellent example of its use is in medicine and that this relates well to forensic science. In 1995, the *Journal of Evidence-Based Medicine* published its first articles on evidence-based medicine (EBM). Sackett's (1997) description that "the practice of evidence-based medicine is a process of life-long, self-directed learning" echoes the statement in the first paragraph of this section. The EBM process applies the following criteria:

1. formulate answerable questions
2. use the best evidence to answer questions
3. critically appraise the evidence for its validity and usefulness
4. integrate this appraisal with expertise and apply it in practice
5. evaluate the implementation or performance (Sackett, 1997)

Like medicine, forensic science has similar issues when approaching a problem because both disciplines analyze past events. A forensic professional uses this evidence-based approach by developing answerable questions about the crime scene or evidence. They use the best evidence (a literature review alongside objective evidence from the scene) and critically appraise that evidence while integrating their expertise. Evidence-based practice only occurs when an individual combines their expertise with the best available external evidence, and it has been suggested that neither alone is enough (Greenhalgh, 2014; Sackett, 1997). In several forensic disciplines, this becomes problematic as these fields, such as bitemark and footwear analyses, may not possess sufficient research literature to support an evidence-based approach.

THE REASON FOR REASONING

The difference between science and non-science (e.g., history-based or religious) disciplines can be attributed to the use of the scientific method

(Lohr et al., 2015; Mahner, 2007). The activities of scientists—such as the use of observation, **deductive** and **inductive reasoning**, experimentation, and hypothesis testing—can vary depending on the research. Above all, this process provides a way of judging whether the conclusions are scientific or non-scientific (Andersen & Hepburn, 2016). This distinction is just as important for forensic science, so that we can differentiate between common-sense, experiential, and intuitive decisions and those decisions (expert opinions) made from evidence-based knowledge (Sangra, Roach, & Moles, 2010).

Whether a scientific statement is true or false has been an inescapable difficulty throughout time and has significant implications for forensic science (Gauch, 2012). The importance of truth in forensic science was judiciously presented by Justice Steven Goudge (2008) in his inquiry into forensic pathology in Ontario. In his report, the first best practice suggested to forensic pathologists is to "think truth," using terms like *objectivity, independence,* and *an evidence-based approach.* As forensic professionals, our own views about the role of science and our knowledge of science will directly influence our analysis and articulation of the evidence (Andersen & Hepburn, 2016). Providing scientific expert evidence is dependent on an intricate array of skill sets and knowledge, such as critical thought, problem solving, and reasoning.

It is important to understand the separation of the scientific method and the products of science. As scientists, our end goal is to provide knowledge, conclusions, predictions, and controls, but this should not be confused with the scientific method. Also, meta-methodology—the values or reasoning behind a specific methodology—cannot be considered scientific method (Andersen & Hepburn, 2016). Scientific method is the process that is used to create the product.

THE SCIENTIFIC METHOD

The scientific method is "a method of procedure that has characterized natural science since the 17th century, consisting in systematic observation, measurement, and experiment, and the formulation, testing, and modification of hypotheses" (Oxford English Dictionary, 2018).

Aristotle (384–322 BC) was one of the first philosophers to use observation as a means of finding the truth about nature, and he observed and reported on many natural phenomena, such as the stars and animals. The development of natural science in this era contributed to subsequent conceptualizations of observation and deduction (Gauch, 2012).

Deductive reasoning is "top-down" logic (see table 2.2). Simply put, deductive reasoning works from the general to the specific, and conclusions about a specific case are made from general knowledge. This type of reasoning can be useful for expanding our knowledge on existing information; however, deductive reasoning may not be so useful when considering new theories or evidence. An extreme example would be as follows:

Premise 1: Every person has fingerprints.
Premise 2: Every person will leave fingerprints at a scene.
Conclusion: Every scene contains human prints. (Gauch, 2003; Noon, 2009)

Simple observations are critical to science; however, they are not enough for concise conclusions. Therefore, a more complex approach is required. The observance of evidence at a crime scene does not necessarily provide information to the judicial system. A piece of evidence may have probative value, standing on its own, or it could be meaningless without scene context or further analyses. The complexity of evidence recognition in relation to the multifaceted scene means that a crime scene investigator (CSI) must be able to identify the interconnectivity of this evidence at the time. This is accomplished by using complex reasoning that either relates or does not relate all the exhibits to the reconstruction of events that occurred within the crime scene. To infer beyond an observation, a crime scene analysis must be based in the scientific method and not just deductive reasoning.

Conversely, inductive reasoning is "bottom-up" logic. This type of reasoning works from specific observations to generalizations or theories. Let's revisit our earlier Premise 1: Every person has fingerprints. If every time we examined a scene and found fingerprints, this would be an observation that supports the conclusion that every scene contains human prints (Gauch, 2003).

Many scientific philosophers—including Albertus Magnus or Albert the Great (1206–80), Thomas Aquinas (1225–74), Robert Grosseteste (1175–1253), Roger Bacon (1214/1220–92), William of Ockham (1287–1347), Andreas Vesalius (1514–46), and Giacomo Zabarella (1533–89)—investigated and described the concepts of observation and induction over the medieval period, exploring how to apply this in scientific inquiry (Laudan, 1968). This led to the scientific revolution, where dramatic advances occurred within multiple disciplines to develop beyond deductive and inductive reasoning (Kuhn, 1962). Shaler (2012) suggests that both reasoning models are likely used by CSIs, by shifting back and forth between observation and hypotheses while examining a scene. Unfortunately, if the CSI does not have a scientific background, they may be using intuition or experience in their application of reasoning, and this can create a gap or risk in evidence decision making.

Abductive or retroductive reasoning is taking a sample set of observations and coming up with the most likely explanation for the set (your conclusion is a best guess). This is typical everyday decision making and the subconscious application of the scientific method. In scientific research, when comparing deduction and abduction, abduction is the best predictor for the development of research hypotheses (Romesburg, 1981).

Roger Bacon (1214/1220–92) was the first to discuss the repeating cycle of observation, hypothesis, experimentation, and validation, which are the foundations of the scientific method. As Bacon was a philosopher, one of the first persons to put this method into practice was Galileo Galilei (1564–1642) during the Renaissance period (the age of enlightenment for scientific discovery). René Descartes's (1596–1650) *Discourse on Method* was an autobiography of the path that guided his scientific reasoning. This contributed to the development of the scientific method. Descartes was also the founder of the Cartesian measurement system (Descartes, 1956).

Table 2.2. Summary of Reasoning Methods

Reasoning Method	Summary of Method
Deduction	Works from the general to the specific (your conclusion is guaranteed; Gauch, 2003).
Induction	Works from specific observations to generalizations or theories (your conclusion is likely; Gauch, 2003).
Abduction or retroduction	Taking a sample set of observations and coming up with the most likely explanation for the set (your conclusion is a best guess; Romesburg, 1981).

Sources: In table

 Hypothesis →

Instructional Pop Out

If you haven't read the original Sherlock Holmes stories written by Sir Arthur Conan Doyle, you have likely watched Benedict Cumberbatch or Robert Downey Jr. play the role in the most recent renderings of the great fictional private detective. Sherlock's approach to reasoning gives us an understanding of the use (and misuse) of induction and deduction.

Although Sherlock is known as the master of deductive reasoning, he often uses inductive reasoning. He starts with specific observations, like the physical observation of a person, and then makes a general/broad conclusion—for example, the person is a banker.

In fact, from a forensic science perspective, Sherlock's reasoning is flawed because he learns the results first, then indicates what led to the result. He describes this as "backward reasoning." As previously stated, though, deductive reasoning is "top-down" logic, working from the general to the specific. The reason Sherlock's logic works is because in the end, he is always right; this is easy to accomplish in a fictional book but it is an unknown in the real world. For example, Sherlock drew conclusions about Dr. Watson when he first met him:

> Here is a gentleman of the medical type, but with the air of a military man. Clearly an army doctor, then. He has just come from the tropics, for his face is dark, and that is not the natural tint of his skin,

for his wrists are fair. He has undergone hardship and sickness, as his haggard face says clearly. His left arm has been injured: He holds it in a stiff and unnatural manner. Where in the tropics could an English army doctor have seen much hardship and got his arm wounded? Clearly in Afghanistan. (Doyle, 1903)

In the end he is right, but his logic is flawed—this is not deduction, it is reasoning backwards. He indicates the results and from that makes an inference (Young, 2018). In forensic science we must use forward reasoning: collect evidence, test hypotheses, and attempt to come up with the best answer at that time.

Another significant figure in the development of the scientific method was Francis Bacon (1561–1626), who discussed controlled experimentation within his publication *Novum Organum*. Like Galileo, Bacon disliked the academic philosophy that was being taught in universities and believed in a more applied approach to science. Repeatability and disciplined strategies in science were developed by Robert Boyle (1627–91) (Gauch, 2003; Gower, 1997; Oster, 1993; Spier, 2002; Taton, 1964).

William Whewell (1794–1866), John Herschel (1792–1871) (father of William James Herschel), Richard Jones (1790–1855), and Charles Babbage (1791–1871) should also be mentioned, not for their direct development of the scientific method but for their help in shaping science as we know it today. In her book *The Philosophical Breakfast Club*, Laura Snyder (2011) writes about how these four scientists met as undergraduates at the University of Cambridge, developing ideas that changed the history of science. Four major revolutionary changes that they inspired were an evidence-based method (induction), science for the public good, new scientific institutions, and external research funding.

Falsification and Hypothetico-Deduction

Karl Popper was a famous scientific philosopher who discussed falsification, a concept now widely accepted by the scientific community, within his work *The Logic of Scientific Discovery* (Popper, 1959). He concluded that all scientific theories and laws must be falsifiable. A positive result of an experiment could never confirm a theory but a negative result would refute (falsify) a theory.

> According to Popper (1934/1959), science works through a process of testing hypotheses, or hypothetico-deductive logic, based on the attempt to exclude possibilities by falsification. Popper's analysis moved beyond **positivism** by accepting that scientific knowledge is tentative and open to review as more evidence comes in. So, even the experimental method, the "gold standard" for research, does not automatically offer generalisable "objective" knowledge. (Taber, 2009)

Carl Hempel (1967) and Imre Lakatos (Hilborn & Mangel, 1997) also wrote about falsification, validation, and the use of multiple hypotheses. Their philosophy is that multiple hypotheses should be tested against each other while attempting to falsify each hypothesis. Hempel wrote that scientific inquiry could be empirical, natural or social, or non-empirical. One important concept that he conveys is that when experimental control is impossible, we can still test the hypothesis non-experimentally by seeking out or waiting for case examples.

Hypothetico-deductive reasoning is the use of cyclical patterns of observation and reasoning (the scientific method) to test explanations. This process remains subconscious for most adults who have developed formal reasoning skills (abstract thinking and testing hypotheses), but biases and omissions can cloud judgment (Lawson, 2013; Moore & Rubbo, 2012).

A practitioner who is completing a forensic analysis should be using advanced (hypothetico-deductive) reasoning while attempting to reduce bias. This involves falsifying multiple hypotheses (the hypothesis and alternatives) while testing them against each other and the data, but never outright rejecting a hypothesis, because science is dynamic and new information (data or evidence) can change an opinion.

The following example illustrates how the concept could be used at a crime scene to test hypotheses.

Intuitively the crime scene analyst develops an idea or a question regarding an event or piece of evidence within a scene. This is the formulation of a crime scene hypothesis. See the following list of examples of crime scene hypotheses:

- this tire tread came from that tire
- this footwear impression came from that shoe
- this bloodstain came from that person
- this bloodstain pattern was created by this event
- this bullet came from that gun

In science we cannot prove a hypothesis; however, we can make every attempt to reject it by attempting falsification of the hypothesis. Appropriate experimentation or testing, gathering of evidence and prior peer-reviewed research knowledge can assist in rejecting a hypothesis. If we fail to reject the hypothesis, then that hypothesis is the best answer at that time and what we can supply as a conclusion to the courts. This answer is not categoric and can change, though. Alternative hypotheses should be formulated, with further attempts to reject. If we fail to reject an alternative hypothesis, then we can reject the original hypothesis, but new evidence may be presented to update these decisions. While this process is used by many forensic scientists and CSIs, it is sometimes difficult to articulate how this method is applied (Inman & Rudin, 2001).

OTHER CONCEPTS TO THINK ABOUT

Laws and Theories

A law is defined as a rule that is made to govern something. Scientific laws are discovered, but they do not explain why and how something works. An example of this would be **Newton's Law of Gravity**—we do not know how or why gravity works. Scientific theories are invented to explain laws; a theory is "a set of principles on which the practice of an activity is based" (Oxford English Dictionary, 2018). Scientific laws and theories are falsifiable, meaning—like everything in science—they are never proven; they are simply the best information that we have to date. Continual hypothesis testing, observation, and experimentation may change or disprove theories and laws. Scientific laws can be considered patterns in nature that someone has observed, and the theories explain these laws. Uniqueness and persistency are examples of basic laws within forensic identification (e.g., friction ridge analysis), and there are theories that support these laws (Langenburg, 2011; Yamashita, 2010).

Data

Quantitative and qualitative data provide the raw information for interpretation in a scientific process. These data are collected in different ways, such as through random or controlled sampling. Qualitative data is collected by observation, while quantitative data is collected by measurement (Inman & Rudin, 2001). Generally, the core sciences, such as biology, chemistry, and physics, use quantitative data. Social sciences like cultural anthropology or sociology tend to use qualitative analysis for research.

Many areas within forensic science, particularly comparison analysis, rely on both quantitative and qualitative research to underpin the various disciplines. From a forensic analysis perspective, we should rely on robust data collection from either quantitative or qualitative approaches or a combination of both methods.

Parsimony

The principle of parsimony is also called the principle of simplicity, principle of economy, and Ockham's razor. Developed by William of Ockham (1285–1347), it states that "the simpler a theory or explanation is, the less is the chance of error" (Musgrave, 1973). This principle relates directly to the scientific method and forensic work by requiring experts to keep hypotheses to a minimum and use the most economical solution (Gauch, 2003; Musgrave, 1973).

Law of Superposition

Nicholas Steno (1638–86) developed the law of superposition, which states that older material will be underneath more recent (Dupras,

Schultz, Wheeler, & Williams, 2006; Geikie, 1962). This concept is used within forensic archeology and can relate to other areas of forensics when we are attempting to sequence events.

Provenience and Context

Provenience refers to the location of an item in three-dimensional space. Context is the association of an item with other objects, in time and space (the object is in situ). Context is easily lost in a scene (Dupras et al., 2006). The following case study on using the scientific method in bloodstain pattern analysis (BPA) stresses the importance of provenience (knowing the exact location of a bloodstain) and context (how the bloodstains or bloodstain patterns are associated).

Paradigm Shifts

The reason for the paradigm shift in forensic science was discussed in chapter 1. Thomas Kuhn's work on *The Structure of Scientific Revolutions* (1962) provides significant insight into paradigm shifts, and many of the concepts from his writings parallel the present forensic science condition. According to Kuhn (1962), the paradigm shift is just the beginning of change within science and the shift is questioning the way science is being conducted within a specific discipline. This has happened in many fields of scientific inquiry; a well-known paradigm shift is the shift from medieval physics to Newtonian physics.

It is important to recognize that the paradigm shift in forensic science occurred because the outside scientific and judicial communities had questioned the reliability and the scientific validity of many disciplines within forensic science. As scientists, we should view this paradigm shift as a positive event because it is an indicator of the maturation of a scientific discipline.

Forensic Evidence Analysis

Evidence analysis in forensic science consists of the following concepts: transfer; identification; individualization; association between source and target; reconstruction; and divisible matter (Inman & Rudin, 2002).

Divisible matter is a newer concept developed by Inman and Rudin to help explain **physical match** evidence. They believe that a basic understanding of how matter divides and the result of this division are essential knowledge for the forensic practitioner. The subsequent sections will discuss these concepts.

Identification and Individualization

Dr. Paul Kirk (1963), a pioneering forensic scientist at the University of California, Berkeley, defined identification as "referring only to placing the object in a restricted class"; therefore, a forensic examiner who has identified (placing an object in a class) something would only be supplying common knowledge. To help the administration of justice, the forensic examiner attempts individualization (reducing the class to a single individual or item) or as closely as possible within the current science (Inman & Rudin, 2002).

Every Contact Leaves a Trace

Edmund Locard was a forensic scientist who developed the first official police crime laboratory in Lyon, France. Locard (1934) is also well known for the Locard's exchange principle. The exchange principle states that every contact leaves a trace—each contact provides a combination of the identification of the source material, the activity leading to transfer, and the persistence of the trace (Crispino et al., 2011).

The following section on bloodstain pattern analysis will provide an example of how some of the methods discussed can be applied to forensic fieldwork.

A CASE STUDY ON THE SCIENTIFIC METHOD: BLOODSTAIN PATTERN ANALYSIS

This section explains the scientific analysis of a bloodstain pattern from a CSI's perspective. We will be analyzing a bloodstain **impact pattern** (see figure 2.1) to scientifically locate the area of origin of that impact

Figure 2.1. Analysis of a Bloodstain Impact Pattern

Photo credit: Mike Illes

to a blood source. Quantitative and qualitative data will be used for this analysis, and information will be presented on the use of a number of scientific principles, theories, and laws. We will also explore the peer-reviewed research that helps explain and provide information on the underpinnings of the analysis, although some areas within this type of analysis still require research. Finally, we will critically discuss this issue in the context of the current forensic science environment.

> **Instructional Pop Out**
>
> Learn the definitions for bloodstain pattern analysis and about the Organization of Scientific Area Committees (OSAC): www.nist .gov/topics/forensic-science/ osac-organizational-structure

Pattern Recognition

Pattern recognition is the essential first step in bloodstain pattern analysis; we can test a hypothesis within pattern recognition. The hypothesis for this exercise would be that the spatter is an impact pattern created by an object impacting a wet blood source. It possesses the following characteristics:

- there are numerous directional bloodstains within the pattern
- the directional stains radiate from an area of origin
- the geometry of the stains allows for measure
- a three- or two-dimensional origin can be located using known scientific techniques

The hypothesis would be tested by alternative or competing hypotheses (and data), such as the following:

1. the spatter is secondary staining created by a **drip pattern**
2. the spatter is secondary staining created by a **projected pattern**

The use of peer-reviewed and scene research can provide the information required to accept or reject each hypothesis. Remember, we are always attempting to falsify each hypothesis and then accept the best explanation at that time with the information available. Nothing should be stated as definitive.

Pattern recognition is accomplished using a set of basic principles: the use of observational data (qualitative) and repeatability. The analyst relies on laboratory observational data that they or other analysts have collected over a number of years. Crime scene patterns are compared to those created under a controlled laboratory environment. The concept of repeatability was established in the 1660s by Robert Boyle. Although this concept was developed for experimental research, it is very applicable to forensic analysis.

To date, the OSAC research subcommittee has collected 84 articles or books that provide information on pattern recognition (National Institute of Standards and Technology, 2018). While this area of BPA is intuitive, it requires quantitative/qualitative research validation. A court case in 2006 in the United States has shown the need for a clear methodology for pattern recognition. In this case, five BPA experts for the prosecution presented evidence that identified a particular pattern as impact spatter, while five defence experts recognized the pattern to be a transfer (Kozarovich, 2006). There is a need for a standardized method for pattern recognition against which opinions can be tested. However, in regard to assessing an impact pattern, there is a quantitative measure that we will describe.

Data Collection

At this stage the pattern has been qualitatively identified, but we can use quantitative analysis to see if we can estimate an area of origin, which is unique to an impact pattern. Quantitative data should be collected (known as **directional analysis**) to establish the area of origin, which will also help validate the observational data (recognition of the pattern). If the individual bloodstains have a clear geometric shape, they can be measured, and a three-dimensional area of origin can be located. If the stains do not possess sufficient detail for measurement, perhaps only stain directionality can be determined. A two-dimensional analysis (convergence area) may be completed in this case.

There are several scientific principles, theories, and laws that have aided in establishing the assessment of directional analysis. They are listed below:

- **Cartesian coordinate system**—René Descartes
- Provenience and context (see figure 2.2)
- Isaac Newton's three laws of motion
- Directional analysis—Dr. Alfred Carter
- **Reynolds' number (Re)**—Osborne Reynolds
- **Weber number (We)**—Moritz Weber
- **Trigonometry**

The purpose of this case study is not to discuss each principle, theory, and law; however, a simplistic explanation of fluid dynamics as it relates to a blood droplet in flight will be helpful. When a weapon strikes

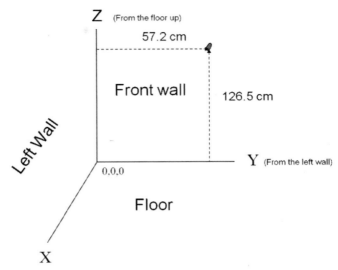

Figure 2.2. Three-Dimensional Provenience of a Bloodstain
Source: Illes & Boué, 2011

a blood source, single blood droplets will form as spheres and move from the source through the air until they hit a surface. The droplets will continue on a single flight path and will be affected by gravitational force and air resistance. Upon impact with the surface, the droplets will become single bloodstains. Trigonometry can be used to trace backward the straight flight path of these stains.

Data can be collected from these bloodstains and analyzed to calculate a three-dimensional estimation of the area of origin. The quantitative data provides for a robust scientific analysis and conclusion supporting our hypothesis that the spatter is an impact pattern created by an object impacting a blood source. This also allows us to falsify the alternative hypotheses: that the spatter is a secondary staining created by a drip pattern or that the spatter is a secondary staining created by a projected pattern, as a single area of origin cannot be found for these patterns.

The analysis of the area of origin for this impact pattern provides for the following:

- standardized methodologies that have been peer reviewed
- known error rates—stain measurement, stain selection (Illes & Boué, 2011; Rowe, 2006; Wells, 2006)
- analysis that is generally accepted by the scientific community
- testing that is falsifiable, testable, and repeatable

As a precaution, the analysis should be independently double-blind peer reviewed by a qualified bloodstain pattern analyst, who would complete a full review and re-analyze the raw data.

SUMMARY

The information provided in this chapter should help with understanding how evidence-based practice and the scientific method should be used in forensic science inquiry. We reviewed some basic scientific concepts, such as the difference between common-sense intuition and scientific explanations, as well as knowledge and information and how they are relevant to forensics. For deeper confidence in the scientific method and its application, we presented a detailed examination of the reasoning, falsification, hypothetico-deduction, and philosophers behind this science. Other scientific concepts as they related to forensics were tied into the case study.

This evidence-based theme will continue throughout the book, and having the knowledge supplied in this chapter will help you to later apply it. The next chapters provide information on how to put this approach to use.

Della Wilkinson

Personal Profile

Della Wilkinson manages the Scientific Technical Support group in the RCMP's Integrated Forensic Identification Services and has been providing scientific and technical support to the forensic identification community since 1992. She has been the recipient of several research grants (totalling C$1.5 million) on topics ranging from recovering fingerprints from human skin to finding physical evidence in the aftermath of a chemical or biological attack. She has accumulated 41 peer-reviewed publications, 28 technical reports, 67 conference papers, and two patents. Dr. Wilkinson contributed a chapter titled "Friction Ridge Detection from Challenging Crime Scenes" to the third edition of Lee and Gaensslen's *Advances in Fingerprint Technology*. In response to concerns about the courts' role in assessing scientific expert evidence, the chief pathologist of Ontario hosted multidisciplinary discussions in 2012 to assess potential gaps in Canadian forensic science. Dr. Wilkinson co-authored the chapter on forensic physical sciences in the resulting report, which outlined a path forward. She is a regular lecturer for the RCMP's Advanced Forensic Identification Training Course and has lectured at both the Canadian and Ontario Police Colleges. Dr. Wilkinson has supervised 18 undergraduate thesis research projects, co-supervised three graduate students, and been external examiner on four PhD examinations. She was an adjunct professor with the University of Toronto's Forensic Science Program from 2005 to 2014. She has also been involved with standards development as a member of the Scientific Working Group on Friction Ridge Analysis, Study and Technology (SWGFAST) and is currently funded by the National Institute of Standards and Technology (NIST) to participate on the Organization of Scientific Area Committees (OSAC) Friction Ridge Subcommittee. Dr. Wilkinson is a founding member of the

Canadian Friction Ridge Working Group (CanFRWG), a member of the editorial board of the *Journal of Forensic Identification*, and past editor of *Identification Canada* (2002–12). She likewise acts as a reviewer for several forensic science journals, including *Forensic Science International*. In January 2017, she was an expert witness in *R. v. Bornyk*, the first court challenge to fingerprint evidence in Canada, where she described the scientific research into fingerprint practices. Dr. Wilkinson is the recipient of the Canadian Identification Society's Edward Foster Award (2011) and the Queen's Diamond Jubilee Medal (2013) for contributions to forensic science in Canada. Dr. Wilkinson obtained a first-class honours degree from Sussex University (1986) and a PhD (in organometallic chemistry) from Cambridge University, UK, in 1990.

Q. How Did You Get Into Forensic Science?

Upon completing my PhD, I applied to the UK Royal Society for a fellowship to continue my research at the National Research Council (NRC) of Canada, where I had been accepted as a post-doctoral fellow. I was awarded the Royal Society fellowship but upon my arrival at the NRC learned that I was also the recipient of a Summit fellowship. I toyed with the idea of living the high life but common sense prevailed and I decided to delay my Royal Society award until the following year. During my first year at the NRC, I came to realize that I was more interested in applying science to practical problems and began looking at different opportunities within the NRC. My husband, who worked in the NRC's aerospace laboratory, suggested that I speak with the folks at the Canadian Police Research Centre (CPRC). When you knock on someone's door with a year's salary tied to you (my Royal Society fellowship), most people are happy to invite you in. During our discussions I asked the CPRC if they had any problems that a synthetic chemist could help with. I was introduced to Dr. John Watkin, who had developed the Luma-Lite and the Watkin CA vacuum chamber. John was looking at fluorescent dyes for cyanoacrylate-treated fingerprints and was a wonderful mentor who gave me many opportunities to provide input and engage with RCMP officers. Within a year we had

Continued

developed a potentially interesting fluorescent dye for fingerprints and I began to work more closely with members of the RCMP's Forensic Identification Research and Review Section (FIRRS). By this time I was hooked on forensic identification, and working with Dr. Brian Yamashita made work a lot of fun. Over the course of time, the RCMP created two research scientist positions within FIRRS and I was lucky enough to win a position. My career in forensics wasn't really planned but I love connecting scientific solutions to policing problems.

Q. What Is Your Role as a Forensic Scientist?

My career has encompassed research, technology transfer to practitioners, international and national standards development, provision of expert testimony to provincial supreme courts, and training and real-time client support with police officers—specifically, guidance and direction with respect to evidence collection at challenging crime scenes.

One example of the diverse research projects that I have played a part in over the years is the use of forensic stable isotope ratio mass spectrometry (FIRMS) as a means to link people together in time and place. Stable isotopes from food and water are sequentially and permanently incorporated into hair, and because water and food isotopes reflect their geographical source, a record of location and time are captured in our hair. I orchestrated the collection of hundreds of water, hair, and protein samples by RCMP members across Canada. The legacy of this research is a sustainable database maintained by the University of Ottawa's Ján Veizer Stable Isotope Laboratory. Police officers can submit samples from unidentified human remains for FIRMS analysis, some of which revealed that unidentified human remains were not from a member of the local community. To ensure that the results of RCMP research reach the end user, I employ a technology-transition model, where success from laboratory-based research is followed by field testing or validation studies situated in the operational environment in which the new method(s) must perform. An example is when chlorofluorocarbon (CFC) solvents were banned due to their impact on the environment. RCMP research contributed to the global development of non-CFC-based amino-acid reagents, used for the detection of latent fingerprints on porous surfaces such as paper. After demonstrating that the new formulations showed improved performance compared to the original CFC-based reagents, I coordinated a national field trial that observed performance of the new formulations in casework. This resulted in the RCMP adopting new environmentally friendly formulations. Travel is part of my work, resulting from presenting research at national and international conferences, participating in standards development work, or through training. Finally, on a rare occasion, I provide testimony in court.

Q. What Kind of Equipment Do You Use?

Our laboratory houses equipment that would be found in operational forensic identification units and includes humidity and vacuum chambers for treating non-porous exhibits with superglue, and humidity ovens for heating porous surfaces after treatment with chemicals that react with the sweat residue in fingerprints and forensic light sources. However, forensic research is multidisciplinary, so I have regularly found myself collaborating with scientists in other fields such as microbiologists, chemical weapons experts, DNA biologists, and chemists, where equipment ranges from DNA sequencers to mass spectrometers.

QUESTIONS TO PONDER

1. In your own words, write down your understanding of evidence-based practice.
2. Why do scientific explanations differ from common sense?
3. Define *knowledge* and *information*. How do they apply to forensic science?
4. Why is scientific research required in forensics?
5. How did the key scientific philosophers' work contribute to the process of reasoning?
6. What is the connection between scientific reasoning and forensic science?

GLOSSARY

abductive or retroductive reasoning: using a sample set of observations to come up with the most likely explanation for the set (your conclusion is a best guess) (Romesburg, 1981).

ACE-V: an acronym for analyze, compare, evaluate, and verify, which is a method for analyzing friction ridge impressions (NIJ, 2011).

Cartesian coordinate system: a system that assigns a pair of numerical coordinates in a plane to a point (Descartes, 1956).

deductive reasoning: "top-down" logic that works from the general to the specific (your conclusion is guaranteed) (Gauch, 2003).

directional analysis: pertaining to bloodstain patterns, a mathematical procedure developed by Dr. Fred Carter. It finds the directions in space (virtual strings) that point from the bloodstains to a spot directly above the location of the blood source (Carter, 2001).

domain knowledge: knowledge that is specific to a discipline or field of study.

drip pattern: a bloodstain pattern resulting from a liquid that dripped into another liquid; at least one of the liquids was blood (AAFS, 2017).

evidence-based practice: the integration of scientific research evidence, forensic science experience, and the available evidence from a scene (Carter, 2015).

hypothetico-deductive reasoning: the use of cyclical patterns of observation and reasoning (the scientific method) to test explanation (abstract thinking, testing of hypotheses) (Lawson, 2013).

impact pattern: a bloodstain pattern resulting from an object striking liquid blood (AAFS, 2017).

inductive reasoning: "bottom-up" logic that works from specific observations to generalizations or theories (your conclusion is likely) (Gauch, 2003).

Newton's Law of Gravity: the law that states that any two objects exert a gravitational force of attraction on each other (Newton, 1833).

physical match: the process of comparing the physical properties of two objects to see if they fit together (e.g., two torn pieces of tape).

positivism: the basic assertions of positivism are (1) that all knowledge regarding matters of fact is based on the "positive" data of experience and (2) beyond the realm of fact is that of pure logic and pure mathematics (Feigl, 2018).

projected pattern: a bloodstain pattern resulting from the ejection of a volume of blood under pressure (AAFS, 2017).

Reynold's number (Re): a dimensionless number ("a number representing a property of a physical system, but not measured on a scale of physical units" [Dictionary.com, 2018]) that is used in fluid dynamics to predict flow patterns. It is used in bloodstain pattern analysis research (Attinger et al., 2013).

trigonometry: the branch of mathematics dealing with the relations of the sides and angles of triangles and with the relevant functions of any angles (Oxford English Dictionary, 2018).

Weber number (We): a dimensionless number ("a number representing a property of a physical system, but not measured on a scale of physical units" [Dictionary.com, 2018]) that is used in analyzing fluid flows where there is an interface between two different fluids; it is used in bloodstain pattern analysis research (Attinger et al., 2013).

NOTE

1. Robert Thorton was a British, Canadian, and US physicist who worked on the Manhattan Project.

FURTHER READINGS

Copeland, K., & James, K. (2016). "My College Education Has Come from My Participation in the Forensics Team": An Examination of the Skills and Benefits of Collegiate Forensic Participation. *Speaker and Gavel, 53*(2), 3.

Crispino, F. (2008). Nature and Place of Crime Scene Management within Forensic Sciences. *Science and Justice, 48*, 24–28.

Crispino, F., Rossy, Q., Ribaux, O., & Roux, C. (2015). Education and Training in Forensic Intelligence: A New Challenge. *Australian Journal of Forensic Sciences, 47*(1), 49–60. doi:10.1080/00450618.2014.906655

Gauch, H. G. (2012). *Scientific Method in Brief.* Cambridge: Cambridge University Press.

Gower, B. (1997). *Scientific Method: An Historical and Philosophical Introduction.* London: Routledge.

Grivas, C. R., & Komar, D. A. (2008). Kumho, Daubert, and the Nature of Scientific Inquiry: Implications for Forensic Anthropology. *Journal of Forensic Sciences, 53*(4), 1–6.

Hilborn, R. A. Y., & Mangel, M. (1997). Alternative Views of the Scientific Method and of Modeling. In R. A. Y. Hilborn & M. Mangel (Eds.), *The Ecological Detective: Confronting Models with Data* (pp. 12–38). Princeton: Princeton University Press.

Langenburg, G., Champod, C., & Wertheim, P. (2009). Testing for Potential Contextual Bias Effects during the Verification Stage of the ACE-V Methodology When Conducting Fingerprint Comparisons. *Journal of Forensic Sciences, 54*(3), 571–582.

Moore, S. (2009). Science Found Wanting in Nation's Crime Labs. *New York Times*, February 4.

Musgrave, L. (1973). William of Ockham, 1280–1349. *History Today, 23*(9), 625–632.

Neumann, C. (2007). Computation of Likelihood Ratios in Fingerprint Identification for Configurations of Any Number of Minutiae. *Journal of Forensic Sciences, 52*(1), 54–64.

Nichols, R. (2007). Defending the Scientific Foundations of the Firearms and Tool Mark Identification Discipline: Responding to Recent Challenges. *Journal of Forensic Sciences, 52*(3), 586–594.

Noon, R. K. (2009). *Scientific Method: Application in Failure Investigation and Forensic Science.* Boca Raton: CRC Press.

Platt, J. R. (1964). Strong Inference. *Science, 146*(3642), 347–353.

R. v. Mohan. (1994). *Her Majesty the Queen versus Chikmaglur Mohan.* 2 SCR 9, No. 23063.

Saviano, J. (2006). The Pursuit of Objectivity in the Examination of Forensic Science. *Journal of Forensic Identification, 56*(6), 877–884.

United Nations. (2009). Crime Scene and Physical Evidence Awareness for Non-Forensic Personnel. New York: United Nations Office on Drugs and Crime. https://www.unodc.org/documents/scientific/Crime_scene_awareness__Ebook.pdf

REFERENCES

AAFS. (2017). Terms and Definitions in Bloodstain Pattern Analysis. American Academy of Forensic Sciences. Retrieved from https://www .aafs.org/about-aafs/

Andersen, H., & Hepburn, B. (2016). Scientific Method. In E. N. Zalta (Ed.), *Stanford Encyclopedia of Philosophy*. Retrieved from https://plato .stanford.edu/entries/scientific-method/

AsapSCIENCE. (2019). Brain Tricks—This Is How Your Brain Works. Retrieved from https://www.youtube.com/watch?v=JiTz2i4VHFw

Attinger, D., Moore, C., Donaldson, A., Jafari, A., & Stone, H. A. (2013). Fluid Dynamics Topics in Bloodstain Pattern Analysis: Comparative Review and Research Opportunities. *Forensic Science International*, *231*(1–3), 375–396.

Bordens, K. S., & Abbott, B. B. (2011). *Research Design and Methods: A Process Approach*. New York: McGraw-Hill.

Carter, A. L. (2001). The Directional Analysis of Bloodstain Patterns: Theory and Experimental Validation. *Canadian Society of Forensic Science Journal*, *34*(4), 173–189. doi:10.1080/00085030.2001.10757527

Carter, K. (2015). Evidence-Based Medicine. *Townsend Letter*, February–March.

Champod, C., Lennard, C., Margot, P., & Stoilovic, M. (2004). *Fingerprints and Other Ridge Skin Impressions*. Boca Raton: CRC Press.

Crispino, F., Ribaux, O., Houck, M., & Margot, P. (2011). Forensic Science—A True Science? *Australian Journal of Forensic Sciences*, *43*(2–3), 157–176. doi:10.1080/00450618.2011.555416

Descartes, R. (1956). *Discourse on Method* (2nd ed.). New York: Liberal Arts Press, Inc.

Dictionary.com. (2018). Dimensionless Number. Retrieved from https:// www.dictionary.com/browse/dimensionless-number

Doak, S., & Assimakopoulos, D. (2007). How Do Forensic Scientists Learn to Become Competent in Casework Reporting in Practice: A Theoretical and Empirical Approach. *Forensic Science International*, *167*(2–3), 201–206. doi:http://dx.doi.org/10.1016/j.forsciint.2006.06.063

Doyle, A. C. (1903). *A Study in Scarlet / The Sign of Four.* London: Smith, Elder & Company.

Dupras, T. L., Schultz, J. J., Wheeler, S. M., & Williams, L. J. (2006). *Forensic Recovery of Human Remains: Archaeological Approaches.* Boca Raton: CRC Press.

Edmond, G., Thompson, M. B., & Tangen, J. M. (2013). A Guide to Interpreting Forensic Testimony: Scientific Approaches to Fingerprint Evidence. *Law, Probability and Risk, 13*(1), 1–25. doi:10.1093/lpr/mgt011

Evans, E. M. (2018). Bridging the Gap: From Intuitive to Scientific Reasoning: The Case of Evolution. In K. Rutten, S. Blanke, & R. Soetaert (Eds.), *Perspectives on Science and Culture* (pp. 131–148). West Lafayette: Purdue University Press.

Evans, J. S. B. (2010). *Thinking Twice: Two Minds in One Brain.* Oxford: Oxford University Press.

Feigl, H. (2018). Encyclopaedia Britannica: Positivism. Retrieved from https://www.britannica.com/topic/positivism

Found, B., & Edmond, G. (2012). Reporting on the Comparison and Interpretation of Pattern Evidence: Recommendations for Forensic Specialists. *Australian Journal of Forensic Sciences, 44*(2), 193–196.

Gauch, H. G. (2003). *Scientific Method in Practice.* New York: Cambridge University Press.

Gauch, H. G. (2012). *Scientific Method in Brief.* New York: Cambridge University Press.

Geikie, A. (1962). *The Founders of Geology.* New York: Dover Publications, Inc.

Goudge, S. T. (2008). *Inquiry into Pediatric Forensic Pathology in Ontario.* Toronto: Ministry of the Attorney General.

Gower, B. (1997). *Scientific Method: An Historical and Philosophical Introduction.* London: Routledge.

Greenhalgh, T. (2014). *How to Read a Paper: The Basics of Evidence-Based Medicine.* Hoboken: John Wiley & Sons.

Hempel, C. G. (1967). *Philosophy of Natural Science.* Upper Saddle River: Prentice Hall.

Hilborn, R. A. Y., & Mangel, M. (1997). Alternative Views of the Scientific Method and of Modeling. In R. A. Y. Hilborn & M. Mangel (Eds.),

The Ecological Detective: Confronting Models with Data (pp. 12–38). Princeton: Princeton University Press.

Illes, M., & Boué, M. (2011). Investigation of a Model for Stain Selection in Bloodstain Pattern Analysis. *Canadian Society of Forensic Science,* *44*(1), 1–12.

Inman, K., & Rudin, N. (2001). *Principles and Practice of Criminalistics: The Profession of Forensic Science.* Boca Raton: CRC Press.

Inman, K., & Rudin, N. (2002). The Origin of Evidence. *Forensic Science International, 126*(1), 11–16.

Karson, M., & Nadkarni, L. (2013). *Principles of Forensic Report Writing.* Washington: American Psychological Association.

Kirk, P. L. (1963). The Ontogeny of Criminalistics. *Journal of Criminal Law, Criminology & Police Science, 54*, 235.

Koehler, J. J. (2018). How Trial Judges Should Think about Forensic Science Evidence. *Judicature, 102*, 28–38.

Kozarovich, L. (2006). Expert Credibility Could Decide Camm Case. *News and Tribune,* February 17. Retrieved from https://www.newsandtribune .com/news/local_news/expert-credibility-could-decide-camm-case/ article_d3073fd5-5a19-5091-9b96-b6005698078e.html

Kuhn, T. S. (1962). The Structure of Scientific Revolutions. In O. Neurath (Ed.), *International Encyclopedia of Unified Science* (FUS II–2). Chicago: University of Chicago Press.

Langenburg, G. (2011). Scientific Research Supporting the Foundations of Friction Ridge Examinations. In *The Fingerprint Sourcebook* (pp. 1–27). Washington: National Institute of Justice. Retrieved from http://www .nij.gov/pubs-sum/225320.htm

Langenburg, G. (2012). A Critical Analysis and Study of the ACE-V Process (Doctoral dissertation). University of Lausanne.

Laudan, L. (1968). Theories of Scientific Method from Plato to Mach. *History of Science, 7*(1), 1–63. doi:10.1177/007327536800700101

Lawson, A. E. (2013). Hypothetico-Deductive Method. In R. Gunstone (Ed.), *Encyclopedia of Science Education.* Dordrecht: Springer. doi:10.1007/978-94-007-6165-0_260-1

Leake, L. J. (2007). A Guide to Producing an Evidence-Based Report. University of Toronto.

Locard, E. (1934). *La police et les méthodes scientifiques.* Paris: Presses
    universitaires de France.

Lohr, J., Gist, R., Deacon, B. J., Devilly, G., & Varker, T. (2015). Science
    and Non-Science Based Treatments for Trauma Related Stress
    Disorders. In S. O. Lilienfeld, S. J. Lynn, & J. M. Lohr (Eds.), *Science
    and Pseudoscience in Clinical Psychology* (pp. 277–321). New York:
    Guilford Press.

Mahner, M. (2007). Demarcating Science from Non-Science. In D. Gabbay,
    P. Thagard, & J. Woods (Eds.), *General Philosophy of Science: Focal Issues*
    (pp. 515–575). New York: Elsevier.

Mnookin, J. L. (2010). The Courts, The NAS, and the Future. *Brooklyn Law
    Review, 75*(4), 1–67.

Moore, J. C., & Rubbo, L. J. (2012). Scientific Reasoning Abilities
    of Nonscience Majors in Physics-Based Courses. *Physical Review
    Special Topics—Physics Education Research, 8*(1). doi:10.1103/
    PhysRevSTPER.8.010106

Musgrave, L. (1973). William of Ockham, 1280–1349. *History Today, 23*(9),
    625–632.

NAS. (2009). *Strengthening Forensic Science in the United States: A Path
    Forward* (T. N. A. Press Ed.). Washington: National Academy of
    Sciences.

National Institute of Standards and Technology. (2018). OSAC: Bloodstain
    Pattern Analysis Subcommittee. Retrieved from https://www.nist.gov/
    topics/forensic-science/bloodstain-pattern-analysis-subcommittee

Newton, I. (1833). *Philosophiae Naturalis Principia Mathematica* (Vol. 1).
    London: G. Brookman.

NIJ. (2011). *The Fingerprint Sourcebook.* Washington: National Institute of
    Justice. Retrieved from http://www.nij.gov/pubs-sum/225320.htm

Noon, R. K. (2009). *Scientific Method: Application in Failure Investigation and
    Forensic Science.* Boca Raton: CRC Press.

Oster, M. (1993). Biography, Culture, and Science: The Formative Years of
    Robert Boyle. *History of Science, 31*(2), 195.

Oxford English Dictionary. (2018). Scientific Method / Theory /
    Trigonometry. Retrieved from https://en.oxforddictionaries.com/

Pacheco, I., Cerchiai, B., & Stoiloff, S. (2014). *Miami-Dade Research Study for the Reliability of the ACE-V Process: Accuracy & Precision in Latent Fingerprint Examinations.* Unpublished report.

Popper, K. (1959). *The Logic of Scientific Discovery.* New York: Routledge.

Romesburg, H. C. (1981). Wildlife Science: Gaining Reliable Knowledge. *Journal of Wildlife Management, 45*(2), 293–313.

Rowe, W. F. (2006). Errors in the Determination of the Point of Origin of Bloodstains. *Forensic Science International, 161*(1), 47–51.

R. v. Bornyk. (2015). *Regina versus Timothy Dale Bornyk.* BCCA 28, CA 041377.

R. v. Bornyk. (2017). *Regina versus Timothy Dale Bornyk.* BCSC 849, X0-76411.

R. v. Millard. (2018). *Regina versus Dellen Millard,* ONSC 4410, CR-16-50000176-0000

R. v. Natsis. (2018). *Her Majesty the Queen v. Christy Natsis.* ONCA 425, C61328.

Sackett, D. L. (1997). Evidence-Based Medicine. *Seminars in Perinatology, 21*(1), 3–5. doi: https://doi.org/10.1016/S0146-0005(97)80013-4

Sangra, B., Roach, K., & Moles, R. (2010). *Forensic Investigations and Miscarriages of Justice: The Rhetoric Meets the Reality.* Toronto: Irwin Law.

Shaler, R. C. (2012). *Crime Scene Forensics: A Scientific Method Approach.* Boca Raton: CRC Press.

Sjerps, M. J., & Berger, C. E. H. (2012). How Clear Is Transparent? Reporting Expert Reasoning in Legal Cases. *Law, Probability and Risk, 11*(4), 317–329. doi:10.1093/lpr/mgs017

Snyder, L. J. (2011). *The Philosophical Breakfast Club.* New York: Random House.

Spier, R. (2002). The History of the Peer-Review Process. *Trends in Biotechnology, 20*(8), 357–358.

Taber, K. (2009). *Progressing Science Education: Constructing the Scientific Research Programme into the Contingent Nature of Learning Science.* Dordrecht: Springer.

Taton, R. (1964). *History of Science: The Beginning of Modern Science.* New York: Basic Books.

Taylor, S., Dutton, E., Aldrich, P., & Dutton, B. (2012). *Application of Spatial Statistics to Latent Print Identifications: Towards Improving Forensic Science Methodologies*. Washington: Department of Justice.

Tierney, L. (2013). Analysis, Comparison, Evaluation, and Verification (ACE-V). In P. J. Saukko & M. M. Houck (Eds.), *Encyclopedia of Forensic Sciences* (pp. 69–73). Waltham: Academic Press.

Triplett, M., & Cooney, L. (2006). The Etiology of ACE-V and Its Proper Use: An Exploration of the Relationship between ACE-V and the Scientific Method of Hypothesis Testing. *Journal of Forensic Identification, 56*(3), 345–355.

Wells, J. K. (2006). Investigation of Factors Affecting the Region of Origin Estimate in Bloodstain Pattern Analysis (Master's thesis). Christchurch: University of Canterbury.

Wertheim, P. A. (2000). Scientific Comparison and Identification of Fingerprint Evidence. *The Print, 16*(5).

Williams, A. (2015). *Forensic Criminology*. London: Routledge.

Yamashita, B. (2010). *Statistics, the Scientific Method and Forensic Identification*. Ottawa: Royal Canadian Mounted Police.

Young, T. W. (2018). *The Sherlock Effect: How Forensic Doctors and Investigators Disastrously Reason Like the Great Detective*. Boca Raton: CRC Press.

CHAPTER 3

Critical Thinking in Forensic Science

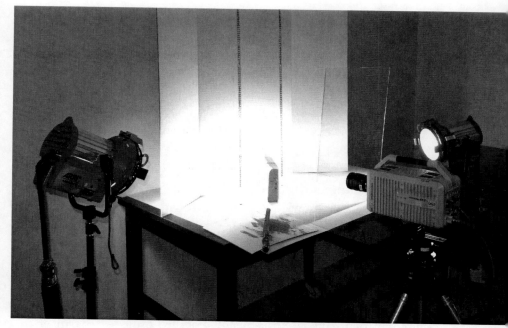

High-Speed Videography Set-Up for Researching Blood in Flight
Photo credit: Mike Illes

Critical thinking is a desire to seek, patience to doubt, fondness to meditate, slowness to assert, readiness to consider, carefulness to dispose and set in order; and hatred for every kind of imposture.
—*Francis Bacon (1605)*

The development of evidence-based practice, reasoning skills, critical thinking, reading skills, and problem-solving skills are interrelated. We will explore the research that defines and supports critical thinking, including notions of rationality, honesty, open-mindedness, discipline, judgment, and how these factors are integral to forensic investigations. There are four general reasons for learning and using critical thought, according to Hughes and Lavery (2015):

- We are flooded with information in our media-rich society. A simple Internet search on a given topic provides a plethora of data that may or may not be trustworthy.
- We are constantly bombarded by arguments designed to change our minds.
- Critical thinking builds intellectual self-respect.
- Thinking critically makes it easier to persuade others.

Problem solving is closely connected to critical thinking and integrates respecting and incorporating multiple perspectives in questioning one's beliefs and knowledge. Problem solving includes making sound arguments through planning, using domain knowledge, and scrutinizing solutions (Choi & Lee, 2008).

Forensic science as a discipline is predicted to be applied very differently over the coming decades versus its historical and current approach. Robertson and Roux (2018) have summarized this evolution in their article "The Forensic Scientist of the Future—Are Universities Prepared?" In the article, they challenge universities that teach forensic science to look toward the future using terms like *trans-disciplinary expertise* and ***forensic intelligence***. The authors suggest that technological advances will change forensic science such that most forensic scientists will shift from being specialists to generalists, with a relatively lower number of specialists working in an office environment analyzing **big data**. Whether the forensic scientist is a specialist in one field of study or a generalist, there will always be a requirement for key skills. Critical thought and problem solving are part of these essential skill sets.

CRITICAL THINKING

We start this chapter with a case study. This scenario is meant to make you think critically about the case and how to problem solve the issues presented. This is a "reverse chapter" process that will explore a scenario before discussing the research and methods behind critical thought and problem solving. Domain knowledge will be supplied to you to consider when thinking about the questions presented. This demonstrates the multidisciplinary nature of forensic science and the need for general and domain knowledge in the various fields of study.

Exercise 3.1: Critical Thinking as a Forensic Biologist

There were a homicide and an attempted murder at a residence in a small village just west of North Bay, Ontario. An ex-boyfriend attended a woman's home on New Year's Eve with a loaded **shotgun**. The woman was in her living room with her current boyfriend when the shooter entered the home. He shot the woman in the shoulder and the boyfriend in his leg. They were both mobile but bleeding. The injured boyfriend ran out of the house by the front door and the woman ran out the back door. The shooter followed the woman, taking a second shot, which grazed the right side of her head, as she exited the door. The pursuit continued, and the woman attempted to hide under the front porch of the residence. The shooter found her and killed her with a fatal shot to the head. The shooter re-entered the residence and proceeded to cut his wrist while walking throughout the house. The North Bay Police attended the scene, taking the shooter into custody and providing hospital treatment.

The Ontario Provincial Police (OPP) Forensic Identification Unit processed the scene for the North Bay Police and called a BPA expert to examine and interpret the bloodstain evidence. The BPA expert found 75 bloodstain patterns and collected 150 blood samples to be analyzed by the Centre of Forensic Sciences (CFS).

In this scenario you are employed as a forensic biologist within the biology section of the CFS. The BPA expert has contacted you about the submission of the 150+ blood samples (including samples from the victim, survivor, and accused) to your unit for DNA analysis. Consider the following questions.

Can You Identify the Problem?

This first question may be difficult for someone who hasn't worked within the forensic community in Canada. If you work or have worked in the field or in a laboratory and have had experience in processing samples, the issue may be obvious—people like forensic biologists working for the CFS or forensic identification officers/BPA experts would possess the domain knowledge required to identify a problem in this evidence submission scenario.

The first piece of information required is knowing what a CFS forensic biologist does. They complete body fluid identification (blood, semen, saliva) and DNA profiling in cases involving crimes against persons and property, such as break and enters, sexual assaults, and homicides. In this case scenario, the BPA expert is contacting the laboratory to complete blood identification on the samples they collected from the homicide scene. The scene clearly falls within the mandate of the CFS biology section—but the problem is the size of the sample set to be examined. The reason for the problem comes down to resources and practicality. There are a limited number of employees to complete the submissions (11,573 cases received in 2008/09) (MCSCS, 2007) and limited budgets for DNA extraction; it is also not likely that all the samples need analysis.

Why Is This Important?

It is obvious that the case is important from a social justice perspective, and a homicide falls under the mandate of the CFS. What needs to be teased out is which samples are important to help with the scientific analysis. Case-specific knowledge and domain knowledge are required to ascertain which samples are logically most important. The BPA expert and biologist review all samples, finding that 100 of the samples are repeats taken as backup samples. These samples are stored just in case there are issues such as contaminants, a **low copy number** (an insufficient amount of DNA), or **mixed DNA** within the first samples tested. Therefore, from the initial 150 blood samples, we can cut our sample set to 50. Upon further review, combining scene information on the bloodstain pattern type, another 15 samples can be eliminated. Being able to recognize bloodstain patterns offers knowledge and additional information that aids in making defendable, robust decisions, such as making assumptions on the owner of a blood sample based on a blood pool where the victims had been located. The remaining bloodstain patterns are reviewed in the context of the scene. The biologist and BPA expert agree on 15 samples in addition to one sample from the victim, the accused, and the deceased, each for comparison purposes.

Further critical thought questions to consider:

- How do you know this is the right decision?
- What crucial information or perspective are you missing?
- What else should you consider?
- Can you explain your decision to the police, your supervisor, or the lawyers involved?
- What evidence supports your decision?
- What might happen if you miss a sample?
- How will these decisions affect the client or case result?
- How will you re-evaluate the process upon completion of your casework?

Write out your answers to each question and discuss with a fellow student, an instructor, or a practitioner.

The questions examined in the previous exercise are the type that a person using critical thinking in forensic science may ask themselves. This exercise aimed to make you think about the key components of critical thought: recognizing the problem (interpretation), analyzing alternatives or perspectives, synthesizing the information (evaluation), exploring assumptions (inferences), taking action, and re-evaluating (University of Lethbridge, 2018). Critical thinking is "purposeful, self-regulatory judgment that drives problem-solving and decision-making" (Quitadamo et al., 2008).

Critical thinking skills are developed over time and are improved through post-secondary education (Halpern, 2013; University of Lethbridge, 2018); moreover, critical thinkers are active, can solve problems well, and possess logical frameworks to process information (Choi & Lee, 2008; Goertel, 2018; Golding, 2011; SFU, 2017). Research on reasoning skills used by CSIs has indicated that higher education, specifically at the graduate level, enhances reasoning skills, which relates directly to critical thinking (Halpern, 2013; Dwyer et al., 2015).

Dan Kurland's (2010) website, www.criticalreading.com, provides another view of what it may take to be a critical thinker. He reviews topics such as rationality, self-awareness, honesty, open-mindedness, discipline, and judgment, and then summarizes who is a critical thinker.

Who Is a Critical Thinker?

Rationality
We are thinking critically when we rely on reason rather than emotion; require evidence, ignore no known evidence, follow evidence where it leads; and are concerned more with finding the best explanation than being right, analyzing apparent confusion and asking questions.

Self-Awareness
We are thinking critically when we weigh the influences of motives and bias and recognize our own assumptions, prejudices, biases, or point of view.

Honesty
We are thinking critically when we recognize emotional impulses, selfish motives, nefarious purposes, or other modes of self-deception.

Open-Mindedness
We are thinking critically when we evaluate all reasonable inferences; consider a variety of possible viewpoints or perspectives; remain open to alternative interpretations; accept a new explanation, model, or paradigm because it explains the evidence better, is simpler, or has

fewer inconsistencies or covers more data; accept new priorities in response to a reevaluation of the evidence or reassessment of our real interests; and do not reject unpopular views out of hand.

Discipline

We are thinking critically when we are precise, meticulous, comprehensive, and exhaustive; resist manipulation and irrational appeals; and avoid snap judgments.

Judgment

We are thinking critically when we recognize the relevance and/or merit of alternative assumptions and perspectives and recognize the extent and weight of evidence.

In Sum,

- Critical thinkers are by nature skeptical. They approach texts with the same skepticism and suspicion as they approach spoken remarks.
- Critical thinkers are active, not passive. They ask questions and analyze. They consciously apply tactics and strategies to uncover meaning or assure their understanding.
- Critical thinkers do not take an egotistical view of the world. They are open to new ideas and perspectives. They are willing to challenge their beliefs and investigate competing evidence.

Critical thinking enables us to recognize a wide range of subjective analyses of otherwise objective data and to evaluate how well each analysis might meet our needs. Facts may be facts, but how we interpret them may vary.

Who Is Not a Critical Thinker?

By contrast, passive, non-critical thinkers take a simplistic view of the world.

- They see things in black and white, as either-or, rather than recognizing a variety of possible understandings.
- They see questions as "yes" or "no," with no subtleties.
- They fail to see linkages and complexities.
- They fail to recognize related elements.

Non-critical thinkers take an egotistical view of the world.

- They take *their* facts as the only relevant ones.
- They take *their* own perspective as the only sensible one.
- They take *their* goal as the only valid one.

Can you think of someone you know who isn't a critical thinker according to these principles?

Considering Critical Thinking at the Crime Scene

This section explores the Canadian forensic identification officer system. Crime scene work is governed by institutional protocols, instructions, worksheets, operating procedures, and police orders. For the purpose of this chapter, they are referred to as standard operating procedures (SOPs). These SOPs are written instructions that explain routine tasks or repetitive activities completed by that agency. SOPs, when followed, allow for the following:

- minimized variation and promotion of quality through consistent procedural implementation
- compliance with organizational and governmental requirements
- they are useful as a part of a personnel training program
- minimization of miscommunication and prompt handling of safety concerns
- valuable input for reconstructing project activities when no other references are available
- they are useful as checklists by inspectors when auditing procedures
- a reduction in work effort

- improved comparability, credibility, and legal defensibility (EPA, 2007)

The use of SOPs can create a highly structured environment that reduces deviation from a specific process or task. Do you think that crime scene work can become task-oriented by following procedures with little exercise in critical thought or problem solving?

In policing, where most Canadian crime scene work is completed, this issue of only following SOPs can be worsened by a highly structured paramilitary culture. The nature of the work also provides an environment that may support the development of an array of biases. Standard police tactics are sometimes based on a sixth sense or feeling, and after some time, officers become very good at reading potentially troublesome situations. However, these circumstances may also be measured by prior situational biases (Charman et al., 2017; Edmond et al., 2017; Granér & Kronkvist, 2015; Lum & Isaac, 2016; Whitman & Koppl, 2010). Historically, police forensic identification officers in Canada were hired as police officers, worked on the road, developed an interest in forensics, and were then hired for that specialty. The officers may or may not have a science background, but due to hiring practices they became forensic scene examiners. The combination of police culture and these officers' lack of scientific training presents an opportunity to consider alternative approaches. In recent years, several progressive police services have recognized that the hiring system of forensic scene examiners could be improved and have begun to hire forensic science graduates as identification technicians/assistants within their forensic identification units.

Conversely, in forensic identification, whether civilian or police, experience and SOPs are relied upon to get through negative experiences. Henry (2004) explains some of the reasoning behind the way that forensic investigators function in his research in the crime scene unit (CSU) within the New York Police Department. He suggests that the reason forensic investigators are capable of coping with extremely disturbing, violent, and grotesque scenes is because the work environment is structured in a highly organized way that narrowly defines duties and delegates specific tasks to certain individuals; this, along with learned psychomotor skills (taking thousands of photographs), helps restore order upon attendance. This structured environment (following SOPs) is essential for making it through a horrific scene that extends over days or weeks of work. Further, the objective application of the scientific method can provide a process to help offset the stress induced by a violent crime scene. However, we should always be conscious that a highly structured work setting may not lend itself to critical thought. Therefore, someone trained post-secondarily in forensic science and the use of the scientific method will be better equipped to handle these issues in highly structured organizations and to think critically once experience is gained.

PROBLEM SOLVING

The formulation of the problem is often more essential than its solution, which may be merely a matter of mathematical or experimental skill.
—*Albert Einstein (Boyer, Einstein, & Infeld, 1938)*

Problem Types

There are two basic types of problems: well-structured and ill-structured problems. Well-structured problems are simple to solve, and there are known rules and clear goals. The main skill sets that are required to solve well-structured problems are justification skills and domain knowledge. On the other hand, ill-structured problems are more complex, with many uncertainties that may include multiple and conflicting problem contexts, perspectives among different stakeholders, diverse solutions or no solution, and multiple criteria for solution assessment (Choi & Lee, 2008; Shin, 2003).

These are the problems that forensic practitioners face each day in their work. Table 3.1 provides the essential skills or factors that influence the general performance of solving ill-structured problems. The table also compares the skills required for critical thought and how they match with ill-structured problem-solving skills. Following this, we present an experiential exercise (3.2) using the multiple skills that have been discussed thus far, including the use of hypothesis testing from chapter 2.

Table 3.1. A Comparison of Critical Thinking and Problem-Solving Skills

Critical Thinking Skills	Problem-Solving Skills or Factors
1. Skills and abilities involved in knowing how (or being able) to evaluate or analyze (Facione, 1990; Siegel, 1988)	1. Epistemological beliefs—respecting and incorporating multiple perspectives and questioning one's beliefs and knowledge (Harrington et al., 1996; Perry, 1968 [1999]; Schraw et al., 1995)
2. Disposition and the tendency or preparedness to engage in critical thinking, such as being reasonable or analytical (Ennis, 1987; Perkins, Jay, & Tishman, 1993; Siegel, 1988)	2. Metacognition—planning and monitoring solutions and processes (Brown et al., 1983; Shin et al., 2003)
3. A sophisticated epistemic understanding involving the insight that critical thinking is about constructing and evaluating reasoned judgments, not about finding the one right answer or just swapping opinions (Kuhn, 1999; Perry, 1970)	3. Justification/argumentation skills—reconciling conflicting interpretations and solutions with sound arguments (Cho & Jonassen, 2002; Jonassen, 1997; Shin et al., 2003; Voss et al., 1991)
4. To employ and fulfil criteria for what counts as successful critical thinking (Bailin et al., 1999a, 1999b)	
5. An understanding of the subject matter under contemplation (McPeck, 1981)	4. Domain knowledge (Bransford 1993; Chi et al., 1988; Shin et al., 2003)

Source: Choi & Lee, 2008; Golding, 2011

Exercise 3.2: Case Study in Forensic Leadership

This exercise is more complex, as we would like you to synergize your knowledge of how to test hypotheses (the scientific method) with critical thinking and problem-solving skills. The scientific method provides a systematic approach to solving everyday problems, and we can develop and test situational hypotheses to help us work through these problems. Because the scientific method is cyclical, we can continue to test several hypotheses until a solution is found to answer the problem.

Imagine you are a police officer leading a group of specialty forensic units in a larger metropolitan police department. The units have developed

organizational silos and do not communicate very well. The members work well within their given teams but not so well with the other small teams. The possible answers to each question are supplied in the appendix. Remember, problem solving can have multiple solutions or no solution.

> Question 1: Define the problem(s) in this case.
> Question 2: How would you solve the problem(s)?
> Question 3: What are the possible solutions that could help with the problem(s)?

Like a research experiment, test each situational hypothesis one at a time. The introduction of multiple solutions to the problem at one time can confuse employees. More importantly, it will be difficult to ascertain the solution that helped with the problem. Therefore, implement one idea at a time and review the outcome(s) (test the hypothesis).

SUMMARY

Research supports the concept that the development of critical thought and problem-solving skills takes time and can be acquired in the post-secondary environment. By supplying knowledge on these skill sets, this chapter can be considered a jump-start to their development. We have reviewed who is a critical thinker and who is not, along with the key components of critical thought: recognizing the problem (interpretation), analyzing alternatives or perspectives, synthesizing the information (evaluation), exploring assumptions (inferences), acting, and re-evaluating.

After defining critical thinking and problem-solving, we looked closely at how the skill sets used to solve ill-structured problems relate to those of a critical thinker. Two forensic case scenario exercises were presented to generate thought on the type of questions a critical thinker may ask and how to integrate the use of the scientific method with critical thought and problem-solving skills. Our discussion of critical thought at the crime scene reflects the importance of scientific training for this discipline.

Shari Forbes

Personal Profile

Shari Forbes is a professor and holds a Canada 150 Research Chair in forensic thanatology at the Université du Québec à Trois-Rivières. She was formerly an Australian Research Council future fellow in the Centre for Forensic Science at the University of Technology Sydney (UTS) in Australia. She was the founding director of the Australian Facility for Taphonomic Experimental Research (AFTER), the first "body farm" to open in Australia and the southern hemisphere. Professor Forbes's research focuses on chemically profiling the odour of forensic evidence using comprehensive two-dimensional gas chromatography. Her research aims to enhance the training of scent-detection canines used for safety and security purposes. She has more than 80 publications in this field and has been awarded C$6.5 million in competitive research funding. She has supervised more than 60 graduate students and early-career researchers in forensic science. Her expertise is regularly requested to assist police with locating and recovering buried or concealed evidence, including human remains, drugs, weapons, and currency. Professor Forbes completed a bachelor of science (honours) in applied chemistry and forensic science and a PhD (forensic chemistry) at UTS. She was the founding director of the Forensic Science program at the University of Ontario Institute of Technology (now known as the Ontario Tech University) and held that post from 2005 to 2012 while also holding a Canada Research Chair in decomposition chemistry.

Photo credit: Anna Zhu

Q. How Did You Get Into Forensic Science?

I really enjoyed science during school and enjoyed reading crime novels in my spare time. When it came time to choose a university degree,

Continued

I decided to combine both passions and choose a career that allowed me to apply science to real-world problems. Forensic science was an obvious choice because it was clear to me how this career could benefit society. I studied my undergraduate forensic science degree from 1996 to 1999, prior to *CSI*, *Bones*, and all the other TV shows that made forensic science popular. At the time, very few people understood what forensic scientists did and most people assumed I would be a forensic pathologist. My degree was an applied chemistry and forensic science degree, which meant I focused on the chemical analysis of trace evidence. In our final year, we had to choose an honour's research project and I decided to choose a project that investigated why bodies in a cemetery in Sydney, Australia, were not decomposing as they should. It was a fascinating problem that employed chemistry, geology, and taphonomy, and it was the reason I decided to continue with doctoral studies in this field. My doctoral research focused on understanding the decomposition and preservation effects that can occur in forensic burials, with a particular focus on adipocere formation. Following many years of research and with a desire to stay in this field, I naturally transitioned into academia so that I could teach and conduct research in forensic chemistry and taphonomy. I have been an academic at universities in Australia, the US, and Canada since 2005.

Q. What Is Your Role as a Forensic Scientist?

My main role is to be the director of a "body farm," a colloquial term used to describe human taphonomy facilities. These facilities allow forensic scientists, police, and other law enforcement to better understand the process of human decomposition in their local environment. We conduct research, teaching, and training to investigate the physical, chemical, and biological processes of decomposition. Much of our work is aimed at recreating scenarios commonly encountered in death investigations. This can include missing persons, victims of homicide, victims of mass disasters, as well as human rights atrocities. Through my research, I am trying to understand the way that dogs locate different types of forensic evidence (such as drugs, explosives, and human remains). I have the opportunity to train with detection dogs and their handlers and use this knowledge to enhance their success when deployed operationally. I also teach forensic science to undergraduate and graduate students, and I encourage them to pursue research in forensic taphonomy as it is still considered a relatively new field and there is a lot of research that we need to do to better assist police with death investigations.

Q. What Kind of Equipment Do You Use?

My area of expertise is a little unusual in that I conduct both fieldwork and laboratory work. My fieldwork involves environmental air sampling, which uses sorbent tubes to trap the odour for subsequent analysis in the laboratory. The sorbent tubes are thermally desorbed into a gas chromatograph–mass spectrometer (GC–MS) to separate and identify the hundreds of compounds that comprise an odour. I also use solid phase microextraction (SPME) to collect the volatile compounds of smaller samples such as illicit drugs and explosives. SPME can also be thermally desorbed into GC–MS. When I am working operationally rather than for research, I am using the detector dogs as my screening tool because they can search large areas quickly. We are often looking for human remains that have been intentionally concealed so once a suspect area is identified, we might use ground penetrating radar to further investigate a potential burial or look at vegetative and soil indicators. Hence, the equipment I use is very diverse.

QUESTIONS TO PONDER

1. What are the four general reasons for learning and using critical thought?
2. Why is critical thought important in forensic science?
3. How do critical thought and problem-solving skill sets connect?
4. Define critical thought.
5. Define an ill-structured problem. Why is it relevant to forensic practitioners' work?

6. When problem solving the issue in exercise 3.2 in this chapter, why would you implement one idea/solution at a time?

GLOSSARY

big data: a large volume of data that can come in different forms, such as structured or unstructured (Song et al., 2016).

forensic intelligence: the relating of forensic evidence with other intelligence information to assist with the proactive recognition of criminal activity (Raymond & Julian, 2015).

low copy number: this type of DNA profiling is a technique sensitive enough to analyze just a few cells (less than 100 picograms [pg] of DNA or the equivalent of the DNA contained in 15 to 17 diploid cells) (Gill, 2001). This concept of use was developed at the Forensic Science Service (FFS) UK.

mixed DNA: a DNA sample profile result indicating more than one individual (National Human Genome Research Institute, 2018).

organizational silo: a group within an organization more loyal to the group than to the employer, resulting in a lack of trust, poor or no information sharing, and no interaction among working groups (Serrat, 2017).

shotgun: a long gun that uses shot shells to discharge multiple pellets or a solid projectile (slug) at the same time from its barrel.

FURTHER READINGS

Dwyer, C. (2017). Domain Generality vs. Specificity. *Psychology Today*, November 27.

Dwyer, C. P., Boswell, A., & Elliott, M. A. (2015). An Evaluation of Critical Thinking Competencies in Business Settings. *Journal of Education for Business*, *90*(5), 260–269.

Dwyer, C. P., Hogan, M. J., & Stewart, I. (2014). An Integrated Critical Thinking Framework for the 21st Century. *Thinking Skills and Creativity*, *12*, 43–52.

Fakayode, S. O., Mayes, J. P., Kanipes, M. I., Johnson, D., & Cuthbertson, E. L. (2017). Promoting Student Learning in Criminal Justice, STEM, and Forensic Science: Aggie Sleuth Initiative (AggieSI)-Guided Inquiry Learning Experience. *Journal of Criminal Justice Education, 28*(2), 192–206.

Greiff, S., Wüstenberg, S., Csapó, B., Demetriou, A., Hautamäki, J., Graesser, A. C., & Martin, R. (2014). Domain-General Problem-Solving Skills and Education in the 21st Century. *Educational Research Review, 13*, 74–83.

Hall, S. (2017). Practise Makes Perfect: Developing Critical Thinking and Writing Skills in Undergraduate Students. Paper presented at the Proceedings of the 3rd International Conference on Higher Education Advances.

Hayes, D. (2014). Let's Stop Trying to Teach Students Critical Thinking. The Conversation, August 8. Retrieved from http://theconversation.com/lets-stop-trying-to-teach-students-critical-thinking-30321

Moore, T. J. (2011). Critical Thinking and Disciplinary Thinking, A Continuing Debate. *Higher Education Research and Development, 30*(3), 261–274. doi:10.1080/07294360.2010.501328

Nargundkar, S., Samaddar, S., & Mukhopadhyay, S. (2014). A Guided Problem-Based Learning (PBL) Approach: Impact on Critical Thinking. *Decision Sciences Journal of Innovative Education, 12*(2), 91–108. doi:10.1111/dsji.12030

Stephenson, N., & Sadler-McKnight, N. (2016). Developing Critical Thinking Skills Using the Science Writing Heuristic in the Chemistry Laboratory. *Chemistry Education Research and Practice, 17*(1), 72–79.

Wass, R., Harland, T., & Mercer, A. (2011). Scaffolding Critical Thinking in the Zone of Proximal Development. *Higher Education Research and Development, 30*(3), 317–328. doi:10.1080/07294360.2010.489237

REFERENCES

Boyer, C., Einstein, A., & Infeld, L. (1938 [1961]). *The Evolution of Physics: The Growth of Ideas From Early Concepts to Relativity and Quanta* (2nd ed.). Cambridge: Cambridge University Press.

Charman, S. D., Kavetski, M., & Mueller, D. H. (2017). Cognitive Bias in the Legal System: Police Officers Evaluate Ambiguous Evidence in a Belief-Consistent Manner. *Journal of Applied Research in Memory and Cognition*, 6(2), 193–202.

Choi, I., & Lee, K. (2008). Designing and Implementing a Case-Based Learning Environment for Enhancing Ill-Structured Problem Solving: Classroom Management Problems for Prospective Teachers. *Educational Technology Research and Development*, 57(1), 99–129.

Dwyer, C. P., Boswell, A., & Elliott, M. A. (2015). An Evaluation of Critical Thinking Competencies in Business Settings. *Journal of Education for Business*, 90(5), 260–269.

Edmond, G., Towler, A., Growns, B., Ribeiro, G., Found, B., White, D., Ballantyne, K., Searston, R. A., Thompson, M. B., Tangen, J. M., Kemp, R. I., & Martire, K. (2017). Thinking Forensics: Cognitive Science for Forensic Practitioners. *Science and Justice*, 57(2), 144–154.

EPA. (2007). *Guidance for Preparing Standard Operating Procedures (SOPs)*. Washington: Environmental Protection Agency.

Gill, P. (2001). Application of Low Copy Number DNA Profiling. *Croatian Medical Journal*, 42(3), 229–232.

Goertel, R. A. (2018). *Critical Thinking and Reading. The TESOL Encyclopedia of English Language Teaching*. Wiley Online Library. Retrieved from https://doi.org/10.1002/9781118784235.eelt0469

Golding, C. (2011). Educating for Critical Thinking: Thought-Encouraging Questions in a Community of Inquiry. *Higher Education Research and Development*, 30(3), 357–370.

Granér, R., & Kronkvist, O. (2015). *The Past, the Present and the Future of Police Research: Proceedings from the Fifth Nordic Police Research Seminar*. Retrieved from http://www.diva-portal.org/smash/get/diva2:798355/FULLTEXT01.pdf

Halpern, D. F. (2013). *Thought and Knowledge: An Introduction to Critical Thinking*. Psychology Press.

Henry, V. E. (2004). *Death Work: Police, Trauma, and the Psychology of Survival*. New York: Oxford University Press.

Hughes, W., & Lavery, J. (2015). Critical Thinking: An Introduction to the Basic Skills, 7th ed., Peterborough: Broadview Press.

Kurland, D. (2010). How the Language Really Works: The Fundamentals of Critical Reading and Effective Writing. Retrieved from www .criticalreading.com

Lum, K., & Isaac, W. (2016). To predict and serve? *Significance, 13*(5), 14–19.

MCSCS. (2007). *Centre of Forensic Science: Annual Report.* Chapter 4, Section 4.02. Toronto: Ministry of the Solicitor General.

National Human Genome Research Institute. (2018). 15 for 15: Enhanced Forensics. Retrieved from https://www.genome.gov/dna-day/15-for-15/ enhanced-forensics

Quitadamo, I. J., Faiola, C. L., Johnson, J. E., & Kurtz, M. J. (2008). Community-Based Inquiry Improves Critical Thinking in General Education Biology. *CBE—Life Sciences Education, 7*(3), 327–337.

Raymond, T., & Julian, R. (2015). Forensic Intelligence in Policing: Organisational and Cultural Change. *Australian Journal of Forensic Sciences, 47*(4), 371–385.

Robertson, J., & Roux, C. (2018). The Forensic Scientist of the Future— Are Universities Prepared? *Australian Journal of Forensic Sciences, 50*(4), 305–306.

Serrat, O. (2017). Bridging Organizational Silos. In *Knowledge Solutions: Tools, Methods, and Approaches to Drive Organizational Performance* (pp. 711–716). Singapore: Springer.

SFU. (2017). Critical Thinking in University. Simon Fraser University Library. Retrieved from https://www.lib.sfu.ca/about/branches-depts/ slc/learning/thinking/critical-thinking-university

Shin, N., Jonassen, D. H., & McGee, S. (2003). Predictors of Well-Structured and Ill-Structured Problem Solving in an Astronomy Simulation. *Journal of Research in Science Teaching, 40*(1), 6–33. doi:10.1002/tea.10058

Song, M.-L., Fisher, R., Wang, J.-L., & Cui, L.-B. (2016). Environmental Performance Evaluation with Big Data: Theories and Methods. *Annals of Operations Research, 270*(1–2), 459–472.

University of Lethbridge. (2018). How Do I Teach Critical Thinking? Retrieved from http://www.uleth.ca/teachingcentre/ how-do-i-teach-critical-thinking

Whitman, G., & Koppl, R. (2010). Rational Bias in Forensic Science. *Law, Probability and Risk, 9*(1), 69–90.

CHAPTER 4

How to Critically Review a Published Journal Article

Building Forensic Science on the Shoulders of Giants

Photo credit: Mike Illes

I was taught that the way of progress was neither swift nor easy.
—*Marie Curie (1867–1934) (The Nobel Prize, 2019)*

In this chapter, we focus on published journal articles: your initial appraisal, their parts, the peer-review process, and how to interpret them. To help you approach such a review, we have selected a published journal article on bloodstain pattern analysis (BPA) that was written by one of the authors of this book. The article, "Investigation of a Model for Stain Selection in Bloodstain Pattern Analysis," was published in 2011 and discusses a theoretical model with little real-world application. If you are interested in a second article on how the theoretical model can be applied by a bloodstain pattern analyst at the crime scene, see the article by Illes and Stotesbury (2015) titled "Development of an Application Method for a Zone Stain Selection Model in Bloodstain Pattern Analysis" in the *Canadian Society of Forensic Science Journal.*

Reviewing a **scientific journal** article requires critical assessment, beginning with an initial appraisal of the author(s) (such as their previous publications and associated institution), whether the publication is current (if it is a book, are you reading the latest edition?), the journal title, and the publisher (Bordens & Abbott, 2011).

The front page from the article (shown on the following page) provides the general information that is required to begin your assessment. This gives us an idea if the information in the article is worth reading and using in our research.

THE INITIAL APPRAISAL

The first author's name within an article is normally accepted as the lead author of the paper. In the article presented, author M. Illes was the lead and core researcher. In the interest of brevity, we will investigate the background of the first author of the article presented; however, when conducting an initial appraisal, it may be critical to do a similar evaluation of all contributing authors. An Internet search of "Mike Illes" provides information of his affiliation with the Trent University Forensic Science Department. It also offers background knowledge of his forensic science practitioner and management experience, along with some previously published journal articles.

Can. Soc. Forensic Sci. J. Vol. 44. No. 1 (2011) pp. 1–12

Investigation of a Model for Stain Selection in Bloodstain Pattern Analysis

M. Illes[1] and M. Boué [2]

Abstract

The selection of spatter stains from an impact pattern is the foundation by which the estimation of the area of origin is derived. In this paper we establish bloodstain selection criteria based on a statistical model. The model is constructed with data collected from several impact patterns created within a laboratory environment. The response variable considered is the distance between the known source and the estimated trajectory emanating from a stain; the explanatory variables are impact angle, glancing angle, zone location of the stain on the wall, and distance from the source to the wall. The model obtained indicates that zone location is relevant for improving accuracy, and that stains with any alpha angles can be used to calculate an area of origin estimation. Results from a validation study for the stain selection rules derived from the model are presented and analysed.

Résumé

La sélection de taches d'éclaboussures d'un dessin d'impact est la fondation par laquelle l'estimation de la région d'origine est tirée. Dans ce papier nous établissons des critères de sélection de taches de sang basés sur un modèle statistique. Le modèle est construit avec les données recueillies de plusieurs dessins d'impact créés dans un environnement de laboratoire. La variable de réponse considérée est la distance entre la source connue et la trajectoire estimée provenant d'une tache; les variables d'explication sont l'angle d'impact, l'angle d'un coup d'œil, l'endroit de la zone de taches sur le mur et la distance de la source au mur. Le modèle obtenu indique que l'endroit zonal est pertinent pour améliorer l'exactitude et que les taches avec n'importe quels angles alpha peuvent être utilisées pour calculer une région d'estimation d'origine. Les résultats d'une étude de validation pour les règles de sélection de tache tirées du modèle sont présentés et analysés.

[1] To whom correspondence should be addressed. Department of Forensic Science, Trent University, 1600 West Bank Drive, Peterborough, ON, K9L 1Z7. E-mail: mikeilles@trentu.ca
[2] Department of Mathematics, Trent University, Peterborough, Ontario

1

Because this is an article on BPA, we want to assess whether the author has a publication history in bloodstain pattern analysis and could be considered an expert in this discipline. Searching further, we find that there are numerous journal articles written by the author on the discipline. Some of the most recent are listed here:

- (2019). Validation of Sherlock, a Linear Trajectory Analysis Program for Use in Bloodstain Pattern. *Canadian Society of Forensic Science Journal*, *52*(2), 78–94 (with A. Orr, J. Beland, & T. Stotesbury).
- (2019). Luminol Reagent Control Materials in Bloodstain Pattern Analysis: A Silicon Sol-Gel Polymer Alternative. *Forensic Chemistry*, *12*, 91–98 (with S. Polacco, P. Wilson, A. Vreugdenhil, & T. Stotesbury).
- (2016). Novel Technological Approaches for Pedagogy in Forensic Science: A Case Study in Bloodstain Pattern Analysis. *Forensic Science Policy & Management: An International Journal*, *7*, 87–97 (with T. Stotesbury, C. Bruce, & R. Hanley-Dafoe).
- (2015). A Commentary on Synthetic Blood Substitute Research and Development. *Journal of Bloodstain Pattern Analysis*, *31*(2), 3–6 (with T. Stotesbury, P. Wilson, & A. Vreugdenhil).
- (2015). An Impact Velocity Device Design for Spatter Pattern Generation with Considerations for High-Speed Video Analysis. *Journal of Forensic Sciences*, 1–8 (with T. Stotesbury, & A. Vreugdenhil).
- Review Article (2015). Confounding Factors of Fly Artefacts in Bloodstain Pattern Analysis. *Canadian Society of Forensic Science Journal*, *48*(4), 215–224 (with S. Langer).

We check several web pages and find information on Illes's global teaching work, as well as years of crime scene and BPA technical and managerial work. From our more in-depth Internet search, we can see that this individual's practitioner and teaching experiences span many years.

The author currently works for the Trent University Forensic Program, and a review of this program indicates that it has existed since 2004, with significant student growth and the subsequent launch of the first Canadian master's program in forensic science in 2018. Trent University is a mid-sized university with a diversity of undergraduate departments and graduate research opportunities. It appears that the author has worked at the university since the early 2000s while also working as a forensic practitioner and manager for the Ontario Provincial Police (OPP). His role in the OPP was diverse, ranging from general forensic identification duties to leading the OPP bloodstain pattern analyst program.

Next, we review the journal in which the article was published, Canada's most read forensic journal: *Canadian Society of Forensic Science Journal*. Reviewing information on this journal, we find that it has a double-blind peer-review process (in which the author[s] and peer reviewer[s] are not known to each other), which is considered the optimal review methodology (Fiske & Fogg, 1990; Mahoney, 1977; Peters & Ceci, 1982). However, a journal **impact factor** could not be found for this journal. An Internet search of forensic science journal impact factors indicates that few are available or low compared to other more prestigious and widely used scientific journals. The journal impact factor is based on the number of times articles in a journal are cited annually; however, its use has been criticized in recent years (Moustafa, 2015). The journal impact factor that was developed by Garfield in 1955 (Garfield, 1955) has become controversial, as it is an indicator of journal prestige and reputation with no experimental data to support its claims (Callaway, 2016; Diamandis, 2017; Garfield, 2006; Moustafa, 2015).

The *Canadian Society of Forensic Science Journal* was purposely selected, as it is the only forensic science journal published in Canada. Our hope is that this will encourage Canadian forensic science students and practitioners to support this journal as Canadian Society of Forensic Science members and to submit their **manuscripts** to the journal. The Canadian Identification Society (2018) also publishes research studies, in addition to providing information and news to police services, through their primary publication source: *Identification Canada.*

Instructional Pop Out

Visit the Canadian Society of Forensic Science website: www.csfs.ca

THE PARTS AND INTERPRETATION OF AN ARTICLE

Before we accept what has been presented in the publication, it is important to understand the purpose of each part of a journal article. Once each part has been defined, we will continue our dissection of the journal article entitled "Investigation of a Model for Stain Selection in Bloodstain Pattern Analysis." Prior to assessing the parts of a journal article (abstract, introduction, methods and materials, results, discussion, and conclusion), though, it is important to note that the least effective way to read a scientific article is from start to finish. We suggest the following sequence: abstract, introduction, discussion, conclusion, results, and then method. This provides an opportunity to decide if the article is interesting and relevant to your research objectives and saves time during the research process. The following is a brief description of each article part and an analysis of each in the sample article.

Abstract

The abstract introduces the context of the manuscript, briefly explains the authorial approach to the problem, and lists the article's main conclusions. The abstract does not contain data and cannot generally be trusted, as it is a brief interpretation of the research. It can tell you if the paper is relevant to your topic. The abstract of the sample article (Illes & Boué, 2011) is as follows:

Abstract

The selection of spatter stains from an impact pattern is the foundation by which the estimation of the area of origin is derived. In this paper we establish bloodstain selection criteria based on a statistical model. The model is constructed with data collected from several impact patterns created within a laboratory environment. The response variable considered is the distance between the known source and the estimated trajectory emanating from a stain; the explanatory variables are impact angle, glancing angle, zone location of the stain on the wall, and distance from the source to the wall. The model obtained indicates that zone location is relevant for improving accuracy, and that stains with any alpha angles can be used to calculate an area of origin estimation. Results from a validation study for the stain selection rules derived from the model are presented and analysed.

In this abstract, the first few sentences succinctly describe the purpose of the research: to establish bloodstain selection criteria based on a theoretical model. The researchers clearly state that they have developed a model based on several variables that influence the selection of stains from an impact bloodstain pattern. They then sum up their main conclusion—that the model can help with accurately estimating the area of origin and that they validated the model.

Introduction

The introduction provides background information, such as a literature search, the reason(s) that the authors performed the study, where the work fits in the grand scheme of the topic, and a clear statement of the hypotheses and their testability.

Introduction

The selection of spatter stains from an impact pattern is the starting point for the estimation of a pattern's area of origin via Directional Analysis (1–3). Given that findings regarding the area of origin have the potential to implicate or eliminate a suspect in a criminal investigation (4, 5), it is vitally important that bloodstain analysts have at their disposal criteria for spatter stain selection that yield reliable estimates. The purpose of this paper is to establish and validate bloodstain selection criteria based on a statistical model. The model is constructed with data collected from several impact patterns created within a laboratory environment. Every stain from every pattern was considered in the analysis (except for stains with a glancing or gamma angle between 90° and 270°), including near circular upward directional stains. Our objective is to develop criteria that allow the use of a wide assortment of stains.

Area of origin calculations ultimately depend on the intersections of trajectories retraced from the selected spatter stains. Consequently, the response variable used to quantify the predictive ability of a stain is the distance between its known source and the estimated trajectory emanating from the stain. The stain characteristics considered as explanatory variables are all ones that can be measured at a crime scene: the impact or alpha angle, the glancing or gamma angle (the angle measured on the wall between the main axis of the stain and the vertical), and the zone location of the stain on the wall (the zone variable is described in detail below). The true horizontal distance from the source to the wall is also included in the analysis. Although this variable is not readily available at a crime scene (it is one of the variables that must be estimated), it is included in the model to account for the increase in error as the distance travelled by the blood droplets increases (6).

At present, spatter stain selection criteria based on impact angles are mainly supported by studies of single blood droplets falling due to gravity onto an angled surface (7–9). Previous work addressing the ability to determine the area of origin for individual spatter stains was discussed in (10). However, only a sample of stains in the created patterns was considered, and the analysis of stain characteristics was done graphically. To the best of our knowledge, this is the first study of stain characteristics which involves all the available stains in an impact pattern and which results in a statistical model.

This introduction provides background information on the importance of calculating an accurate estimation of the area of origin along with a short literature review on the topic. Generally, a reader can expect a more in-depth review, but this review is limited—likely from the focus of one technique in a highly specialized field of study that does not have a large body of researchers. As stated in the abstract, the researchers repeat their reasoning for the study in the introduction, which can be interpreted as testing the hypotheses: establishing and validating bloodstain selection criteria based on a statistical model. If true, then criteria can be developed that allow the use of a wide assortment of stains. The purpose of the study and how it fits into BPA is clearly stated, with evidence to support the originality of their research: this is the first study of stain characteristics that involves all the available stains in an impact pattern and that results in a statistical model.

Methods and Materials

This section should contain a detailed description of the methods and materials used. It will allow the reader to replicate the study and assess if the methods are appropriate for testing the hypotheses. Are the analyses appropriate for the data and hypotheses, and were the data collected in a way that was unbiased? (See chapter 7 for a detailed description of research design.)

Methods

Pattern Creation

This study required that the location of the impact site be known with precision. Therefore, impact patterns were created with a striking device expressly designed for that purpose.

The striking device was set up as follows (see Figure 1). First, a wooden base was constructed and a concave basin large enough to hold the required amount of blood was sanded in the centre of its top face. Next, a 0.635 cm hole was drilled into the top and a metal rod was hammered into the hole. Finally, a striking weight was fashioned by jamming two 0.635 cm hexagonal nuts into two 1.27 cm nuts. One of the smaller nuts extended 3–4 cm out from the end surface of the large nut, thus creating a striking area of 1.3 cm.

Figure 1. Producing an Impact Pattern with the Striking Device

Prior to the strike, the target surface (smooth white paper) was prepared with a template for measuring zone location (Figure 2). The template consisted of a pair of perpendicular axes with origin at the known y-z coordinates of the site of impact, and with horizontal axis parallel to the floor. Each of the two upper quadrants was divided into three 30° zones, labelled as A1–A3 (clockwise) on the upper left quadrant, and B1–B3 (counter-clockwise) on the upper right quadrant. The lower quadrants were not of interest since they will necessarily contain downward moving spatter stains, which are not included in the analysis.

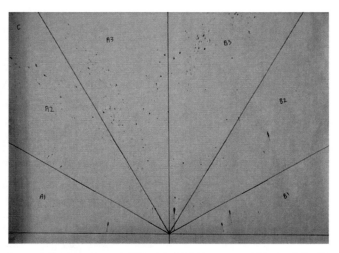

Figure 2. Impact Pattern Target "C" with 30° Zones and Marked Radii

Data Collection

Six impact patterns were created by striking 5 mL of sheep's blood with the striking device. The blood contained 1% sodium fluoride, which acted as an anticoagulant. The literature suggests that the chemical and physiological differences between human and bovine, equine, swine, and sheep blood are minimal (11, 12). The studies within the literature concentrated on impact angle calculation, impact spatter comparison, reproducibility, viscosity, and colour comparison. These studies concluded that there were no significant differences between animal and human blood.

In every instance, the impact location was known and recorded. For every upward moving stain in each of the six patterns, the following procedure was conducted. A 2 cm scale was placed beside each stain, and a plumb line and identification number were placed near the stain. The y and z two-dimensional stain location on the target surface was measured and recorded, together with its zone location. Upon image digitization of the stain, both the impact and the glancing angles were measured within BackTrack™ Images, and the stain location information was transcribed into the program. Version BTW_45_MIP of BackTrack™ Win (13) was used to calculate the distance between the known source and the estimated trajectory emanating from the stain.

Model Development

We next describe the linear model from which spatter stain selection rules will be derived. As explained earlier, estimations for area of origin depend on the intersections of trajectories retraced from selected stains. Accordingly, the response variable used here to measure the predictive ability of a stain is the distance between the known source and the estimated trajectory emanating from the stain—the shorter the distance, the better predictive ability of the stain. (Henceforth, we shall refer to this variable simply as distance to the source.) The explanatory variables considered are the source's horizontal distance to the wall and the stains' impact angles, glancing angles, and zone locations.

Removal of Outliers

Outliers are extreme values that can have a dramatic effect on the parameter estimations of a linear model. In the context of impact patterns, outliers occur when certain stains are more affected by gravity and by air resistance than the rest of the stains in the pattern, resulting in greater impact angles upon contact with the target surface (confirmation of these effects using high speed video can be found in [14]). The identification and removal of these outliers is necessary in the process of constructing a linear model.

Any spatter stain whose distance to the source was beyond 3 standard deviations from the mean for all stains (4.838 ± 3*3.671 cm) was recognized as a potential outlier and examined individually within the context of the complete pattern. Adhering to accepted practices and general experience in the field, potential outliers falling into any one of the following three groups were categorized as true outliers and thus removed from any further analysis:[3]

- near circular stains outside of the convergence area;
- directional stains with a different shape (width and length ratio) than the majority of the stains in the region close to them; and
- downward directional stains (which should not have been in the data set to begin with).

In total, 32 stains were removed, all of them stains that would not normally be selected by a forensic practitioner (10).

The Model

Table 1 presents the average distances to the source tabulated by zone for all 2,095 usable stains. We can see from the table that zones A3 and B3 have the shortest average distance for most patterns, with distances becoming larger as the true distance from the source to the wall (x) increases. For small values of x (patterns B and D), the means within all zones are small, with mean values in zones A3 and B3 being very close to those in zones A2 and B2.

In order to test whether the observed differences were in fact statistically significant, regression computations were performed using the statistical package R (15). Among all the models investigated involving the four predictors (impact angle, glancing angle, zone location, and distance to the wall), with and without interactions, the model that was considered the best fit was a Box-Cox Transformation Model (16) with $\lambda = 0.32$.[4]

---

[3] We note that these characterizations can be applied in a practical setting without knowledge of the true location of the source.

[4] For $\lambda \neq 0$, the Box-Cox transformation of y is given by $(y^\lambda - 1)/\lambda$.

Table 1. Average Distances Tabulated by Zone

Target	Zone	Average Distance	Standard Deviation	X Value	Target	Zone	Average Distance	Standard Deviation	X Value
A	A1	10.99	5.02		D	A1	5.03	2.26	
A	A2	6.06	2.87		D	A2	4.45	3.15	
A	A3	4.81	2.39		D	A3	4.74	3.22	
A	B3	4.26	1.97	25.9	D	B3	3.92	2.43	21.3
A	B2	5.34	2.2		D	B2	4.73	2.2	
A	B1	11.4	2.82		D	B1	10.06	2.81	
B	A1	3.33	1.36		E	A1	6.48	2.67	
B	A2	3.74	2.77		E	A2	4.37	3.03	
B	A3	3.53	2.74	17.8	E	A3	4.01	2.76	27.7
B	B3	3.53	2.4		E	B3	3.43	1.59	
B	B2	4.79	4.14		E	B2	4.52	1.99	
B	B1	5.69	3.78		E	B1	10.77	4.77	
C	A1	7.44	3.76		F	A1	12.25	1.4	
C	A2	5.72	2.96		F	A2	8.14	3.71	
C	A3	4.65	2.97	34.2	F	A3	5.99	3.41	43.1
C	B3	4.68	2.51		F	B3	5.11	2.99	
C	B2	5.27	2.27		F	B2	5.71	4.27	
C	B1	11.39	2.05		F	B1	12.75	0.9	

The regression output can be found in Table 2, with dummy variables defined for each zone as

Table 2. Parameter Estimation Results

Coefficients:	Estimate	Std. Error	t value	Pr(>|t|)
(Intercept)	1.237	0.026	45.88	< 2e-16
A2	0.084	0.022	3.78	0.000161
A1	0.199	0.036	5.58	2.66e-08
B3	-0.005	0.016	-0.30	0.761948
B2	0.093	0.026	3.58	0.000356
B1	0.477	0.053	8.93	< 2e-16
x	0.0107	0.0009	11.93	< 2e-16

Residual standard error: 0.3078 on 2088 degrees of freedom
Multiple R-squared: 0.1172, Adjusted R-squared: 0.1147
F-statistic: 46.19 on 6 and 2088 DF, p-value: < 2.2e-16

$$A2 = \begin{cases} 1, & \text{if in } A2 \\ 0, & \text{if not} \end{cases}$$

$$A1 = \begin{cases} 1, & \text{if in } A1 \\ 0, & \text{if not} \end{cases}$$

$$B3 = \begin{cases} 1, & \text{if in } B3 \\ 0, & \text{if not} \end{cases}$$

$$B2 = \begin{cases} 1, & \text{if in } B2 \\ 0, & \text{if not} \end{cases}$$

$$B1 = \begin{cases} 1, & \text{if in } B1 \\ 0, & \text{if not} \end{cases}$$

When all of these zone variables are 0, the stain is found in zone A3, which is considered the baseline.

The authors provide sufficient information to replicate this study by dividing each step into a section within the methods: pattern creation, data collection, and model development. The first two sections of the methods specify how the patterns were created, describing how to build the striking device used. The impact pattern target surface with template, blood material used, number of patterns, stain data collection procedure, and software analysis are each detailed.

The model development section explains the linear framework from which spatter stain selection rules were derived. The response variable and explanatory variables considered are provided with an explanation of outlier stains in the pattern, why they need to be removed, and a detailed removal procedure. The statistical model used, analytical software, data, and analysis have been provided.

Results and Discussion

The results are the essence of the paper—what you should be interested in. The results should not contain any interpretation (e.g., whether or not the hypotheses are rejected). This section contains the empirical data that was used to test the hypotheses.

Results and Discussion

The regression results displayed in Table 2 give rise to the following linear model:

$$d^{0.32} = 1.24 + 0.08\ A2 + 0.2\ A1 + -0.005\ B3 + 0.09\ B2 + 0.5\ B1 + 0.01\ x \qquad [1]$$

Analysis of the model's coefficients allows us to state the following conclusions:

1. n average, stains in zones A3 and B3 have better predictive ability than stains in the other zones.

The coefficient for zone B3 is not significantly different than zero, so that the average distance to the source in zone B3 is the same as that of the baseline (zone A3). Moreover, the coefficients for all other zones are highly significant, positive, and increasing in magnitude as we move outward in both directions away from the central zones.

Therefore, stains in other zones have greater average distance to the source (and hence lower predictive ability) than those in zones A3 and B3. Since the coefficients for A2 and B2 are very similar, the average increase in distance in zones A2 and B2 is estimated as being the same. The greatest increase occurs in the lower zones A1 and B1, with the largest average distance estimated for zone B1. (We note that the experimental data support our hypothesis that zones A1 and B1 would have the largest average distances. We do not have an explanation for the difference observed between these two zones, however, other than the possible effect of the method of pattern creation, which consistently gave rise to patterns with fewer stains in zone B1 than in any other zone.)

2. verage predictive ability of stains decreases as the distance between the source and the wall increases.

The coefficient for x (the true distance from the source to the wall) is positive and highly significant. Therefore, average distance to the source for all stains in a pattern is greater if the source is farther away from the wall. This confirms the fact that estimation is less accurate for patterns whose source of origin is far from the wall.

3. Stains with all alpha and gamma angles can be used for area of origin estimation.

Model [1] does not include the impact angle or the glancing angle. We have opted for this model with fewer variables since for a more general model, impact angle was found to be just slightly significant (coefficient = -0.001 and p-value = 0.025), and glancing angle was not significant at all. The lack of effect of a stain's alpha and gamma angles on its predictive ability indicates that any upward directional stain can be used for area of origin analysis. In particular, since the alpha angles considered were between 11.5° and 90°, all stains with angles within these values can be considered for estimation. Even stains with alpha angles above 60° are acceptable (142 stains used in the data analysis were above 60°), contradicting the suggestions derived from studies of single blood droplets falling due to gravity onto an angled surface (7–9, 17, 18).

The adequacy of model [1] rests on the assumption that errors are normally distributed with constant variance. This assumption was in fact strongly supported by diagnostic plots involving the residuals. Nevertheless, a tree-based regression analysis (19) was performed to bypass the normality assumption and strengthen our conclusions. The classification of zones resulting from this non-parametric technique is displayed in Figure 3. It can be observed that the classification coincides precisely with that discussed in conclusion 1 above. Conclusions 2 and 3 are also consistent with other tree-based regression results obtained but not included here.

Rules for Stain Acceptance

The conclusions derived from model [1], combined with the outlier removal criteria discussed earlier, suggest the following rules for spatter stain acceptance:

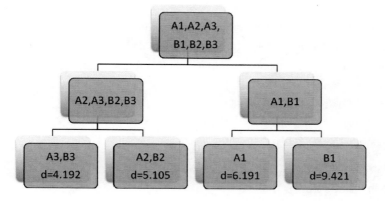

Figure 3. Tree-Based Regression Analysis by Zone. The Number in Each Branch Represents the Estimated Distance to the Source within the Corresponding Zones

i.   Accept stains that are located in the upper zones (A3 and B3) including nearly circular stains from the centre of the convergence.
ii. Reject all downward directional stains.
iii. If there is a directional stain with a different width and length ratio within a group of stains (a suspected outlier), measure the alpha angle for each stain within the group. Average the alpha angles of all stains excluding the suspected outlier. If the alpha angle of the outlier is 5° or more than the mean value, reject the stain.

In the context of this paper, these rules are to be applied after a preliminary set of stains has been selected by the analyst using the currently accepted methods (as described in [10]). In accordance to the rules, stains are accepted or removed and new stains are incorporated, resulting in a modified set of stains to be used for estimation. Theoretically, this modified set should have a better predictive ability than the original one, thus resulting in a more accurate estimation of area or origin. This claim was tested under laboratory conditions, and the results of the validation experiments are discussed in the next section.

We note that in the setting of this paper (where the zone location is known without error for each stain), the acceptance rules can only be validated as a training tool for teaching spatter stain selection to bloodstain pattern analysts. The development and validation of a workable application will require further investigation beyond the scope of this paper.

Model Validation

Data Collection

Four field operational bloodstain analysts were selected to assist in this validation project. They are forensic practitioners with experience ranging between three and seven years of bloodstain pattern analysis (BPA) field work. Prior to participating in this project, all four of them had completed extensive study on impact pattern analysis, including a full understudy training program consisting of basic pattern recognition, advanced BPA, mathematics, and physics (20). The expectation was that they possessed the skills and knowledge for selecting stains with high predictive ability and provide an accurate estimation of an area of origin. If this training model could assist such experienced individuals in improving their estimates, then the validation could be considered successful.

Four impact patterns were created using the striking device described earlier.[5] The known three-dimensional blood-source impact locations were recorded and secured by the researcher/trainer but were not revealed to the analysts. Each analyst was given one impact pattern and was asked to select a set of stains from which to estimate the area of origin using the Backtrack™ Suite of Programs. Upon completion of the selection, each analyst was provided with the following list of instructions:

1. Complete Backtrack™ Suite of Programs analysis.
2. Calculate the auto or manual CPxy and manual z three-dimensional coordinates.
3. Mark a + on the target, indicating the y, z known location (data on the known source will be provided at this time).

---

[5] It must be noted that four different patterns were used to collect data, one supplied to each analyst. The use of a single pattern would have biased the analysts' choices as it was passed on.

4. Photograph the overall pattern.

5. Place the photographic image of the pattern and Backtrack™ end view onto an MS Office Word document.

6. Place the provided overlay (marked zones and radii) onto both images at the known y, z location.

7. Accept stains according to the zone and alpha angle acceptance rules:

    a. Accept stains that are located in the upper zones (A3 and B3).

    b. If available, select and measure nearly circular stains from the centre of the convergence area within zones A3 and B3.

    c. Reject all downward directional stains.

    d. If there is a directional stain with a different width and length ratio within a group of stains (a suspected outlier), measure the alpha angle for each stain within the group. Average the alpha angles of all stains excluding the suspected outlier. If the alpha angle of the outlier is 5° or more than the mean value, reject the stain.

    e. Review the trajectory data for any obvious outliers and remove the outliers.

8. Recalculate the auto CPxy and manual z.

These instructions were followed by the analysts under the guidance of the researcher/trainer, so that bloodstains were removed or added as required and a new estimation of area of origin was obtained from the modified set. By providing the analysts with direction, it was possible to validate the clarity of the instructions themselves at the same time that data for validating the method was collected.

After all the steps had been completed, the information available from each analyst consisted of: (a) the known source location for their pattern; (b) the area of origin estimation from the first analysis; and (c) the area of origin estimation after following the stain acceptance rules. Items (a) to (c) regarding a fifth pattern were also collected. This pattern was analysed by a student with no BPA experience. The results were not included in the statistical test but are discussed in the conclusion.

Results of Validation

The area of origin estimations from the original analysis and those from the re-analysis after implementing the stain acceptance rules were compared to the known source locations. The error values, their means, and their differences are displayed in Table 3.

Table 3. Validation Study Comparison Data

Target	Known Value	BPA	Error	BPA after rules	Error	Error Difference
A	X = 27 Y = 55 Z = 60	X = 22.1 Y = 53.5 Z = 65.9	$\Delta X = 4.9$ $\Delta Y = 1.5$ $\Delta Z = 5.9$	X = 20.8 Y = 54.1 Z = 64.9	$\Delta X = 6.2$ $\Delta Y = 0.89$ $\Delta Z = 4.9$	$\Delta X = -1.3$ $\Delta Y = 0.61$ $\Delta Z = 1.0$
B	X = 33 Y = 39.5 Z = 60	X = 26.9 Y = 38.9 Z = 70.4	$\Delta X = 6.1$ $\Delta Y = 0.6$ $\Delta Z = 10.4$	X = 24.3 Y = 37.8 Z = 67.7	$\Delta X = 8.7$ $\Delta Y = 1.7$ $\Delta Z = 7.7$	$\Delta X = -2.6$ $\Delta Y = -1.1$ $\Delta Z = 2.7$
C	X = 40.5 Y = 36.5 Z = 60	X = 41.4 Y = 39.1 Z = 68	$\Delta X = 0.9$ $\Delta Y = 2.6$ $\Delta Z = 8$	X = 39.8 Y = 36.2 Z = 67	$\Delta X = 0.7$ $\Delta Y = 0.3$ $\Delta Z = 7$	$\Delta X = 0.2$ $\Delta Y = 2.3$ $\Delta Z = 1.0$
D	X = 30.5 Y = 53 Z = 60	X = 26.5 Y = 52.1 Z = 70.6	$\Delta X = 4$ $\Delta Y = 0.9$ $\Delta Z = 10.6$	X = 25.2 Y = 52.1 Z = 66.5	$\Delta X = 5.3$ $\Delta Y = 0.9$ $\Delta Z = 6.5$	$\Delta X = -1.3$ $\Delta Y = 0$ $\Delta Z = 4.1$
E (student)	X = 35 Y = 49.5 Z = 60	X = 31.3 Y = 47.4 Z = 74.8	$\Delta X = 3.7$ $\Delta Y = 2.1$ $\Delta Z = 14.8$	X = 28 Y = 48.3 Z = 64.5	$\Delta X = 7$ $\Delta Y = 1.2$ $\Delta Z = 4.5$	$\Delta X = -3.3$ $\Delta Y = 0.9$ $\Delta Z = 10.3$
Average (A-D only)			$\Delta X = 3.975$ $\Delta Y = 1.4$ $\Delta Z = 8.725$		$\Delta X = 5.23$ $\Delta Y = 0.95$ $\Delta Z = 6.52$	$\Delta X = -1.255$ $\Delta Y = 0.45$ $\Delta Z = 2.205$

It can be seen that application of the stain acceptance rules resulted in improved accuracy in the estimation of the z coordinate, with estimated z values closer to the source in all four patterns. Moreover, there was little or no improvement in the estimation of the x and y coordinates.

A student's t-test was used to test whether the improvement in estimation was significant (Table 4). The improvement in the estimation of the z value is significant (p-value = 0.03036), suggesting that the stain acceptance rules can help obtain more accurate estimations of height when attempting to estimate an area of origin. However, improvement in estimation for the x and y coordinates was not significant (P > 0.1).

Table 4. Student's t-Test for the Stain Selection Rules Validation Study (Targets A-D Only)

	x Value	y Value	z Value	3D
Mean error by analyst	3.975	1.4	8.725	9.928
Mean error after model	5.23	0.95	6.52	8.793
Δ	-1.255	0.45	2.205	1.135
P-value	0.9416	0.2847	0.0304	.0972

The authors decided in their article to combine the results and discussion. Depending on the formatting requirements of a specific journal, the discussion can occur within the results section or in the conclusions. The results and discussion section for this article provides data from Box-Cox regression and tree-based regression models that support the finding that, on average, stains in zones A3 and B3 have better predictive ability than stains in the other zones, average predictive ability of stains decreases as the distance between the source and the wall increases, and stains with all alpha and gamma angles can be used for area-of-origin estimation. This information combined with the outlier removal criteria provides rules for spatter stain selection within impact patterns. The model was validated by doing a field test using four field operational bloodstain analysts. The student t-test comparing the analysts' first area of origin and using the new model provided p-values that support an improvement in area of origin estimations using the new model.

Instructional Pop Out

See the following links for further explanation of statistics and probability. These links should also be referenced when reviewing chapter 6, The Use, Misuse, and Absence of Statistics in Forensic Science Casework.

Statistics How To: www.statisticshowto.com/probability-and-statistics/

Conclusion

This is the authorial interpretation of the data and should not influence your views.

Conclusions

The comparison between the known source locations and the area of origin estimations both before and after implementing the stain selection rules validates the model for improving the estimation of the z value. Consistently, estimation of the z value from the modified set of stains outperformed the original estimation, resulting in a statistically significant improvement. The re-selection of stains incorporated a wider range of alpha angles for spatter stains within specific zones. In particular, stains with angles close to 90° but within zones A3 and B3 and near the area of convergence were incorporated after implementing the stain selection rules. The observed improvement indicates that the use of such stains is acceptable, in disagreement with the conclusions derived from studies of single droplets.

The estimation of the x and y coordinates does not improve after implementing the stain acceptance rules. We attribute this to the fact that the estimation of the x and y coordinates using BPA is not dependent on alpha angles, on the one hand, and is quite robust to outliers, on the other. An in-depth study of the robustness of BPA using Directional Analysis will appear elsewhere (21).

The stain selection rules have assisted four experienced bloodstain analysts in computing a more accurate height estimation of the area of origin. This would support the utility of the selection rules as a tool in the training of new bloodstain analysts, particularly when considering the large increase in accuracy achieved by the student who had no prior bloodstain selection experience (see results for Target E in Table 3). Moreover, this study has also validated the instructional technique used within the research.

The article's conclusions indicate that the research validates the stain selection model, improving the estimation of the z value, and that circular (90°) stains can be used for analyzing an impact pattern. Further, the analyst validation study supports the utility of the model presented.

When considering this interpretation, it is important to think about the results and that those data presented support the findings of the research.

Acknowledgments

Acknowledgments

The authors would like to thank Dr. Paul Wilson, Dr. Christopher Kyle, Dr. Joanna Freeland, and Theresa Stotesbury of Trent University, Dr. Brian Yamashita of the Royal Canadian Mounted Police (RCMP), Dr. David Baldwin of the Midwest Forensics Resource Center (MFRC), and Dr. Michael Taylor of the Institute of Environmental Science and Research Limited (ESR). We also thank the Ontario Provincial Police (OPP), notably George Miller, Gord Lefebvre, Scott Hlady, David Sibley, and Trevor McLeod for their time and expertise in completing this research. We also extend a special thank you to Alice Czitrom for her assistance with data collection and to Dr. Alfred Carter of Forensic Computing of Ottawa for developing version BTW_45_MIP of the BackTrack™ software upon our request.

References

A review of the references within an article can help with furthering research on the topic. The reference section in a published article can be used as an indicator of the quality of the research article being reviewed. In fact, it is common practice for research scientists to first check the citations of an article for quality and authors before or as part of their initial appraisal.

Reference lists include both primary and secondary sources. Primary sources are full research reports with details necessary to duplicate the study, while secondary sources summarize information (e.g., a book). Another benefit of the reference section is that it can be used when completing a literature review on a topic that you may be investigating.

An active bloodstain pattern analyst would be aware of the many researchers (Carter, Kish, Knocks, Raymond, and Reynolds) used in the reference section and that they are well known in the discipline. This can offer some confidence to the reviewer that the authors of the article being reviewed have used reliable primary and secondary sources.

References

1. SWGSTAIN. Scientific Working Group on Bloodstain Pattern Analysis: Recommended Terminology. *Forensic Sci. Comm.* 2009; *11* (2): 1.
2. Carter, A. L. The Directional Analysis of Bloodstain Patterns: Theory and Experimental Validation. *Can. Soc. Forensic Sci. J.* 2001; *17* (4): 173–189.
3. Carter, A. L. Carter's Compendium for Bloodstain Analysis with Computers: Directional Analysis of Bloodstain Patterns. Forensic Computing of Ottawa Inc. 2001; 1–8.
4. *Daubert et al. v. Merrell Dow Pharmaceuticals Inc.* 1993, United States Supreme Court; 9–17.
5. *R. v. Mohan.* 1994, Supreme Court of Canada, File no. 23063; 1–36.
6. James, S. H., Kish, P. E., and Sutton, P. E. *Principles of Bloodstain Pattern Analysis: Theory and Practice*; CRC Press: Boca Raton, FL, 2005; 224.
7. McGuire, J. A., and Rowe, W. F. Uncertainty in the Estimated Angles of Impact of Freely Falling Blood Drops. Presented at: 57th Annual Meeting of the American Academy of Forensic Sciences, New Orleans, LA, 2005.
8. Willis, C., Piranian, A. K., Donaggio, J. R., Barnett, R. J., and Rowe, W. F. Errors in the Estimation of the Distance of Fall and Angles of Impact Blood Drops. *Forensic Sci. Int.* 2001; *123* (1): 1–4.
9. Reynolds M., Franklin, D., Raymond, M. A., and Dadour, I. Bloodstain Measurement Using Computer-Fitted Theoretical Ellipses: A Study in Accuracy and Precision. *J. Forensic Ident.* 2008; *54* (4): 469–484.
10. Wells, J. K. Investigation of Factors Affecting the Region of Origin Estimate in Bloodstain Pattern Analysis, M.Sc. Thesis, University of Canterbury, Christchurch, 2006: 121–173.
11. Christman, D. V. A Study to Compare and Contrast Animal Blood to Human Blood Product. *International Association of Bloodstain Pattern Analysts News,* 1996; *12* (2): 10–25.

12. Raymond, M. A., Smith, E. R., and Liesegang, J. The Physical Properties of Blood - Forensic Considerations. *Science & Justice*, 1996; *36* (3): 153–160.

13. Carter, A. L. BackTrack/Win Version 4.50, in BTW_45_MIP, A-A1, Editor. 2009; Ottawa.

14. Illes, M. B. Investigation of a Model for Stain Selection and a Robust Estimation for Area of Origin in Bloodstain Pattern Analysis, M.Sc. Thesis 2011, Trent University, Peterborough, ON, 2011.

15. R Development Core Team. R: A Language and Environment for Statistical Computing. R Foundation for Statistical Computing, Vienna, Austria, 2009. http://www.R-project.org (accessed in 2009).

16. Faraway, J. J. *Linear Models with R*; CRC Press: Boca Raton, FL, 2005; pp. 109–110.

17. Knock, C., and Davison, M. Predicting the Position of the Source of Blood Stains for Angled Impacts. *J. Forensic Sci.* 2007; *52* (5): 1044–1049.

18. Pace, A. The Relationship between Errors in Ellipse Fitting and the Increasing Degree of Error in Angle of Impact Calculations. *International Association of Bloodstain Pattern Analysts News*, 2005; *21* (3): 12–14.

19. Maindonald, J., and Braun, J. *Data Analysis and Graphics Using R—an Example-Based Approach, Second Edition,* Cambridge Series in Statistical and Probabilistic Mathematics; Cambridge University Press: New York, 2007; pp. 350–374.

20. Ministry of Community Safety and Correctional Services, Editor. *Bloodstain Pattern Analyst Understudy Program*, Ontario Police College: Aylmer, ON, 2005, pp. 1–11.

21. Illes, M. B., and Boué, M. The Robustness of Estimation for Area of Origin in Bloodstain Pattern Analysis via Directional Analysis, To be published.

PEER REVIEW

> Nothing in life is to be feared, it is only to be understood. Now is the
> time to understand more, so that we may fear less.
> —Marie Curie (Benarde, 1973)

Peer review is a process in which an independent qualified reviewer assesses a researcher's work. It has a long history in academia—dating to the 1600s—where several scientific societies, such as the Royal Society (see www.royalsociety.org/about-us/history/), began reviewing manuscripts to be published. In academic journal reviews, the process is used to "evaluate the scientific merit and suitability for publication," while forensic report reviews can be for technical issues (e.g., following institutional guidelines) and for scientific validity (e.g., are the conclusions scientific and evidence-based?) (Ferreira et al., 2016). Peer review can be single blind, where the reviewer or author are known to the other, or double blind, where the reviewer and author are unaware of each other.

The peer review of academic journals has been extensively researched and many authors indicate the positive attributes of the system; however, like any system, there are negative features as well. We will first explore these positive attributes and negative features by summarizing some of the research literature on the academic journal peer-review process. Second, we will discuss the practitioner peer-review process and the ancillary differences from academic peer review.

Academic Journal Review

Generally, peer review works very well and should be done. The process is not perfect, though, and there can be reviewer bias such as that indicated in the research by Mahoney (1977). He found that the reviewers did tend to be biased within their own theoretical beliefs on a topic (e.g., evolution versus creation). Peters and Ceci (1982) found that if researchers were named within the manuscript (single-blind review), the reviewers showed bias. It was also suggested by Fiske and Fogg (1990) that there was little agreement between reviewers in their study (Bordens & Abbott, 2011).

Another interpretation of the peer-review process was presented in a review paper by Ferreira and colleagues (2016). This was a critical analysis of the peer-review system as it related to evolution and biology journals; however, it can easily relate to any scientific discipline. These researchers completed a comprehensive historical investigation on the system; they reviewed how peer review has progressed since the 1600s, specifically how several technological advances have influenced this progression. The researchers found that advancements such as print, the specialization of science, the pressure in academia to "publish or perish," and the Internet have each played a significant role in changing the peer-review process. It seems that the advancement of technology has placed this academic process in an archaic state.

Forensic Report Review

Scientific journals have been using peer review for many years and it should be an important part of any forensic reporting system. The long history of peer review within academia has provided significant information on the process (Garfield, 1955). What can we learn from this history and how should peer review be conducted in forensic reporting?

There are differences between academic peer review used by a scientific journal and the peer review that is used by forensic practitioners for scientific report writing. In the latter type of peer assessment, there may be multiple levels of review within an organization; however, in general, most forensic practitioners are required to complete a technical peer review of their reports. Some organizations go beyond this and use double-blind peer review systems along with administrative reviews (a review performed by a supervisor).

Significant research has been conducted specifically on why peer review should be done in forensic science reporting; it is suggested that peer review can provide a "methodological solution for ineffective and unethical forensic science assessment, promoting integrity, quality, and confidence in justice" (Welner et al., 2012). Furthermore, a blind peer review by a qualified practitioner can provide interpretations that are free from contextual information and bias (Zajac et al., 2015). This can be particularly important in the policing environment, where contextual information is freely available to forensic practitioners within that system. This evidence, along with the vast number of journals using peer review, supports its use; however, a balance between pragmatism and scientific process may be necessary in forensic science practice. An example would be the debate surrounding the need to complete a full double-blind peer review on every **elimination fingerprint** that was individualized at a crime scene. This is likely not a practical approach or even a possibility in a busy forensic identification unit.

We further discuss peer review in chapter 9, The Key to Effective Communication in Forensic Science, and how it is an essential part of the forensic report system.

SUMMARY

In summary, we have learned how to conduct an initial appraisal of a journal article by critically reviewing authors' credentials, such as other publications and their associated institutions. We discussed the need to know if the publication is current and the importance of the publisher. Second, we looked at the parts of a journal article and how to interpret each. Reviewing the abstract of the provided journal article introduced us to the context of the article, a brief explanation of the authorial approach to the problem, and the main conclusion of the article. We found that the introduction provided background information, such as the relevant literature on the research conducted, why the authors performed the study, a clear statement of the hypotheses and their testability, and how this work fits into the forensic science community. The third part was on methods and materials, finding that the article reviewed contained details of the methods used and that these appeared to be appropriate. We found that the analyses were appropriate for those data and the hypotheses and also that those data were collected in an unbiased manner. We then examined the essence of the article—the results. We found that the sample article contained core data and some interpretation of those data. Finally, we reviewed the article's conclusion, which provided a broader view of the interpretation of these data and information on the direct relevance of the results to the forensic bloodstain community. The references for the paper were very specific to the forensic BPA community.

Amanda Lowe

Personal Profile

Amanda Lowe worked as a forensic toxicologist with the Centre of Forensic Sciences prior to taking a forensic research analyst position with the Ontario Provincial Police (OPP). She was formerly a project and research analyst within the Office of the Chief Coroner for Ontario and a forensic services technologist within the Ontario Forensic Pathology Service. Throughout her career, she has contributed to the advancement of forensic science by performing audits of regional

Photo credit: Melina Larizza

pathology units, developing data extraction tools to examine groupings of deaths, presenting recommendations to prevent future similar deaths, and testifying as an expert witness in toxicology for death investigations and criminals matters (in the Ontario Court of Justice and Superior Court of Justice). Amanda's educational background includes a bachelor of science in forensic science honours degree from Trent University, a master of science degree in applied bioscience with a specialization in forensic chemistry from the University of Ontario Institute of Technology and continuing education in pharmacology from the University of Toronto.

Amanda's Path to Forensic Science

Amanda was drawn to forensic science as she enjoyed core science courses but also wanted to do hands-on fieldwork. During her undergraduate degree, she completed a variety of science, forensic, and law courses, which fuelled her passion for investigation and finding solutions to complex

Continued

problems. Her education at Trent University, her volunteering in the Natural Resources DNA Profiling and Forensic Centre preparing samples for analysis, and her work within the OPP on a bloodstain pattern analysis project led her to complete graduate research that included in-lab analysis and fieldwork throughout Ontario. This research involved the burial of clothed pig carcasses as human body analogs, use of ground penetrating radar (GPR) as a means of detecting clandestine gravesites in a variety of soil textures, the exhumation of the carcasses at regular intervals for the collection of samples of soil, textiles, and tissue, and the analysis of those samples. Her work involved using diffuse reflectance infrared Fourier transform spectroscopy (DRIFTS), attenuated total reflectance—Fourier transform infrared (ATR-FTIR) spectroscopy and gas chromatography—mass spectrometry (GC-MS) to detect fatty acid composition and breakdown as a means of estimating time since burial. Within her toxicology work, Amanda performed and directed the analysis of biological and non-biological samples for the presence and quantification of alcohol, drugs, and poisons using a variety of analytical instrumentation, including gas chromatography–flame ionization detection (GC–FID) and liquid chromatography–tandem mass spectrometry (LC–MS/MS).

Amanda's Role as a Forensic Scientist

As part of the Forensic Identification Services, Amanda's role is to advance the future of forensic identification in the largest police service in Ontario through ensuring members are properly trained, equipped with the latest and most beneficial technological advancements, and able to make recommendations regarding methods to adopt. In order to gain an appreciation for the work completed by uniformed members, Amanda attends death and crime scenes alongside the officers and works closely with regional identification units.

QUESTIONS TO PONDER

1. What is the main purpose of an abstract?
2. What is the difference between a manuscript and a published journal article?
3. How does the number of authors influence your view of the quality of a journal article?
4. Why are the results so important in a journal article?
5. Name the parts of a journal article.
6. What is the significance of peer review and why is it beneficial?

GLOSSARY

Canadian Society of Forensic Science (CSFS): a non-profit professional organization incorporated to maintain professional standards and to promote the study and enhance the stature of forensic science as a distinct discipline (Canadian Society of Forensic Science, 2018).

elimination fingerprint: exemplars of friction ridge skin detail of persons known to have had legitimate access to an object or location (NIJ, 2011).

impact factor: the number of times a research article is cited in a particular year in a journal (Callaway, 2016).

manuscripts: in the context of this chapter, research papers that have not been published.

peer review: the process of having a manuscript reviewed by experts in a specific discipline to be sure the research meets the required standards before publication (Voice of Young Science, 2012).

scientific journal: a periodical that advances science by the peer review of manuscripts on research. Scientific journals generally contain research papers, review articles, technical notes, and case reports (Canadian Society of Forensic Science, 2018).

FURTHER READINGS

Greenhalgh, T. (2014). *How to Read a Paper: The Basics of Evidence-Based Medicine*. Hoboken: John Wiley & Sons.

Janick-Buckner, D. (1997). Getting Undergraduates to Critically Read and Discuss Primary Literature. *Journal of College Science Teaching, 27*(1), 29–32.

Relman, A. S., & Angell, M. (1989). How Good Is Peer Review? *New England Journal of Medicine, 321*(12), 827–829. doi:10.1056/nejm198909213211211

Smith, R. (2006). Peer Review: A Flawed Process at the Heart of Science and Journals. *Journal of the Royal Society of Medicine, 99*(4), 178–182.

University of Minnesota Libraries. (2014). How to Read a Scholarly Journal Article. Retrieved from https://www.youtube.com/watch?v=t2K6mJkSWoA

Voice of Young Science. (2012). Peer Review: The Nuts and Bolts. Sense about Science. Retrieved from http://senseaboutscience.org/voys/

Wood, M., Roberts, M., & Howell, B. (2004). The Reliability of Peer Reviews of Papers on Information Systems. *Journal of Information Science, 30*(1), 2–11. doi:10.1177/0165551504041673

REFERENCES

Benarde, M. A. (1973). *Our Precarious Habitat*. W. W. Norton & Company.

Bordens, K. S., & Abbott, B. B. (2011). Research Design and Methods: A Process Approach. New York: McGraw-Hill.

Callaway, E. (2016). Publishing Elite Turns against Impact Factor. *Nature, 535*(7611), 210–211.

Canadian Identification Society. (2018). Journal Issues. Retrieved from http://www.cis-sci.ca/journals

Canadian Society of Forensic Science. (2018). About—Promoting Forensic Science in Canada. Retrieved from https://www.csfs.ca/about/

Diamandis, E. P. (2017). The Journal Impact Factor Is Under Attack—Use the CAPCI Factor Instead. *BMC Medicine, 15*(1), 9.

Ferreira, C., Bastille-Rousseau, G., Bennett, A. M., Ellington, E. H., Terwissen, C., Austin, C., ... Murray, D. L. (2016). The Evolution of Peer Review as a Basis for Scientific Publication: Directional Selection towards a Robust Discipline? *Biological Reviews, 91*(3), 597–610.

Fiske, D. W., & Fogg, L. F. (1990). But the Reviewers Are Making Different Criticisms of My Paper! Diversity and Uniqueness in Reviewer Comments. *American Psychologist, 45*(5), 591–598.

Garfield, E. (1955). Citation Indexes for Science. *Science, 122*, 108–111.

Garfield, E. (2006). Citation Indexes for Science: A New Dimension in Documentation through Association of Ideas. *International Journal of Epidemiology, 35*(5), 1123–1127.

Illes, M., & Boué, M. (2011). Investigation of a Model for Stain Selection in Bloodstain Pattern Analysis. *Canadian Society of Forensic Science, 44*(1), 1–12.

Illes, M., & Stotesbury, T. (2015). Development of an Application Method for a Zone Stain Selection Model in Bloodstain Pattern Analysis. *Canadian Society of Forensic Science Journal, 49*(1), 19–25. doi:10.1080/00 085030.2015.1108541

Mahoney, M. J. (1977). Publication Prejudices: An Experimental Study of Confirmatory Bias in the Peer Review System. *Cognitive Therapy and Research, 1*(2), 161–175.

Moustafa, K. (2015). The Disaster of the Impact Factor. *Science and Engineering Ethics, 21*(1), 139–142.

NIJ. (2011). *The Fingerprint Sourcebook*. Washington: National Institute of Justice. Retrieved from http://www.nij.gov/pubs-sum/225320.htm

The Nobel Prize. (2019). Marie Curie—Biographical. Retrieved from https://www.nobelprize.org/prizes/physics/1903/marie-curie/biographical/

Peters, D. P., & Ceci, S. J. (1982). Peer-Review Practices of Psychological Journals: The Fate of Published Articles, Submitted Again. *Behavioral and Brain Sciences, 5*(2), 187–255.

Voice of Young Science. (2012). Peer Review: The Nuts and Bolts. Sense about Science. Retrieved from http://senseaboutscience.org/voys/

Welner, M., Mastellon, T., Stewart, J. J., Weinert, B., & Stratton, J. M. B. (2012). Peer-Reviewed Forensic Consultation: Safeguarding Expert Testimony and Protecting the Uninformed Court. *Journal of Forensic Psychology Practice*, *12*(1), 1–34.

Zajac, R., Osborne, N., Singley , L., & Taylor, M. (2015). Contextual Bias: What Bloodstain Pattern Analysts Need to Know. *Journal of Bloodstain Pattern Analysis*, *31*(2), 7–16.

CHAPTER 5

What the Literature Says: From Student to Expert

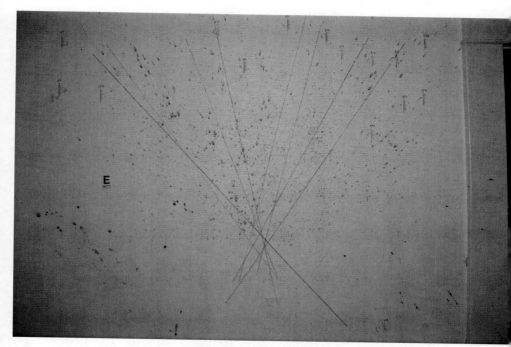

A Two-Dimensional Bloodstain Impact Pattern Analysis
Photo credit: Mike Illes

Science is the knowledge of consequences, and dependence of one fact upon another.
—*Thomas Hobbes (1980)*

A literature review is just like a criminal investigation. As a forensic scientist or investigator, you are required to collect evidence prior to a charge being laid and any attempt at prosecution in court. The same applies to any research project conducted in academia or as a practitioner—you are required to collect all evidence to support what is being said in a manuscript, thesis, dissertation, or forensic report. In this chapter, we define and explore the appropriate use of high- and low-level publication sources, some basic search strategies, accessing the evidence base, types of literature reviews, and the role of the review within research and for the forensic practitioner (Booth et al., 2012).

TYPES OF PUBLICATIONS

Publication sources can be separated into two levels: low and high. A low-level source is not peer reviewed and cannot be counted on for accuracy as it is not necessarily based on testable evidence or fact, whereas a high-level source is peer reviewed and scientifically robust. An example of a low-level source would be a supermarket tabloid; high-level sources consist of scholarly books or scientific journals.

High-level sources can be further separated into primary and secondary source material. Primary sources are full research reports with the details necessary to duplicate the study. They can be found in scholarly journals. Secondary sources are review papers or books that summarize information on a topic and may not be peer reviewed.

For current research and theories regarding a subject, researchers turn to scholarly journals; however, keep in mind that not all journals are created equal and the method of assessment described in chapter 4, How to Critically Review a Published Journal Article, should be followed. You should always consider whether the journal is peer reviewed or not. Peer-reviewed journals have quality control measures in place to minimize the publication of poor research.

A secondary source summarizes information and may consist of a review paper or a book. When conducting a literature review, books and review papers provide a great starting point, if primary sources are listed. We recommend that you make every effort to obtain a copy of the primary source cited in a textbook so that you can critically review the original work. Be aware that books can be written based on **authoritative knowledge** and may not undergo as rigorous a review as works published in scientific journals.

Literature review articles published within a refereed scientific journal can be considered peer reviewed; however, be cautious when analyzing these publications as they are not reporting on new experimental results. These articles discuss research that has been previously published. The rest of this chapter will help you to distinguish between the types and purposes of each literature review.

You should rely most heavily on peer-reviewed primary sources. There are a few simple ways to check if a journal is peer reviewed.

- Check your university or college online library system, as many will provide this information when you search for a journal.
- Check the journal's website—a peer-reviewed journal will provide information on their process. The "instructions for authors" is an excellent place to see if the journal is peer reviewed.
- Conduct an Internet search of the journal.

Exercise 5.1: Sources

Find two examples each of a primary and secondary source by searching the Internet.

BASIC STRATEGY

The strategy for finding relevant literature should include the following steps:

1. Find an initial relevant publication.
2. Use the reference section of that publication to locate other publications.
3. Repeat steps 1 and 2 for each relevant publication identified until you cannot find any more.

4. Use one of the many indexes available at your library or on the Internet. We have provided some sites to get you started:
   a. EBSCOhost, www.ebsco.com/products/research-databases
   b. Google Scholar, www.scholar.google.com/
   c. ScienceDirect, www.sciencedirect.com/
   d. Microsoft Academic, https://academic.microsoft.com/home
   e. Directory of Open Access Journals, www.doaj.org/
   f. PLOS ONE, www.plosone.org/
   g. Science and Technology of Advanced Materials, www.iopscience.iop.org/1468-6996/
   h. JSTOR, www.jstor.org/
5. Repeat the entire process as you find additional and more recent articles.

Exercise 5.2: Sources

Locate each of the following publications, then state whether the publication is a primary or secondary resource and explain your answer.

1. Campbell, A. (2011). *The Fingerprint Inquiry Report.* Edinburgh: APS Group.
2. Eldridge, H. (2011). Meeting the Fingerprint Admissibility Challenge in a Post-NAS Environment. *Journal of Forensic Identification, 61*(5), 430–446.
3. Langenburg, G. et al. (2012). Informing the Judgments of Fingerprint Analysts Using Quality Metric and Statistical Assessment Tools. *Forensic Science International, 219*(1–3), 183–198.
4. Mnookin, J. L. (2010). The Courts, the NAS, and the Future. *Brooklyn Law Review, 75*(4), 1–67.
5. Egli, N., Moret, S., Bécue, A., & Champod, C. (2013). 17th Interpol International Forensic Science Managers

Symposium: Review Papers; Fingermarks and Other Impressions. Lyon: Interpol.

6. Laber, T. L. et al. (2014). *Reliability Assessment of Current Methods in Bloodstain Pattern Analysis.* Washington: National Institute of Justice.

7. Brunetto, Y. et al. (2012). Emotional Intelligence, Job Satisfaction, Well-Being and Engagement: Explaining Organisational Commitment and Turnover Intentions in Policing. *Human Resource Management Journal, 22*(4), 428–441.

8. McDonald, S. P. (2013). Promoting Critical Thought. *Military Review, 93*(3), 79–82.

9. McDermott, P. J., & Hulse-Killacky, D. (2012). Strengthening Police Organizations through Interpersonal Leadership. *FBI Law Enforcement Bulletin, 81*(10), 19–23.

10. Mnookin, J. L. et al. (2011). The Need for a Research Culture in the Forensic Sciences. *UCLA Law Review, 58*(3), 725–779.

The details for each publication can be found in the appendix.

THE REVIEW

A literature review is a "systematic, explicit, and reproducible method for identifying, evaluating, and synthesizing the existing body of completed and recorded work produced by researchers, scholars, and practitioners" (Fink, 2005), and they are used by researchers, students, practitioners, service users, managers, and policymakers. In a review, the investigator systematically looks for all the evidence that can be found on their topic of interest. They then evaluate and synthesize the evidence to identify gaps in knowledge, find the strengths and weaknesses in the literature, facilitate theory development, and meet required future research needs

(Booth et al., 2012; Palmatier et al., 2018; Webster & Watson, 2002). A literature review can be completed in forensic science for several purposes:

1. as part of a thesis, dissertation, or academic work (or it could be the entire document)
2. as a peer-reviewed publication within a scientific journal
3. as research needed for expert reporting or testimony
4. when conducting case-specific research
5. when establishing standard operational procedures

This process provides a level of confidence to the researcher, student, or practitioner that the researched discipline or topic is robust, and they can tell how well a technique, method, or program is working. Further, we can find deficiencies in the literature, see if it is consistent across multiple studies, has unwelcome results, or if the research is transparent (that is, was there sufficient detail provided for a full assessment?) (Booth et al., 2012).

Throughout this book we have discussed the need for evidence-based practice in forensic science, comparing it with the field of medicine in chapter 2. In the early 1990s, health care librarians and information workers began to observe clinicians' reliance on medical literature as evidence-based practice took hold. Literature reviews became an important aspect of research in the health care industry by summarizing the scientific information doctors required to make evidence-based decisions for their patients (Grant & Booth, 2009). There are literature reviews available within the various forensic science journals; a search of "review article" for 2018–19 in *Forensic Science International* revealed 16 reviews.

You will be interested in obtaining and evaluating the research literature in an area of interest, and review articles can help with this search. When starting a scientific research project, conducting a literature review will help with research design, may reveal other questions, and avoids duplication. Grant and Booth (2009) provide a very practical definition of a review: "Gathering research, getting rid of rubbish and summarizing the best of what remains captures the essence of the science of systematic review." For the practitioner, literature research will focus on a specific area of expertise and keep you up to date within your field. It is also essential for evidence-based reporting and providing expert-opinion testimony in a court of law. The practitioner may also be required to complete a literature review for a case-specific research project. The next section outlines a casework example of the utility of systematic literature review within forensic science.

R. v. France: Ruling on Expert Evidence

On July 14, 2013, two-year-old Nicholas Cruz died as a result of septic shock arising from injuries to his intestines by blunt-force trauma. To determine this, an autopsy was performed by a forensic pathologist, and eventually two people were charged with the second-degree murder of Cruz. At the preliminary hearing, the pathologist was called to testify, for the crown attorney, on the cause and mechanism of death. The defence objected to the admissibility of portions of the pathologist evidence in the **voir dire**, specifically:

> (1) whether the blunt-force trauma to the abdomen was deliberately inflicted as opposed to being accidental; (2) whether he could infer that the abdominal trauma was an assault based on the other injuries to Cruz; (3) whether he could testify as to the probabilities of the abdominal injury being accidentally caused; (4) whether he could use terms that might be confusing to the jury, such as injuries being "consistent with" certain causes or the force of the abdominal trauma being "significant"; and (5) the nature of hypothetical questions. (*R. v. France*, 2017)

Ontario Superior Court Justice Anne Molloy provided a ruling on the admissibility of the pathologist's testimony. Although this is an Ontario Superior Court decision, it has not been appealed (other than on sentencing; the defendant "appealed on other grounds" and the appeal was dismissed—see *R. v. France*, 2018) and therefore has not been challenged in a higher court, such as Ontario's Court of Appeal.

The justice cited issues within the evidence tendered, including the expert committing a possible breach of the duty of impartiality to the court, offering extreme and rigid positions and expert opinions without the most rudimentary amount of research or scientific basis, supplying evasive and disingenuous evidence, not having the expertise or doing sufficient research to draw a conclusion on the statistics, exhibiting **professional credibility bias**, overstepping the role of a forensic pathologist and usurping the role of the jury, improperly using wording such as "significant force" and "consistent with," and wandering off their area of expertise.

Instructional Pop Out

The document can be found at http://netk.net.au/Canada/Canada22
.pdf, and we encourage you to read it in full, as Justice Molloy has provided a short outline on the general principles of law governing expert witnesses in Canada.

The following summarizes the literature research issue in this case. The pathologist provided expert-opinion evidence at the preliminary hearing. At this voir dire, the need for a literature review was so that there was sufficient evidence-based information for the pathologist's opinion—specifically, that Nicholas Cruz's intestinal injuries were caused from "a significant force that is present on the front of the abdomen.... It's got to be essentially a blow to the abdomen.... this is actually an area that has been studied in the medical literature. It's in the medical literature you can look up—it's—it's literature around short falls, short falls in childhood. And what we know is that the majority of short falls in childhood are innocuous" (*R. v. France*, 2017). The defence was suggesting that the injuries could have occurred from an accidental fall and not a blow to the abdomen, as suggested by the witness.

According to the court document, the pathologist expert did not complete a literature review on pediatric abdominal trauma prior to the preliminary hearing; however, he wrote a supplementary report prior to the voir dire on January 31, 2017. The report indicated that its purpose was to survey the medical literature on pediatric abdominal trauma and to address the possibility of an accidental fall. Justice Molloy provides a summation indicating that the expert "did not review the medical literature on abdominal injuries prior to his testimony at the preliminary hearing. At the time of the autopsy and when preparing the post-mortem report, he reviewed some literature, but only with respect to abdominal injuries caused by physical abuse" (*R. v. France*, 2017).

The defence produced "a bound volume of 26 scholarly, published articles on abdominal trauma causing injuries to the bowels." The expert "agreed that an accidental cause for the injuries Nicholas sustained was 'possible' but that such a conclusion was misleading in light of the statistical data showing the infrequency of such injuries resulting from falls. He explained that when looking only at the abdominal trauma, it would be reasonable to say that an accidental fall was a 'possible' cause, or that it 'could' have happened that way. However, he stated that medicine and science have a bit more to offer than 'could' based on the medical literature he reviewed on the frequency with which such injuries are caused accidentally. He explained that he approaches cases 'holistically' and therefore did not focus only on the abdominal injury" (*R. v. France*, 2017).

In her analysis of the information on the literature review, Justice Molloy indicated that the review completed by the expert was insufficient and "that he was predisposed to see this case as an assault and failed to keep an open mind on other possible explanations" (*R. v. France*, 2017).

Justice Molloy provides a strong message about the importance of doing a literature review and the necessity for its completeness. In this case, a full review of all the literature could have mediated this court decision. The accusations of professional credibility bias (where an expert has a professional interest in maintaining their own credibility after taking a position) and **confirmation bias** (when a person is attached to a particular outcome, they tend to search for evidence that supports their "desired" conclusion or to interpret evidence in a way that supports it) may have been avoided by performing a thorough review of the literature, coupled with critical thinking and the scientific method to reject an alternative hypothesis (Paciocco, 2009, *R. v. France*, 2017). The expert witness has a responsibility, to society and the judicial system, to reliably be a knowledgeable person in their area of expertise. Therefore, the expert should always consider all of the procurable evidence (searching for the whole truth), using a systematic approach, to help the court understand all possibilities in a case scenario.

On a cautionary note, though, the forensic expert and the courts should not rely too heavily on the scientific literature. The NAS and Goudge reports support an evidence-based approach to the use of published research versus one that is based on experience; however, approaches that place greater dependence on published research literature present some hazards. The introduction of published literature into a trial can be a source of error and misinterpretation. A proper link between the article and case question is important, as journal research articles can be unique to the sample set and variables used within that study. Therefore, it may be inaccurate to apply the results of a single study to the specific court question. Also, the research being referenced may not be accurate or peer reviewed—hence the importance of knowing the process used within the specific journal, as presented in chapter 4. If the research is accurate, it is still possible that it may be misunderstood by the reporting scientist (specifically, if the research is outside of their expertise) and even more so by a non-scientifically trained lawyer (Sangra et al., 2010).

Types of Literature Reviews

There are 14 common literature reviews used within scientific journals. We have listed and summarized each and provided an exercise that will help you critically analyze each type of review.

1. Critical Review
   This review type consists of a wide-ranging search of the literature on a topic while critically evaluating its quality. A critical review can provide an assessment of previous topical work and direct your future research requirements. This approach is not

very systematic or structured, making it a starting point for further evaluation.

2. Integrative Review

   An integrative review incorporates experimental and non-experimental research into a topical investigation. Integrative reviews may combine quantitative and qualitative data.

3. Literature or Narrative Review

   A literature or narrative review is an examination of recently published articles that have been peer reviewed. It typically identifies articles to include in the review but does not analyze data from those articles.

4. Mapping Review/Systematic Map

   This review style is used to identify gaps in the literature of a specific topic by mapping out and classifying research articles. These types of reviews can help practitioners by providing theory on an area of research and to discern whether a more in-depth review is required. Mapping reviews can be considered a type of rapid review and should not replace a full systematic review.

5. Meta-Analysis

   A meta-analysis synthesizes quantitative results from similar research to provide a more detailed account of the results. It is important to analyze the included studies, making sure they are suitably comparable.

6. Mixed-Methods Review

   This type of review can be any combination of review methods (quantitative or qualitative) with a literature review component.

7. Overview

   An overview review is any summary of the literature on a topic. These reviews can be useful to a reader who does not have domain knowledge on certain topics, as they broadly survey the information.

8. Qualitative Systematic Review/Qualitative Evidence Synthesis

   This review style compares qualitative research findings, which can be useful to practitioners by providing qualitative information on areas such as case studies and practitioner-observed considerations.

9. Rapid Review

   Rapid reviews assess what is known about policy or practice in a field of study. Caution should be used when analyzing a rapid review, as limiting the breadth and depth of the search can introduce bias into the process.

10. Scoping Review

    This review assesses the nature and potential size of the available literature and research evidence. It can dictate whether a systematic review is required and should not be used by practitioners in court decision making.

11. State-of-the-Art Review

    The state-of-the-art review is a narrative review that only addresses current research and may offer new perspectives and novel research ideas. These reviews can be useful to someone who is new to a discipline and looking for a novel topic for a research project.

12. Systematic Review

    This is a systematic search, appraisal, and synthesis of all the research evidence on a topic. These reviews are heavily relied upon by researchers and practitioners.

13. Systematic Search and Review

    This review style is the combination of a critical review and a comprehensive searching process. They aim to provide a full image of the available research.

14. Umbrella Review

    An umbrella review compiles information from multiple review articles. (Booth et al., 2012; Grant & Booth, 2009)

Exercise 5.3: Review Article

Locate each of the following review articles, then critically analyze and state the type of review.

1. Krishan, K. et al. (2016). A Review of Sex Estimation Techniques During Examination of Skeletal Remains in

Forensic Anthropology Casework. *Forensic Science International, 261*, 165.e1–165.e8.

2. Maitre, M. et al. (2017). Current Perspectives in the Interpretation of Gunshot Residues in Forensic Science: A Review. *Forensic Science International, 270*, 1–11.

3. Lynöe, N. et al. (2017). Insufficient Evidence for "Shaken Baby Syndrome"—A Systematic Review. *Acta Paediatrica, 106*(7), 1021–1027.

4. Langer, S., & Illes, M. (2015). Confounding Factors of Fly Artefacts in Bloodstain Pattern Analysis. *Canadian Society of Forensic Science Journal, 48*(4), 215–224.

5. Abrami, P. C. et al. (2015). Strategies for Teaching Students to Think Critically: A Meta-Analysis. *Review of Educational Research, 85*(2), 275–314.

6. Pollitt, M. M. (2007). An Ad Hoc Review of Digital Forensic Models. Systematic Approaches to Digital Forensic Engineering (SADFE), Second International Workshop.

7. Swann, L. M., Forbes, S. L., & Lewis, S. W. (2010). Analytical Separations of Mammalian Decomposition Products for Forensic Science: A Review. *Analytica Chimica Acta, 682*(1–2), 9–22.

8. Lupariello, F. et al. (2018). Staged Crime Scene Determination by Handling Physical and Digital Evidence: Reports and Review of the Literature. *Forensic Science International, 288*, 236–241.

Answers for each type of review article in this exercise can be found in the appendix.

How Do You Organize the Literature?

To organize and cite the literature, we recommend using cite-as-you-write programs, such as EndNote, Mendeley, or RefWorks. These programs provide an interface between word processing software and a library of citations that can be retrieved from Internet searching resources and cited directly in a document. The functions within these programs vary and can include a library that organizes citations and the ability to store a copy of each article, figure, image, and table.

SUMMARY

In this chapter, we explored the importance of completing a literature review for research and case analysis/reporting. High- and low-level sources were defined alongside a suggested basic search strategy for finding the best literature, particularly primary literature. A critical lens should be applied to both primary and secondary literature. After outlining the basic review process, we investigated the fourteen types of journal literature reviews. Finally, a court case example was used to reinforce the necessity of systematic literature reviews by the reader.

Alex MacNeil

Personal Profile

As a medical resident currently pursuing a career in forensic pathology, I have yet to gain the breadth of professional experience required to be able to offer advice or professional insight into what is a fascinating and complex forensic subspecialty. It might be more appropriate for me to elaborate on how someone might become interested in such a niche field of work and what steps are necessary in order to train and work as a forensic pathologist.

Q. How Did You Get Into Forensic Science?

I have been directly and indirectly involved in the forensic sciences since attending Trent University in Peterborough, Ontario, as part of the first graduating class of the bachelor's program in forensic science. The program provided exposure to a number of subspecialties within the forensic sciences, which enabled me to explore a variety of interests. I became particularly interested in the subspecialty of forensic anthropology and the use of subtle variations in human anatomy to help identify skeletonized human remains. This interest led me to complete a master of applied science with a focus on forensic anthropology. Forensic anthropologists are tasked with identifying human remains that have undergone the process of decomposition, to the point of skeletonization. Using published data sets that have been collected through precise measurements of skeletal specimens from around the world, forensic anthropologists interpret the subtle anatomic variations in skeletal anatomy to determine specific traits of a deceased individual, such as their height, age, and sex. This information helps to narrow the focus of further investigation in trying to identify deceased individuals. While completing my master's degree, I contributed to published data sets of facial soft tissue depth measurements, which can be used to create facial reconstructions from skeletonized remains. These reconstructions are used to help identify skeletal remains by providing an approximation of what a deceased individual looked like when alive, in the hopes that the reconstruction may be recognized when disseminated to the public. This research experience highlighted for me the ways in which the scientific method can be employed in various forensic applications. The opportunity to apply my previous training in basic sciences to help solve forensic-related problems, such as the identification of human remains, was truly exciting.

During my training in the field of forensic anthropology, I had the opportunity to work directly with a medical examiner service and observed some of the day-to-day work of forensic pathologists. As someone who enjoyed applying principles of human anatomy to forensic investigations, I was absolutely fascinated by the forensic pathologists' employment of autopsy pathology principles as their main investigative tool. Realizing that the field of forensic pathology might be the best fit for my interests, I decided to start on the long road toward training as a forensic pathologist, with the help of some very supportive mentors along the way.

Continued

Q. What Is Your Role as a Forensic Scientist?

In Canada, training to become a forensic pathologist is usually a 10-year process after completing an undergraduate degree: four years of medical school, five years in a pathology residency training program, and one additional year of subspecialty training in forensic pathology. The training completed in medical school offers a broad overview of all aspects of human health and disease, and completion of an MD degree is the requisite step before obtaining specialized training in any field of medicine, including pathology. After medical school, residency training programs offer intensive training in a specific field, and for those who wish to pursue a career in forensic pathology, that field is usually anatomical pathology or general pathology. A resident in a Canadian anatomical pathology training program will spend five years learning how to diagnose a variety of disease processes in surgical pathology specimens that are collected from patients in hospitals and in the community. Residency programs in anatomical pathology also offer some exposure to the subspecialty of forensic pathology, which involves investigating suspicious and unexpected deaths with the use of autopsies and ancillary testing. Upon completion of a residency training program in anatomical pathology, an extra year of training is required in order to work as a forensic pathologist. There are a handful of training programs in Canada that offer this specialized training, known as a "fellowship" in forensic pathology, and many others exist in the US. After completing this intensive 10-year process, one earns the professional moniker of "forensic pathologist" and, in some jurisdictions in Canada, "medical examiner."

Q. What Kind of Equipment Do You Use?

The practice of forensic pathology is often portrayed on television and in movies as a morbid activity relegated to the dark depths of a hospital basement or poorly lit morgue. The reality is that the process is a careful step-by-step approach to collecting information carried out by highly trained pathologists, often working in a team setting with technologists and assistants. Compared to some other forensic subspecialties, the tools of the trade in forensic pathology are rather mundane: a blade, a saw, a pair of shears, and a scale for completing the autopsy; a microscope for examining tissue samples for evidence of disease or injury. More advanced techniques can be and are applied by forensic pathologists, but the tools listed above are the basic tools necessary to perform a complete autopsy. Other forensic specialists are sometimes asked to help with an investigation, including forensic anthropologists, forensic toxicologists, forensic entomologists, forensic dentists, and so on. The collaboration with other forensic science professionals is one of the facets of forensic pathology that makes it such a rewarding field.

I believe that the practice of forensic pathology contributes a great deal to society in general, in part by monitoring and reporting on trends in potentially preventable deaths that may lead to specific interventions to protect individuals from a similar fate (the introduction of seat belts in motor vehicles is a particularly practical example). The work of forensic pathologists also serves to answer specific questions for the family and friends of individuals who pass away unexpectedly, or under suspicious circumstances, offering some amount of closure in a difficult time. The road to becoming a forensic pathologist is a long one, and for good reason, as the questions that require answering are often complex. I do feel, however, that the job of answering these questions makes for a rewarding and worthwhile career.

QUESTIONS TO PONDER

1. Why is it important to conduct a literature review?
2. How do you conduct a literature review?
3. Which is the most robust literature review style?
4. Why do researchers do literature reviews?

GLOSSARY

authoritative knowledge: a person telling others what to believe with no evidence (Bhatta, 2013).

confirmation bias: when a person is attached to a particular outcome, they tend to search for evidence that supports their "desired" conclusion or to interpret evidence in a way that supports it (*R. v. France*, 2017).

professional credibility bias: where an expert has a professional interest in maintaining their own credibility after taking a position (*R. v. France*, 2017).

voir dire: a trial within a trial for determining if evidence should be allowed to be presented in the main trial (Schneider et al., 2007).

FURTHER READINGS

Hart, C. (2018). *Doing a Literature Review: Releasing the Research Imagination*. London: Sage.

Machi, L. A., & McEvoy, B. T. (2016). *The Literature Review: Six Steps to Success*. Thousand Oaks: Corwin Press.

Mitchell, M. D., Guise, J.-M., Robinson, K. A., Umscheid, C. A., Dryden, D. M., Paynter, R. A., ... Hartling, L. (2015). Advancing Knowledge of Rapid Reviews: An Analysis of Results, Conclusions and Recommendations from Published Review Articles Examining Rapid Reviews. *Systematic Reviews, 4*(1), 50.

REFERENCES

Bhatta, B. (2013). *Research Methods in Remote Sensing*. Dordrecht: Springer.

Booth, A., Papaioannou, D., & Sutton, A. (2012). *Systematic Approaches to a Successful Literature Review*. London: Sage.

Fink, A. (2005). *Conducting Research Literature Reviews: From the Internet to Paper*. London: Sage.

Grant, M. J., & Booth, A. (2009). A Typology of Reviews: An Analysis of 14 Review Types and Associated Methodologies. *Health Information and Libraries Journal*, *26*(2), 91–108. doi:10.1111/j.1471-1842.2009.00848.x

Hobbes, T. (1980 [1651]). *Business Ethics the Big Picture: Chapter 3 Contractarianism from Leviathan*. Glasgow: Broadview Press.

Paciocco, D. (2009). Taking a "Goudge" Out of Bluster and Blarney: An "Evidence-Based Approach" to Expert Testimony. *Canadian Criminal Law Review*, *13*(2), 135.

Palmatier, R. W., Houston, M. B., & Hulland, J. (2018). *Review Articles: Purpose, Process, and Structure*. Dordrecht: Springer.

R. v. France. (2017). *Her Majesty the Queen v. Joel France*. ONSC 2040, CR-17-10000034-0000.

R. v. France. (2018). *Her Majesty the Queen v. Joel France*. ONCA 1052, C64020.

Sangra, B., Roach, K., & Moles, R. (2010). *Forensic Investigations and Miscarriages of Justice: The Rhetoric Meets the Reality*. Toronto: Irwin Law.

Schneider, R. D., Bloom, H., & Heerema, M. (2007). *Mental Health Courts: Decriminalizing the Mentally Ill*. Toronto: Irwin Law.

Webster, J., & Watson, R. T. (2002). Analyzing the Past to Prepare for the Future: Writing a Literature Review. *MIS Quarterly*, *26*(2), xiii–xxiii.

CHAPTER 6

The Use, Misuse, and Absence of Statistics in Forensic Science Casework

Searching for the Evidence

Photo credit: Mike Illes

This chapter explores sample cases that used statistics or probability theory in court. We will review the basic statistical concepts discussed within these cases and have supplied an exercise pop out for further study. We will also explore the use of mathematics in several case studies—first in the 1999 murder trial and conviction of Sally Clark in the United Kingdom and then in the application of DNA in wildlife and human court cases in Canada. The reader will learn the benefits and risks in applying statistics or probability from a practitioner's view, with critical scientific discussion surrounding each case.

Statistics is the collection and summarization of numerical data and can be classified as inductive reasoning. An example of a statistical experiment would be tossing a coin 20 times and having it land on "tails" each time. This result can infer propositions such as the most likely outcome of any toss (likely to get a tail) or perhaps the experiment is biased because a two-tailed coin was used. Probability is the study of chance and can be objective—a logical measure of chance—or subjective—the strength of a person's belief in a proposition.

A probability trial means performing a probability experiment once. One trial might include rolling a die. Performing 20 trials might involve, for example, rolling two dice 20 times. An outcome is the observed result of a single trial. Rolling a die may result in a single outcome, a roll of six. The sample space for a probability experiment consists of all the possible outcomes for that experiment. An event consists of one or more possible outcomes from a sample space, and an event can be independent (one event does not impact the probability of the other event) or dependent (the occurrence of one event will alter the probability of the other).

A sample is a set of data collected from a population. It can be collected randomly, which avoids bias in the sampling; in the Sally Clark case summary, however, you will read that a random sample set was not used, making the analysis and testimony on probability inaccurate. Probability of identity (POI) or random match probability (RMP) are terms used in genetics to indicate the probability of drawing an individual at random from the population with a particular combination of alleles (a variation of a gene).

Instructional Pop Out

See the following links for further explanation on statistics and probability.

Statistics How To: www.statisticshowto.com/probability-and-statistics/
UCLA Institute for Digital Research and Education: https://stats.idre
.ucla.edu/other/mult-pkg/whatstat/

THE CASE OF SALLY CLARK

... one of the worst miscarriages of justice in our history.
—*British Parliament (Batt, 2004)*

Sally Clark lived in Cheshire, England; she was a lawyer and mother of one who was convicted in 1999 of killing her first two children. She was jailed for three years and eventually exonerated of these crimes, with the British government indicating that her conviction was "one of the worst miscarriages of justice in the history of the country" (Batt, 2004; Scheurer, 2018; Watkins, 2000). The story begins with the birth of Clark's first son, Christopher, who, at around three months of age, died within the family home. His death was not investigated at the time as it was considered to be of natural causes, possibly from cot death or **sudden infant death syndrome (SIDS)**. Clark had a second son, Harry, who died within two months of his birth. An investigation was initiated into both deaths, which were then regarded as suspicious.

In October 1999, Mrs. Clark stood trial for the murder of her two sons, and most of the evidence was presented by medical professionals. There were no eyewitnesses at the trial as she was alone with the infants at the time of their deaths. There were two expert witnesses who erred when they provided forensic evidence at the trial. The first was a pathologist who was a witness for the prosecution and withheld evidence of an infection in Harry's cerebrospinal fluid. He failed to provide this evidence to other medical witnesses, police, or lawyers at the first trial (Scheurer, 2018; Watkins, 2000).

This is an important ethical issue, not just for this trial but for any practitioner who is handling evidence and providing expert-opinion evidence in a court of law. The job of the expert is to provide a scientific, thorough, evidence-based opinion, and they cannot judge the relevance of the evidence. The outcome of a court case should not be of concern to the forensic scientist. Presenting robust and unbiased scientific evidence should be their main objective. We discuss ethical considerations for forensic science and scientific research in chapter 8, The Importance of Ethics and Impartiality in Forensic Science.

The second forensic error that occurred in this court of law was made by a prominent pediatrician who delivered expert-opinion evidence on the chance of two children from the same family suffering cot death or SIDS. This individual provided statistical evidence supporting that the occurrence of two infant deaths in the Clark family would be highly improbable. This expert opinion was based on a statistical analysis indicating that the chance of two children dying in an affluent family from cot death would be one in 73 million. While the exact effect that this evidence had within the trial is dubious, upon appeal, this error would have likely caused a judge to dismiss the charges (Scheurer, 2018; Watkins, 2000).

There was a serious misunderstanding of probability theory in this case. The witness derived the "one in 73 million" using information from the Confidential Enquiry into Sudden Death in Infancy (CESDI) report. This report concluded that the risk of a child dying of SIDS in a household with none of the risk factors (smoking, age of mother, and family wages) was one in 8,543 live births. This number was multiplied by itself to derive the 73 million. The first mistake is the assumption of independence. When considering that the family did not have any risk factors, an assumption was made that the death of the first child was independent of the second. If the calculation of one in 8,543 is true for one SIDS death, it is not correct to square this number to derive the 73 million for the second death. For this to be true, SIDS deaths must occur randomly without hidden causes. Since the causes of SIDS are unknown, it is therefore impossible for the two deaths to be assuredly independent (Scheuer, 2018). In fact, there was research at the time supporting the notion that cot deaths are not random events and could be connected to family units (Beal & Blundell, 1988; Guntheroth, Lohmann, & Spiers, 1990; Øyen, Skjaerven, & Irgens, 1996; Watkins, 2000).

On January 23, 2002, the president of the **Royal Statistical Society** wrote a letter to the lord chancellor of Britain regarding the use of statistical evidence in court cases and specifically discussing Sally Clark's. In this case, there was public attention on the statistical evidence provided by the medical expert witness, who provided the frequency of SIDS or cot death in families with specific characteristics as one in 73 million. This value had a dramatic impact on media reports for the trial; however, the one in 73 million calculation was invalid, according to the president.

The president of the Royal Statistical Society, along with others, has pointed out two more issues surrounding this evidence: ecological and prosecutor's fallacies.

The idea was that genetic or environmental factors within specific families could make those families more susceptible to SIDS. Therefore, a second case within these families would be more likely. In Sally Clark's case, the facts that no one smoked in the home, that there was at least one wage earner, and that Mrs. Clark was over 27 years of age were each used to indicate a level of risk for SIDS within their family. In this case, epidemiological group data from the CESDI report was applied to an individual. This mistake is known as the **ecological fallacy**. We cannot take data from a group study and apply it stereotypically to a single case.

The trial prosecutor suggested that the deaths of Sally Clark's two children could not be accidental. This was a misinterpretation in logic that is known as the **prosecutor's fallacy**. The fact that two separate events are quite unlikely is of little value and doesn't indicate that a murder occurred. However, the statement of "one in 73 million" was presented to the jury, implying that Clark's innocence was highly improbable and that the guilty verdict would be correct (Green, 2002; Scheuer, 2018).

Although many scientists are familiar with statistical methods, statistics remains a specialized area, and it was suggested by the Royal Statistical Society president that statisticians should be used as experts in the courts when it comes to statistical evidence. The president also suggested that guidelines should be developed for the use of probability theory in criminal cases.

Instructional Pop Out

Much has been written on the Sally Clark case, and we encourage you to read further with a critical and skeptical mind. See the following articles:

"The Case of Sally Clark": www.ncbi.nlm.nih.gov/pmc/articles/PMC 539414/

"Sir Roy Meadow, the Flawed Witness, Wins GMC Appeal": www .telegraph.co.uk/news/uknews/1510798/Sir-Roy-Meadow-the-flawed-witness-wins-GMC-appeal.html

Exercise 6.1: Math

Define the following terms: *statistics, probability, experiment, trial, outcome, sample space, event, random match probability (RMP).*

Helpful resources:

"Probability and Counting Rules": http://math.ucdenver.edu/~ssantori/ MATH2830SP13/Math2830-Chapter-04.pdf

"Basic Probability Rules": https://bolt.mph.ufl.edu/6050-6052/unit-3/ module-6/

WILDLIFE DNA CASE

The importance of statistical rigour in forensic science can also be observed in less mainstream applications—for example, in the application of DNA to wildlife forensic science. Such profiling includes generating evidence to address (1) individual identification; (2) species identification; (3) sex identification; (4) pedigree reconstruction; and (5) population identification. The two applications that will be described in this section are (1) individual identification to determine if a sample associated with an illegal kill site was identical to a sample(s) associated with a suspected poacher; and (2) population identification to assign an animal to a specific population. These databases and statistical approaches demonstrate the need for solid research design (see chapter 7 for a discussion on research design) in evaluating the strength of evidence.

Producing individually specific DNA profiles in wildlife cases commonly uses similar variable genetic loci to those implemented in human studies, specifically microsatellite loci or short tandem repeats (STRs). While human protocols apply tetramer repeat units, wildlife often use dinucleotide loci; however, the general principles are the same in hypervariable loci being combined to generate a unique DNA signature, whether it be human, animal, plant, or otherwise. In human cases, the genotypes of the victim and/or putative criminal are profiled to determine an association to a crime scene: Is the victim's DNA attached to objects associated with the suspected perpetrator, or did the perpetrator leave DNA associated with a crime scene or victim—for example, sperm in a rape case? In wildlife, the most common case relates to poaching, where material from the kill site of a known poached animal is associated with tissue collected from the suspected poacher(s). A common case would be the gut pile of a moose left at the kill site, as dragging the innards out of the woods is cumbersome from an animal that large. The moose may have been killed out of season or the suspected poacher did not have the appropriate tag.

The process would involve sampling the poached moose's DNA for comparison to blood on a rifle, in the cab of a truck, et cetera, or meat that may be packaged in the suspect's freezer. Generating individually specific profiles that are identical then requires a statistical estimation of the strength of that association—specifically, the probability of identity (POI) or the random match probability (RMP).

The estimate of the POI or RMP in humans is often associated with the chance of another person sharing that genotype. The chance is one in the hundreds of millions, billions, or trillions, and that is even when applying specific databases—for example, African-American or Caucasian. These probabilities are often enormous due to increased variability in the tetramer repeats applied to large population sizes globally, with modern gene flow, that maintain higher levels of variability among the targeted loci. In contrast, wildlife populations are becoming more fragmented because of anthropogenic development, thereby structuring populations and reducing their variability in the dinucleotides applied to casework, and these loci also have relatively fewer alleles than tetramer microsatellite loci. Compounding this is the fact that some wildlife taxa are species at risk—potentially maintaining low genetic diversity or having seen population reductions that have decreased their populations' contemporary genetic variability.

Moose are likely the most extreme example of a game species that has relatively low allelic diversity compared to other deer or *Cervidae*. This has been suggested to have resulted from repeated population reductions during the Pleistocene ice age—which has affected genetic diversity and potential population structures so that it is feasible to have more than one moose share a DNA profile by chance given a standard suite of microsatellite loci (e.g., six to eight loci constructing the genotype) (Ball et al., 2011; Wilson et al., 2003).

Newfoundland moose may be the worst-case scenario, as this population was founded a little more than 100 years ago by potentially four but as few as two moose translocated from New Brunswick on two different voyages (Broders et al., 1999; Wilson et al., 2003), and the population has expanded to be in excess of 160,000 animals: a potential by-product of not showing inbreeding depression as a result of repeated ice-age population reductions eliminating detrimental alleles from the species. In any event, a moderate suite of microsatellite loci can generate a POI of one in 50,000 moose, leaving the possibility of three to four animals roaming the province with identical genotypes by chance. Often, the DNA is not the only evidence and can be interpreted in context, but these statistics are realistic for this wildlife population and not at the magnitude of one in billions, as is often cited in human investigations using DNA evidence.

As a result of fragmented or structured wildlife populations, it is advisable to develop DNA databases of unrelated animals of the same species from specific geographies or estimated structured populations to provide the baseline allele frequencies for estimating the probability of identity. Coupling these POI estimates with census population estimates from wildlife surveys can provide a realistic framework for presentation in court. As an example, the POI estimates for moose in a region of Ontario may be one in 100,000, and there are an estimated 25,000 moose in that region; therefore, it is unlikely that another moose with that genotype is inhabiting that region. The downside of the need to implement these comprehensive databases is the investment in profiling representative samples for multiple regions; however, these databases open up the possibility for another wildlife forensic application: the ability to test whether an animal was derived from a specific population by geography or population identification.

Similar to the translocation of New Brunswick moose to Newfoundland more than 100 years ago, Cape Breton moose were translocated from Alberta, and these animals represent a different subspecies (*A. a. andersoni*) than those on the east coast (*A. a. americana*), including neighbouring mainland Nova Scotia. On mainland Nova Scotia, moose are provincially listed as a species at risk and hunting is prohibited. Cape Breton moose are not at risk, and there is a legal hunt for moose on the island. In a study published in *Forensic Science International: Genetics*, Ball and colleagues (2011) presented the approach taken to address the issue of hunters claiming the three moose they possessed were shot on Cape Breton Island while conservation officers suspected the moose were illegally killed on mainland Nova Scotia. To be able to test these alternative hypotheses, significant genetic structure needed to be detected to be able to differentiate mainland Nova Scotian moose from Cape Breton moose. Given the subspecific differences between the two populations as a result of the translocation, this requirement was met, as representative moose could clearly be assigned to one or the other geography. This application does not formally apply a POI or RMP, but assigning an unknown moose to a population requires a statistical approach, and due to the nature of the investigation, multiple approaches were published to validate the interpretation. In the end, the three moose showed a very high statistical probability of originating from the at-risk Nova Scotia mainland population and not the Cape Breton population, as the suspects claimed (Ball et al., 2011).

HUMAN DNA CASE

While wildlife forensic science should incorporate the most representative regional databases possible, with comparisons to the estimated census populations of these regions, human forensic DNA databases typically yield incredibly high random-match probabilities. As a result of these one-in-millions, -billions, or -trillions of probabilities that another person will share the same DNA profile by chance, DNA has been elevated to a "gold standard" to the point where at times it has a perception of being "infallible" (Gill, 2019). There is no doubt that DNA profiling is a highly effective discriminatory tool in forensic science; however, the discipline is not without issues.

One issue relates to the databases used in estimating random-match probabilities as well as the DNA database of offenders that can be applied to "no suspect" or database matches. "No suspect" cases depend solely on a "hit" to an offender database through database-driven investigations (Roth, 2010). The increasing size of DNA databases has provided empirical comparisons of the number of real match profiles. This was exemplified in the early 2000s (when DNA databases were expanding exponentially) by the Puckett case, where a then-elderly man with a prior sex conviction (thereby placing him in an offender database) had a "hit" with a 30-year-old cold case with an RMP of one in 1.1 million (Murphy, 2015; Roth, 2010). First, that two million men of similar age lived in the San Francisco Bay Area indicates other equivalent profiles may have existed in the population at large. Also, at this same time, the Arizona state crime laboratory had identified identical DNA profiles at 9 of 13 forensically informative markers (loci) between a Caucasian individual and an African-American individual, and the RMP of such a match should have been one in more than 750 million and one in 561 billion, respectively (Murphy, 2015). This occurred in a database of less than approximately 65,000 individuals, and upon court-ordered review through the Puckett case, the database also revealed 122 individuals sharing 9 out of 13 loci, with some sharing 10, 11, and 12 markers (Murphy, 2015)—significantly less, empirically, than would be calculated through RMPs. The Puckett case flagged potential early issues with offender databases and their utility, and issues around "database match probabilities" are continually being addressed (Gill et al., 2015). This includes calls to educate forensic scientists, lawyers, and judges on RMP estimations such as "one in a billion" and to be clear that the term "match" is different than a person's actual "identity" in a statistical context (Gill, 2019), particularly as human forensic DNA databases get more populated.

Applying statistical rigour to DNA profiling and associated "matches" is critical for the discipline, and given the increasing sensitivity in DNA detection, other potential limitations are described by Gill (2019) in his commentary "DNA Evidence and Miscarriages of Justice." Specific limitations that are emerging include the fact that DNA other than that of the actual perpetrator of the crime may be profiled in an investigation—due to, say, picking up background DNA existing prior to the crime, a secondary transfer of DNA, and events such as laboratory contamination (Gill, 2019). The Adam Scott case in Exeter, UK (Gill, 2019; Taylor, Kokshoorn, & Biedermann, 2018), demonstrated the issue of laboratory contamination, where Mr. Scott was suspected of committing a sexual offence based on an identical DNA profile that resulted from the testing of swabs of trace sperm samples from the victim. However, evidence emerged corroborating Mr. Scott's explanation of events, and the subsequent investigation of laboratory procedures revealed that a sample of Mr. Scott's from a non-criminal spitting issue a day earlier had been contaminated through a plastic plate inadvertently used for both cases (Gill, 2019; Taylor, Kokshoorn, & Biedermann, 2018). A second example involved David Butler in Liverpool, UK (Gill, 2019; Taylor, Kokshoorn, & Biedermann, 2018), charged with murdering a sex worker based on trace DNA that hit in the UK's DNA database. The defence team of Mr. Butler, who was nicknamed "Flaky," successfully argued that his skin condition resulted in higher than normal shedding of skin cells and secondary transfer to money or another carrier, resulting in his trace material contacting the victim. Ultimately, given the heightened ability to amplify DNA from trace amounts and the increased recent consideration of DNA transfer, to the point of transfer via gloves worn during casework (Goray, Pirie, & van Oorschot, 2019), such scenarios demonstrate the importance of considering multiple hypotheses (as discussed in chapter 2) when applying DNA evidence.

SUMMARY

The experiential learning approach to statistics and probability in this chapter has highlighted the use, misuse, and absence of statistics in forensic science casework. While this book supports the use of probability theory and statistical analysis, extreme caution toward such applications is required by those who use them. We have presented evidence that, even with the best intent, an expert may misuse statistical information. Therefore, we recommend always consulting a statistician in a research design project and prior to completing a forensic report that contains statistical analyses.

Kathy Gruspier

Personal Profile

Kathy Gruspier obtained her BA in near eastern archaeology from Wilfrid Laurier University, her MA in paleopathology and funerary archaeology from the University of Sheffield, her PhD in physical anthropology from the University of Toronto, and her JD from the Faculty of Law, University of Toronto. She is currently the first and only full-time forensic anthropologist in Canada working for the Ontario Forensic Pathology Service. She is an associate professor of laboratory medicine and pathobiology at the University of Toronto.

Kathy has undertaken extensive fieldwork and analysis of human remains in archaeological sites in Italy and Jordan and forensic investigations in Kosovo, East Timor, Cambodia, and Poland. She has been a consulting forensic anthropologist to Ontario's Office of the Chief Coroner since 1992 and advised the Laboratoire de sciences judiciaires et de médecine légale in Quebec. Kathy has published numerous articles in scientific journals and regularly presents papers at international conferences and for continuing education groups and special seminars. She regularly testifies in criminal proceedings and testified for the Goudge Inquiry into Pediatric Forensic Pathology, for which she also wrote a research paper. Her teaching contributions include law courses for forensic science students and forensic science courses for law students, as well as courses in forensic anthropology.

Q. How Did You Get Into Forensic Science?

I first became interested in forensic anthropology (FA) while doing my master's research at the University of Sheffield. I was using fresh bone samples from the medico-legal centre, and the pathologists began to show me "interesting" cases and ask my opinion on bones. I had already excavated and analyzed hundreds of skeletons from the Middle East and was just embarking upon a number of cemetery excavations in Italy. Forensic anthropology seemed to me to be a way to do something useful for society with my knowledge. When I returned to Canada, I approached the then–chief pathologist in Toronto and told him of my interest. It was 1986, and I was not welcomed. Finally, in 1989, I got a break. Crown attorneys were looking for a forensic archaeologist to assist Dr. Clyde Snow in an exhumation and re-analysis of the remains of Christine Jessop. It was a fascinating case, and I ended up in court for the very first time. This was 1990, and it was pre–*R v. Stinchcombe*, the case that changed everything by determining that the Crown had to disclose everything to the defence prior to the preliminary hearing or trial. Needless to say, my first court experience was very lengthy.

Continued

Q. What Is Your Role as a Forensic Scientist?

After the Kaufman Inquiry, which looked into the wrongful conviction of Guy Paul Morin for the murder of Christine Jessop, the Office of the Chief Coroner decided that they had to make some changes and began to call on the services of the forensic anthropologist more often, but still only for completely skeletonized remains. This was in 1992. Prior to that, in the 1980s, they really only called a biological anthropologist for archaeological remains. Drs. Spence and Saunders would get an occasional call, but the chief forensic pathologist in Toronto always did his own anthropology.

From 1992 onward, I shared the FA work in Toronto with Dr. Melbye while continuing to work on archaeological excavations in Italy and Jordan in the spring and summer. The excavation and analysis of archaeological remains allowed me to understand the full spectrum of human variation, which is extremely important if one wants to apply this knowledge to a single set of remains in the medico-legal arena. In the mid- to late 1990s, the age of human rights dawned with the war in Bosnia and Kosovo. This allowed for many FAs to get hands-on training, particularly in the areas of excavating human remains, sorting out commingling, and trauma analysis and interpretation. I was very lucky to be able to be part of the second Canadian team to go to Kosovo and then East Timor. I went back to East Timor a couple of times, working for the UN, and I also did some work in Cambodia. This work allowed me to become very knowledgeable in the analysis of gunshot wounds, sharp force, and blunt-impact trauma.

The use of FA in Ontario expanded dramatically during the 2000s. There were two reasons for this: the appointment of Dr. Michael Pollanen as chief forensic pathologist in 2006, and the Inquiry into Pediatric Forensic Pathology in 2009, which resulted in the formation of the Ontario Forensic Pathology Service (OFPS) that same year. Dr. Pollanen and the OFPS recognized that FA could offer more than just analysis of skeletal remains. A full-time FA position was posted in 2011, and I competed for and was offered the position. In Ontario, we now have one full time and five consulting forensic anthropologists, and there is still too much work!

Q. What Kind of Equipment Do You Use?

FAs use pretty basic equipment. At a scene I rely on forensic identification specialists or traffic reconstructionists to map a scene, as they have the most up-to-date equipment (total stations, 3D scanners, etc.). Every once in a while, they are not available, so I have my basic archaeological mapping tools in my car (line levels, plumb bobs, tape measures, etc.). I designed my lab at the provincial forensic pathology unit in Toronto and I have a number of boiling stations, sinks, an autopsy table, and other things such as Mikrosil for casting toolmarks and superglue for reconstructing skulls. In our new building, we have the luxury of both an MRI and a CT scanner, and all bodies are CT scanned upon arrival. We purchased a Mac computer system and the OsiriX imaging program for the FA lab. This has been my biggest learning curve in the past few years. The FA does all of the identifications, which are accomplished by comparing antemortem and post-mortem imaging. Most people now have CT scans taken during their life, although we do have X-ray facilities if we are sent antemortem X-rays. Learning and working with three-dimensional identification instead of two took some time. The OsiriX program, however, also offers 3D reconstruction capabilities and this led to a fourth-year research project by a Trent University student a couple of years ago where she rendered pubic symphyses of known age at death individuals and applied the Suchey-Brooks method to them. The research was very promising, and there is more to do in this area. My work is extremely varied, and a typical week could include the following:

- Identifying bone pictures that are sent to me from police agencies all over the province. In 2012, we notified all chiefs of police that they could send suspected animal bone photos directly to the FA instead of involving a coroner or taking them to a vet or the local hospital. This has been a very welcome service and in 2018 we answered around 400 inquiries that were identified as animal bones.

Continued

- Liaising with the police, coroner, and cemeteries registrar on found human remains and determining that they are "not of recent forensic interest."
- Attending a scene of found decomposed, skeletal, or burned remains and working with FIS, cadaver dogs, and fire marshals to process the scene and remove the remains.
- Directing traffic services to send remains—either burned or fresh and not extricable at the scene—to the extrication bay at the provincial forensic pathology unit for extrication or excavation by the FA (this specialized bay was also designed by me and allows for vehicles to be removed quickly from accident or homicide/suicide scenes and to have the bodies removed in a controlled environment).
- Assisting at post-mortem exams of unidentified remains in order to determine the group and personal biology of the individual. These cases can be burned, skeletal, decomposed, or fresh.
- Dealing with tips and managing information on all the unidentified remains in Ontario with our partners and stakeholders in the OPP and RCMP; managing multiple fatalities according to the Multiple Fatality Implementation Plan that I created and maintain.
- Receiving and interpreting DNA reports for identification from the Centre of Forensic Sciences in my role as DNA coordinator.
- Boiling remains for trauma analysis and biological profiling.
- Casting toolmarks for toolmark analysis.
- Reconstructing remains for trauma analysis.
- Attending meetings with police, coroners, and scientists, and talking to the press.
- Testifying in court.

For the past number of years, I have also trained fellows in forensic pathology for the Royal College of Physicians and Surgeons, and this is part of my daily work as we often have a number of them in any given year. We have trained both local and international fellows, particularly those from Jamaica, where we have the support of the Raymond Chang Foundation to assist in improving the quality of death investigations in that country. Our 2019 project plan aimed to design a FA training program for suitable candidates from Jamaica, and we hope to be able to make this program available to candidates from any country in the near future. It is my hope that other provinces recognize the need for full-time FAs in their jurisdiction, as many of them certainly have the casework to support this.

QUESTIONS TO PONDER

1. Name three errors that occurred regarding the use of probability theory in the Sally Clark case.
2. If you were conducting research for a criminal case that required the use of statistics, how would you proceed?
3. Can you find another case example online of the "prosecutor's fallacy"?
4. Would you consider Sally Clark's case a miscarriage of justice? Are there other similar cases?
5. Why has DNA been considered a "gold standard" in forensic casework? Why could this be a misleading statement?

GLOSSARY

ecological fallacy: false reasoning that is based on applying aggregate group data to an individual (Green, 2002; Scheuer, 2018).

prosecutor's fallacy: the use of a statistical inference in a court where multiple tests are relied upon to elevate the likelihood that an individual is guilty or innocent (Green, 2002; Scheuer, 2018).

Royal Statistical Society: founded in 1834, it is one of the world's leading organizations to promote the importance of statistics and data (Royal Statistical Society, 2019).

sudden infant death syndrome (SIDS): the unexplained death of an infant who appears to be in good health (Liebrechts-Akkerman et al., 2011).

FURTHER READINGS

Batt, J. (2004). *Stolen Innocence: The Sally Clark Story—A Mother's Fight for Justice*. London: Ebury Press.

Gammell, C. (2007). Alcohol Killed Freed Mother Sally Clark. *Telegraph*, November 7. Retrieved from https://www.telegraph.co.uk/news/uknews/1568567/Alcohol-killed-freed-mother-Sally-Clark.html

Green, P. (2002). Letter from the President to the Lord Chancellor Regarding the Use of Statistical Evidence in Court Cases. Royal Statistical Society, January 23. Retrieved from https://www.rss.org.uk/Images/PDF/influencing-change/rss-use-statistical-evidence-court-cases-2002.pdf

Meadow, R. (2002). A Case of Murder and the BMJ. *British Medical Journal*, *324*(7328), 41–43.

Shaikh, T. (2007). Sally Clark, Mother Wrongly Convicted of Killing Her Sons, Found Dead at Home. *Guardian*, March 17. Retrieved from https://www.theguardian.com/society/2007/mar/17/childrensservices.uknews

Triola, M. F. (2014). *Elementary Statistics*, 13th ed. New York: Pearson Higher Ed.

REFERENCES

Ball, M. C., Finnegan, L. A., Nette, T., Broders, H. G., & Wilson, P. J. (2011). Wildlife Forensics: "Supervised" Assignment Testing Can Complicate the Association of Suspect Cases to Source Populations. *Forensic Science International: Genetics*, *5*(1), 50–56.

Batt, J. (2004). *Stolen Innocence: The Sally Clark Story—A Mother's Fight for Justice*. London: Ebury Press.

Beal, S., & Blundell, H. (1988). Recurrence Incidence of Sudden Infant Death Syndrome. *Archives of Disease in Childhood*, *63*(8), 924–930.

Broders, H., Mahoney, S., Montevecchi, W., & Davidson, W. (1999). Population Genetic Structure and the Effect of Founder Events on the Genetic Variability of Moose, *Alces alces*, in Canada. *Molecular Ecology*, *8*(8), 1309–1315.

Gill, P. (2019). DNA Evidence and Miscarriages of Justice. *Forensic Science International, 294,* e1.

Gill, P., Haned, H., Bleka, O., Hansson, O., Dørum, G., & Egeland, T. (2015). Genotyping and Interpretation of STR-DNA: Low-Template, Mixtures and Database Matches—Twenty Years of Research and Development. *Forensic Science International: Genetics, 18,* 100–117.

Goray, M., Pirie, E., & van Oorschot, R. A. (2019). DNA Transfer: DNA Acquired by Gloves during Casework Examinations. *Forensic Science International: Genetics, 38,* 167–174.

Green, P. (2002). Letter from the President to the Lord Chancellor Regarding the Use of Statistical Evidence in Court Cases. Royal Statistical Society, January 23. Retrieved from https://www.rss.org.uk/Images/PDF/influencing-change/rss-use-statistical-evidence-court-cases-2002.pdf

Guntheroth, W. G., Lohmann, R., & Spiers, P. S. (1990). Risk of Sudden Infant Death Syndrome in Subsequent Siblings. *Journal of Pediatrics, 116*(4), 520–524.

Liebrechts-Akkerman, G., Lao, O., Liu, F., van Sleuwen, B. E., Engelberts, A. C., L'Hoir, M. P., … Kayser, M. (2011). Postnatal Parental Smoking: An Important Risk Factor for SIDS. *European Journal of Pediatrics, 170*(10), 1281–1291. doi:10.1007/s00431-011-1433-6

Murphy, E. E. (2015). The Dark Side of DNA Databases. *The Atlantic,* October 8.

Øyen, N., Skjaerven, R., & Irgens, L. M. (1996). Population-Based Recurrence Risk of Sudden Infant Death Syndrome Compared with Other Infant and Fetal Deaths. *American Journal of Epidemiology, 144*(3), 300–305.

Roth, A. (2010). Database-Driven Investigations: The Promise—and Peril—of Using Forensics to Solve No-Suspect Cases. *Criminology and Public Policy, 9,* 421.

Royal Statistical Society. (2019). Royal Statistical Society—About. Retrieved from https://www.rss.org.uk/RSS/About/RSS/About_the_RSS/About_top.aspx?hkey=e8216e58-513f-4d7c-be9d-f989d9eed036

Scheuer, V. (2018). Convicted on Statistics? *Understanding Uncertainty.* Retrieved from https://understandinguncertainty.org/node/545

Taylor, D., Kokshoorn, B., & Biedermann, A. (2018). Evaluation of Forensic Genetics Findings Given Activity Level Propositions: A Review. *Forensic Science International: Genetics, 36,* 34–49.

Watkins, S. J. (2000). Conviction by Mathematical Error? Doctors and lawyers should get probability theory right. *British Medical Journal, 320*(7226), 2–3. doi:10.1136/bmj.320.7226.2

Wilson, P. J., Grewal, S., Rodgers, A., Rempel, R., Saquet, J., Hristienko, H., … White, B. N. (2003). Genetic Variation and Population Structure of Moose (*Alces alces*) at Neutral and Functional DNA Loci. *Canadian Journal of Zoology, 81*(4), 670–683. doi:10.1139/z03-030

CHAPTER 7
Research Design for the Forensic Science Student and Practitioner

Experiential Learning at Trent University's Crime Scene Training Facility

Photo credit: Mike Illes

Good, sound research projects begin with straightforward, uncompli-
cated thoughts that are easy to read and understand.
   —*John W. Creswell (2014)*

In this chapter, we review the basic concepts of research design and provide forensic research examples for correlational study and experimental design. We'll explore quantitative, qualitative, and mixed-method approaches; the stages of research design; and basic scientific concepts, such as applied versus pure research. We will define case-specific research and discuss the present issues with this type of research as it relates to forensics. We emphasize core research practices like research design types, planning the experiment, conducting literature reviews, and formulating research hypotheses and research questions.

BASIC STAGES OF SCIENTIFIC RESEARCH

The following provides a typical linear scientific approach of how to do research; however, scientific inquiry is often not this straightforward, with researchers continually considering new information, new hypotheses, new problems, and rethinking design. This can make the process nonlinear and more complex (Lanier & Briggs, 2014; Reiff, Harwood, & Phillipson, 2002). Figure 7.1 depicts a more accurate representation of scientific inquiry.

Step 1: Selecting a Research Topic

Topic selection can be an intensive process. The main purpose of conducting research is to provide answers to a novel problem. Therefore, it is imperative to conduct a preliminary literature review on the topic to ascertain if and to what extent it has been researched. It is also important to know if the research is worthwhile and if the problem is testable. It is common at this point in the design for the researcher to start to question everything. Be careful not to make the project focus too large.

It can also be useful at this stage to review the general scientific theories, laws, and philosophy surrounding the topic under investigation.

Step 2: Identifying a Testable Research Question and Hypotheses

Now that you have your research problem, the next step is to develop a testable research question. What is it you would like to research about

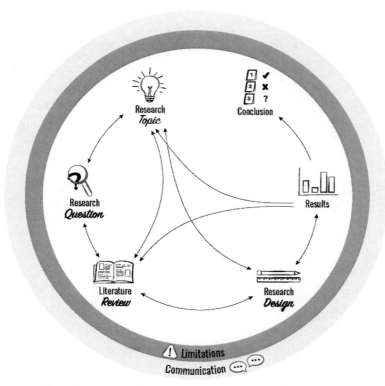

Figure 7.1. An Example of a Nonlinear Approach to Scientific Inquiry

Source: Designed by Sonia Seto, Sonia Seto Studios, www.soniaseto.com

your topic? At this point you should also be developing a testable null hypothesis and alternative hypotheses.

Step 3: Literature Review

A literature review is a "systematic, explicit, and reproducible method for identifying, evaluating, and synthesizing the existing body of completed and recorded work produced by researchers, scholars, and practitioners" (Fink, 2005). Literature reviews are used by researchers, students, practitioners, service users, managers, and policymakers. For an in-depth analysis of the literature review, see chapter 5, What the Literature Says: From Student to Expert.

Step 4: Research Design

Research design is the blueprint of your research and also a complex decision-making process. In this step, the researcher selects methods and techniques that can logically answer the research question. We will provide an in-depth analysis on research design and methods in the remainder of this chapter, including summarizing correlational and experimental research design studies through two forensic science examples.

Step 5: Data

Data can be quantitative, qualitative, or a mixture of both. In this stage you will design the collection process, collect the data, and analyze it. It is important to remember that quantitative and qualitative data are the two broad types of variables. Qualitative data can be broken down further to **nominal** (e.g., employment status, police, or civilian forensic science employees) or **ordinal** (e.g., a scale of confidence level in providing an expert opinion in court), and quantitative data can be **discrete** (e.g., the number of test questions answered correctly) or **continuous** (e.g., temperature). Therefore, the data type will dictate the statistical method employed. Knowing the method ahead of researching means a minimum sample set can be derived for the design. A statistician should be consulted at the start and throughout any research project, as the type of data must agree with the statistical model that will be used to analyze it (Illes & Wilson, 2020). See the following link for help when selecting data types and statistical models: https://stats.idre.ucla.edu/other/mult-pkg/whatstat/.

Step 6: Reporting Results

The results will be a narrative with a combination of graphs, tables, and/ or illustrative figures. This section should provide the data generated from the methods without any interpretation. The interpretation of the results by the researcher can be articulated in the discussion or conclusion.

Step 7: Conclusions and Limitations

The conclusion should pull it all together, indicate the limitations within the study, and suggest future implications and research (Lanier & Briggs, 2014).

TYPES OF RESEARCH DESIGN

Research design can be approached in many ways, especially when considering the different areas of study within the liberal arts and the sciences. The purpose of planning your research in this way is to ensure that your data collection is precise and enables you to logically address the research problem (University of Southern California, 2019). Scientific discovery is not a predetermined linear path, and each discipline has different approaches and challenges when it comes to research design (Reiff et al., 2002). Since forensic science is multidisciplinary, each area of practice may have its own specific research questions to answer and different materials to work with. To further complicate this situation, forensic science also needs to be **transdisciplinary** to define and explore some of the common research questions that may need answering in all disciplines. For instance, disciplines such as toolmark and footwear comparison equally struggle with limited research on the **law of uniqueness** (PCAST, 2016). A transdisciplinary research approach could be beneficial to both practices.

Our earlier review of the NAS report and PCAST directive provided a clear image of the desire for quantitative experimental research design. This would not only support the underpinnings of the various disciplines but also provide statistical information on the discipline being researched. However, there is little or no mention of the use of qualitative research approaches in these documents. This is not surprising when considering that most of the contributing authors are from the core sciences, with little representation from forensic, social, or humanity researchers (NAS, 2009; PCAST, 2016). We agree, when possible, that a quantitative experimental research design with replication should be used in forensic science. However, in those situations where quantitative data is limited or not available and replication is not possible, it would be irresponsible not to consider the use of different types of data sets and research approaches (qualitative and mixed method). In fact, the quantitative tradition can constrain knowledge, and the addition of qualitative data might be crucial to give context, to put a narrative on the experimental and statistical analysis, and to provide a foundation for replication and generalization (Onghena, Maes, & Heyvaert, 2018). The use of qualitative data or a limited-sized data set has a long history in research. Much of sociology research does not use the scientific method and may depend on other approaches such as **observational design**, case study, or **grounded theory** (Hilborn & Mangel, 1997; Platt, 1964; University of Southern California, 2019).

The development of a research project takes expertise, and we endorse a collaborative approach, specifically when forensic practitioners involve expert researchers from academic institutions (Bruce, Flynn, & Stagg-Peterson, 2011; Granér & Kronkvist, 2015; Griffiths, 2014; Kelty & Julian, 2011; Public Safety Canada, 2017; Rojek, Alpert, & Smith, 2012; Steinheider et al., 2012). We maintain that a non-expert should not conduct research without the collaboration of a statistician and seasoned researchers in the area being investigated (Linacre, 2013).

There are numerous research approaches or designs that can be selected. Incorporating the results from multiple other projects that have used different approaches can strengthen your conclusions. This is called research **triangulation**. We present several designs that may be appropriate in the forensic framework.

Experimental with Repetitions

This experimental design allows the researcher to have control over all variables within the design: Dependent variables can be left the same while changing one (independent) variable and testing the hypotheses. This can identify what may have caused something to occur in the research. Repetitions within the experiment provide stronger evidence when suggesting causation. This type of design provides for strong inference and should be used, if viable (Eberhardt & Thomas, 1991). An example of a publication of a forensic science experimental design with repetitions is as follows:

Wells, J., & LaMotte, L. (2017). The Role of a PMI-Prediction Model in Evaluating Forensic Entomology Experimental Design, the Importance of Covariates, and the Utility of Response Variables for Estimating Time Since Death. *Insects, 8*(2), 47. doi:10.3390/insects8020047

Experimental without Repetitions

Experimental repetition provides an estimation of both the experimental error and the main effect of any factor. A lack of replication in an experiment will limit the researcher's ability to address the significance of an experimental result. Therefore, repetition on a large sample set is desirable; however, there are times when this is not possible (Eberhardt & Thomas, 1991). Examples of publications of forensic science experimental designs without repetition are as follows:

Maclean, B., Powley, K., & Dahlstrom, D. (2001). A Case Study Illustrating Another Logical Explanation for High Velocity Impact Spatter. *Canadian Society of Forensic Science Journal, 34*(4), 191–195. doi: 10.1080/00085030.2001.10757528

Rossi, C., Herold, L. D., Bevel, T., McCauley, L., & Guadarrama, S. (2017). Cranial Backspatter Pattern Production Utilizing Human Cadavers. *Journal of Forensic Sciences, 63*(5), 1526–1532. doi:10.1111/1556-4029.13713

Correlational

A correlational study can indicate a relationship between variables and is very useful in determining if sufficient evidence exists to proceed with a full experimental design project; however, this type of study has limitations, specifically when attempting to assign causation. In a full experimental design, changes in one variable may affect another and these effects are not tested to show the level of influence within a correlation design (Bordens & Abbott, 2011). An example of a forensic science correlational study publication is as follows:

Cappelle, D., Neels, H., De Keukeleire, S., Fransen, E., Dom, G., Vermassen, A., ... van Nuijs, A. L. N. (2017). Ethyl Glucuronide in Keratinous Matrices as Biomarker of Alcohol Use: A Correlation Study Between Hair and Nails. *Forensic Science International, 279*, 187–191. doi:10.1016/j.forsciint.2017.08.022

Mixed Methods

Mixed-method research uses both quantitative and qualitative research methods in one study. This approach can provide a depth and breadth of understanding of the research question that may not be available when using a quantitative or qualitative method alone. However, a limitation with using mixed-method research is that you must analyze and collect different data sets. The researcher must also understand the complexity of the process and have knowledge of multiple data collection and analytical methodologies (Lanier & Briggs, 2014; McKim, 2017; Onghena et al., 2018). An example of a forensic science mixed methods research publication is as follows:

Mottershead, T., Khalifa, N., & Völlm, B. (2020). A Mixed-Methods Examination of Patient Feedback Within Forensic and Non-Forensic Mental Healthcare Services. *The Journal of Forensic Psychiatry & Psychology, 31*(1), 106–122. doi:10.1080/14789949.2019.1680726

Exploratory

This design is used to gain background knowledge, to understand how best to proceed in investigating an issue and what research methods may be appropriate, and to develop hypotheses. An exploratory design can be useful in forensic research because it is the study of a research problem when there are few or no earlier studies to reference or rely upon to predict an outcome (University of Southern California, 2019). An example of a forensic science exploratory research publication is as follows:

Pivetti, M., Caggiano, A., Cieri, F., Di Battista, S., & Berti, C. (2017). Support for the Forensic DNA Database and Public Safety Concerns: An Exploratory Study. *The Open Psychology Journal, 10*(1), 104–117. doi:10.2174/1874350101710010104

Cohort

A cohort study involves a subgroup (forensic discipline) of the subject or representative group (forensic community) that has some commonality or similarity. Cohort studies benefit the forensic community because they provide insight for the overall (forensic science) community about information gained from a subgroup (specific forensic discipline). The researcher can also study the effects of something that has already happened—for example, comparing the acceptance of expert-opinion evidence supplied in court based on science to that based on pseudoscience. However, it is difficult to control variables in this design (Devane & Healy, 2011; Glenn, 2005; Talman et al., 2018). An example of a forensic science cohort study publication is as follows:

Conlan, X. A., Harvey, M. L., Gunning, T. K., & Durdle, A. (2019). Forensic Undergraduate Cohort; Job Readiness Curricula. *Australian Journal of Forensic Sciences, 51*(sup1), S243–S246. doi:10.1080/00450618.2019.1568550

Descriptive

Descriptive research is designed to depict the participants or status of a studied phenomenon in an accurate way. It can answer who, what, when, where, and how within a research problem. It does not answer why, though. Three ways of conducting descriptive research are by observations, case studies, or surveys (Garstang et al., 2016; University of Southern California, 2019). An example of a forensic science descriptive research design publication is as follows:

Magalhães, A. F. A., & Caldas, E. D. (2018). Underreporting of Fatal Poisonings in Brazil - A Descriptive Study Using Data from Four Information Systems. *Forensic Science International, 287*, 136–141. doi:10.1016/j.forsciint.2018.03.040

Case Study

A case study is a detailed investigation of a specific research problem, which is useful if little is known about the matter. It can provide an understanding of a complex issue through detailed contextual analysis of a limited number of replications. It could be used in forensic science to extend the knowledge of specific and rare cases, but the researcher must be aware that this design may offer little basis for establishing reliability or generalizability of the findings in a forensic report or court. This type of study may also bias a researcher's interpretation of the findings (see chapter 8 for a discussion on bias and ethics in research), specifically if they have been involved in the crime scene or with case information (University of Southern California, 2019). An example of a forensic science case study publication is as follows:

Shaw, A. (2019). The Role of the Gunshot Residue Expert in Case Review - A Case Study. *Forensic Science International, 300*, 28–31. doi:10.1016/j .forsciint.2019.04.024

Historical or Archival Design

Historical research is very similar to conducting a literature review for court or forensic investigations (see chapter 5 for a detailed description on how to conduct literature reviews). By collecting, verifying, and synthesizing evidence from the past, a researcher or practitioner can establish facts that defend or refute a hypothesis. Historical research is purely descriptive and may provide some interesting trends or correlations. Causal relationships cannot be established (Bordens & Abbott, 2011; University of Southern California, 2019). An example of a forensic science historical design study publication is as follows:

Cardoso, R., Alves, H., Richter, J., & Botelho, M. C. (2017). Parasites in Forensic Science: A Historic Perspective. *Annals of Parasitology, 63*(4), 235–241. doi:10.17420/ap6304.110

Sequential

Sequential design is the use of multiple research projects that are set up in a staged approach. After a research project is completed, the researcher could select their null or alternative hypothesis, or another sample set, for further investigation. In the end this provides a robust conclusion with multiple projects supporting the common research. One benefit of this design is that sample sets are not predetermined (University of

Southern California, 2019). An example of a forensic science sequential study publication is as follows:

Molina, C. M., Pringle, J. K., Saumett, M., & Hernández, O. (2015). Preliminary Results of Sequential Monitoring of Simulated Clandestine Graves in Colombia, South America, Using Ground Penetrating Radar and Botany. *Forensic Science International, 248*, 61–70. doi:10.1016/j .forsciint.2014.12.011

Sampling from Patterns

Sampling from patterns is the analysis of spatial patterns over a selected region. This approach can be useful in forensic science as many disciplines analyze and/or compare patterns, such as in friction ridge and BPA. There are many ways of summarizing pattern data, such as through **moving averages** or **spatial splines** (Eberhardt & Thomas, 1991). An example of a forensic science sampling from patterns publication is as follows:

De Moor, S., Vandeviver, C., & Vander Beken, T. (2018). Are DNA Data a Valid Source to Study the Spatial Behavior of Unknown Offenders? *Science & Justice, 58*(5), 315–322. doi:10.1016/j.scijus.2018.04.003

Mixed-Methods Single-Case Research

Mixed-methods single-case research (MMSCR) may be used to design case-specific forensic research studies. MMSCR is a combination of single-case quantitative experimentation and qualitative case-study methods to answer a research question for a single case. This method is useful for forensic practitioners who wish to answer a research question, in a practical way, that is pertinent to an investigation and the courts. Because pragmatism is philosophically attached to mixed-method research, it is a good pick for solving the real-world problems in forensic investigations. There are two ways of approaching MMSCR: qualitative case studies in which quantitative research components are brought in or single-case experiments that are complemented with qualitative data (Horner et al., 2005; Onghena et al., 2018). An example of a forensic science MMSCR publication is as follows:

Vakhitova, Z., Webster, J., Alston-Knox, C., Reynald, D., & Townsley, M. (2018). Offender–Victim Relationship and Offender Motivation in the Context of Indirect Cyber Abuse: A Mixed-Method Exploratory Analysis. *International Review of Victimology*, *24*(3), 347–366. doi:10.1177/0269758017743073

CASE-SPECIFIC RESEARCH DESIGN

Our conception of case-specific research is the process of answering a case research question that is pertinent to an investigation and to the courts. The fundamental difference between academic research and forensic case-specific research is that the latter examines past events with no knowledge of what happened at the time of the event. Conducting research for a forensic case question can present complications—such as time since the event, research time limits, limited sample sets, uncontrolled variables, quantitative and qualitative data sets, and other unknowns—that can lead to justifying problematic assumptions.

Case-specific research strategies exist within different areas of study (e.g., ecological science); however, these approaches generally apply only to existing problems (Kueffer, 2006). The fundamental difference between case-specific research in these more traditional fields and in forensic science is that forensic research deals with no or limited knowledge of past events. This distinction makes the selection of research methods more complex and problematic, and at this time there is no direction on how to implement this framework. No forensic science studies have yet provided insight on conducting research for case-specific questions and overcoming the inherent challenges with this type of research.

This chapter describes the design of two of our current research projects that investigate some aspect of forensic epistemology. The designs presented in this chapter provide clear examples of a correlational study and an experimental design. The first project, a correlational study, evaluates the use of reasoning by practitioners in the field of crime scene investigation. Many studies support the use of the scientific method within crime scene work, and recent writings have indicated a movement within this discipline from a purely technical to a more scientific approach (Crispino, 2008; Crispino et al., 2011; Ludwig et al., 2012; Shaler, 2012). In fact, Dr. Paul Kirk (1963) suggested that criminalistics needed to evolve to be more scientific in nature. Unfortunately, even within recent studies on the critical skills required by a CSI, such as those by Kelty and colleagues (Kelty, 2011; Kelty & Gordon, 2012; Kelty, Julian, & Robertson, 2011; Kelty, Robertson, & Julian, 2017), the researchers do not address scientific reasoning on a wide-ranging scale. Therefore, no baseline currently exists in the literature that specifically examines what reasoning skills should be essential for a CSI.

This reasoning study directly merges with our second study, which explores the reference point requirements for case-specific research design. We suggest that a forensic practitioner who is called to conduct research must be able to use hypothetico-deductive reasoning and be an expert at research. The second project uses experimental design, showcasing the formulation of a scientific correlational study and experimental design research (and their concepts), which are novel to forensic science. The correlational study and experimental design will be the most prominent types of approaches that you will encounter in the forensic science domain.

Example 1: Forensic Science Correlational Study Design

Here we share a forensic science example of a correlational study that tested the reasoning ability of CSIs. As previously stated, a correlational study is useful in determining if sufficient evidence exists to proceed to a full experimental design project; however, this type of study has limitations, specifically when attempting to assign causation: changes in one variable may affect another, but those effects are not tested to show the level of influence within a correlation design. In the end, the correlation study can indicate a relationship between variables that supports further research (Bordens & Abbott, 2011).

Step 1: Select a Research Topic

The topic of this research was forensic epistemology—testing the reasoning skills of a CSI. (Note: A different statistical approach was used in the original research article.)

Step 2: Identify a Testable Research Question

We tested the following hypotheses (alternative hypotheses were implicit):

Hypothesis: There is a positive relationship between higher education and the ability to apply formal reasoning to crime scene
evidence, resulting in more accurate analyses.

Prediction: If a CSI has a higher education, their reasoning will be
better and they will score higher on the classroom test of scientific reasoning (CTSR).

Hypothesis: Crime scene expert experience plays a less significant role
in the ability to apply formal reasoning to crime scene evidence.

Prediction: If a CSI has a high level of experience, then that experience will not increase their reasoning ability and they will not
do better on the CTSR.

Hypothesis: The employment status of a crime scene expert is not
correlated to one's reasoning ability.

Prediction: If a CSI is employed as a police officer, then their employment status will not increase their reasoning ability and
they will not do better on the CTSR.

Step 3: Literature Review

The literature has indicated that CSIs should be able to use advanced
reasoning skills, such as hypothetico-deductive reasoning (the scientific method), at a crime scene (Crispino, 2008; Crispino et al.,
2011; de Leeuwe, 2017; Harrison, 2006; Horswell & Edwards, 1997;
Jamieson, 2004; Julian, Kelty, & Robertson, 2012; Ludwig, Fraser, &
Williams, 2012; Makin, 2012; Milliet, Delémont, & Margot, 2014;
Perepechina, 2017; Saldivar, 2017; Shaler, 2012). Unfortunately, no one
has conducted extensive tests on active CSIs to assess their level of reasoning (Kelty, 2011; Kelty & Gordon, 2012; Kelty, Julian, & Robertson,
2011; Kelty, Robertson, & Julian, 2017).

We selected education level, employment status (police officer or
civilian crime scene technician), and years of experience as the de-
mographics for this research, because these areas have been subjects
of great debate within the discipline of crime scene investigation

(Baber et al., 2006; Capsambelis, 2002; Department of Justice, 2004; PCAST, 2016; Saldivar, 2017). Researching the correlation between reasoning skills and education, employment status, and years of experience may provide evidence to support certain hiring practices, required reasoning skill sets, and education levels.

Step 4: Research Design
Within this study, we incorporated the CTSR developed by Lawson and colleagues (Lawson, 1978; Lawson, 2004; Lawson, 2005; Lawson et al., 1991; Lawson et al., 2000) to test the reasoning process of research participants. We conducted initial research to provide evidence supporting the validity of this test and its use for our specific research circumstances.

Step 5: Data
To acquire data, we developed and distributed an online survey. Ethics approval was granted by the Trent University Research Ethics Board (REB) (see chapter 8 for further detail on REBs). The completed questionnaire included the 24 multiple-choice reasoning questions developed by Lawson and colleagues (1978), along with additional demographic questions, and it was distributed electronically to crime scene investigation professionals using the Qualtrics software available from Trent University. We also solicited the International Association of Identification (IAI) for approval to distribute a voluntary, anonymous electronic questionnaire to their members. The global membership of this organization consists of active practitioners in the fields of forensic identification, investigation, and scientific examination of physical events (IAI, 2016). With membership registration, individuals provide information on their fields of expertise—thus, a list of members who are CSIs was easily produced. The IAI forwarded the email addresses of active CSI members, providing a comprehensive population for random sampling. Using a random sampling function within Microsoft Excel 2016, 1,400 participants were contacted to participate. A robust random sample set was determined to be 84 individuals ($n = 84$), using power analysis within R (R Foundation, 2018).

Further information on this research design included the following:

- data collected: ordinal variable from a random sample set;
- statistical models used: Spearman's correlational coefficient and a t-test to test the hypothesis;
- power analysis: a power analysis R provided the sample size required to detect the effect of a given size with a given degree of confidence. Therefore, the approximate correlation power calculation (arctangh transformation) is $n = 84$, with r $= 0.3$, sig. level $= 0.05$, power $= 0.8$, where n is the sample size, r is the effect size, and Cohen suggests that r values of 0.1, 0.3, and 0.5 represent small, medium, and large effect sizes respectively; sig. level (significance level) is the probability of finding an effect that is not there, and power is the probability of finding an effect that is there (R Foundation, 2018).

Step 6: Report Results

The results were reported in graphics—in this case, box plots and table formats. The tables provided correlation coefficients and p-values that supported the conclusions.

Step 7: Conclusions and Limitations

This research was one of the first studies that included the use of a CTSR for testing CSIs. It provided exploratory research information (correlation between test scores and education level) that supported further research into the subject, such as ranking the CSIs' test scores by reasoning pattern, which could include proportional reasoning, control of variables, probability reasoning, correlational reasoning, hypothetico-deductive reasoning, and conservation of matter and volume (Hanson, 2016). This could be an experimental design study that assigns causation and could direct pedagogic practice in post-secondary institutions or for practitioner-driven training. The study also supported the use of a CTSR in the forensic science employment pre-test, identifying training gaps and assessing forensic science students and expert witnesses.

It provided valuable knowledge on how education level, employment status, and experience are associated for CSIs. The results could be applied in policy and best practice development. The study was limited to correlation and could not assign causation to the issue, though (Illes, Wilson, & Bruce, 2019).

Example 2: Forensic Science Experimental Design

Step 1: Select a Research Topic

This study will investigate potential strategies for selecting research methods (data types) for case-specific research in three pattern-interpretation disciplines within forensic science.

Step 2: Identify a Testable Research Question

The following hypothesis was tested (the alternative hypothesis is implicit):

> Hypothesis: There will be differences in the effectiveness of research methods when applied to different forensic disciplines.
> Predictions: Given the nature of forensic applications of friction ridge, footwear impression, and bloodstain pattern analysis, we predict that the mixed-method data collection approach will be more effective than the quantitative or qualitative data collection approach.

Step 3: Literature Review

This study's literature review was limited; however, we did find significant discrepancies in how practitioners were conducting case-specific research. The lack of rigorous scientific methodology supported the need for research into this topic.

Step 4: Research Design

We developed three cases from different pattern-interpretation disciplines: a friction ridge analysis, a bloodstain pattern analysis, and a footwear impression analysis. For each case, a series of experiments were created using three different research methods: a quantitative approach (using numeric data), a qualitative approach (using image data), and a mixed-methods approach (using both numeric and image data). These fabricated research cases and data allow for knowledge of the right answer (ground truth) within an invented investigation, thereby eliminating the typical challenges of case-specific research. Electronic files were compiled for each case and research method and forwarded to a forensic practitioner who is an expert within the prescribed discipline.

Step 5: Data

Quantitative data were analyzed using ANOVA, and the qualitative data was sorted and coded using NVivo 12 Suite (NVivo, 2018).

Furthermore, the design included the following:

- data collected: continuous, categorical, and ordinal variables from a random sample set that had random assignment for three research models and three forensic disciplines;
- statistical models used: ANOVA analysis;
- power analysis: a power analysis in R provided the sample size required for a balanced one-way analysis of variance power calculation: $k = 9$, $n = 27$, $f = 0.25$, sig. level $= 0.05$, power $= 0.8$, 9 groups—BPA + FR + FW: $28*9 = 252$. Here, k is the number of groups, n is the sample size, f is the effect size and Cohen suggests that f values of 0.1, 0.25, and 0.4 represent small, medium, and large effect sizes, respectively; sig. level is the probability of finding an effect that is not there, and power is the probability of finding an effect that is there (R Foundation, 2018).

Step 6: Report Results

The results were reported in graphics—in this case, clustered columns and table formats. The tables provided information on whether there was a three-way interaction between the three research methods and three disciplines.

Step 7: Conclusions and Limitations

The evidence from the study supported the use of a mixed-method data collection and analysis approach for case-specific research within forensic science; however, further research is required to tease out appropriate guidelines and methodologies that would be accepted by the global scientific community. More importantly, the results supported a need for forensic science practitioner education in experimental design and the use of the scientific method in case-specific research, specifically for the more complex mixed-methods approaches. This research design is both applied—scientific planning to answer a real-life problem—and pure—extending the knowledge base of a discipline (Illes & Wilson, 2020).

Instructional Pop Out

The following link lists further information on research design:

University of Southern California—Types of Research Designs: https://libguides.usc.edu/writingguide/researchdesigns

SUMMARY

This chapter's main message is to consult with experts—statisticians and domain-specific researchers—when attempting to design and conduct a forensic science research project and for case-specific research. We've provided basic information on the stages of research design as well as multiple approaches that may be useful in your forensic science research. We used two real-life forensic-related examples (correlational and experimental designs) to show how a forensic research scientist would work through these projects. Hopefully this experience has aided you in understanding the critical thought and knowledge that is required to conduct research in forensic science and the need to seek out appropriate experts.

Robert Chisnall

Personal Profile

My journey into forensic science was not conventional. From an early age I was fascinated by science, mathematics, puzzles, and knots. My other pursuits included rock climbing and outdoor activities, and I later became a certified climbing instructor. These interests expanded into testing safety systems and knots as well as extensive reading regarding risk and crisis management. I performed a considerable number of tests, investigating the strength and security of knots, thereby producing data applicable to rescues and climbing.

Photo credit: Margarita Babkova

I did a BSc in biology with a mathematics minor in the 1970s. Teaching climbing and rescue led to a bachelor of education and a master of education in curriculum design and adventure education. Equipped with this experience and training in quantitative and qualitative research, I was primed to become deeply involved in the forensic analysis of knots and ligatures, as well as accident investigation.

Q. How Did You Get Into Forensic Science?

In the late 1970s, I corresponded with Geoffrey Budworth, a British police inspector who's now retired, someone I regard as the father of modern forensic knot analysis and from whom I learned the basics. Among others, we were founding members of the International Guild of Knot Tyers, a worldwide organization of people with recreational and professional interests in knots. In the early 1980s, Budworth put the Toronto Metropolitan Police Department in touch with me concerning several cases involving knots. This was my initial hands-on exposure to forensic evidence. I was subsequently retained by the Crown, and I gave expert testimony for the first time. Unknown to me then, no knot expert had ever given testimony in Canada. This was for the best, because I was quite naive starting out.

Q. What Is Your Role as a Forensic Scientist?

I immediately realized that there was a great deal more to learn. So much was unknown when I began and, despite thousands of hours spent in research and data collection since then, many more questions still require answers. Thus, my part-time career in forensic knot analysis and research began. I discovered over the decades that the scientific literature was lacking, and some self-professed knot experts provided unsupportable opinions and made basic errors. There was too much subjectivity and not enough objectivity. I started formal behavioural research while I was in graduate school in the late 1980s, focusing on tyer handedness and knot-tying behaviour.

Over the following decades, I undertook multiple research projects, several of which have continued, and numerous new projects are pending. Surprisingly, my reading pursuant to forensic knot analysis included hundreds of papers from a diverse array of topics beyond forensic science, all of which inspired my research and provided insights into knot characteristics and tyer behaviour. Relevant subjects included psychology and epistemology; mathematics, particularly topology; physics and engineering; chemistry and biology; medical research; pathology; computer science; and even robotics. My research topics have included tyer handedness and knot chirality, tyer sophistication relative to innate tying habits, external versus self-tying, mathematical modelling of knot security and strength, the combinatorics of factor knots, and knot metrics, variance, and change, to mention a few. I do this self-funded research independently in my spare time.

Q. What Kind of Equipment Do You Use?

Case knot analysis entails exhibit preservation and documentation, precise knot identification, recognition of variance and chirality, detailed

Continued

ligature measurements, the recording of pertinent qualitative information, determining the tying order and function of those knots, and a consideration of tying behaviour. The resources employed in my research and case analyses are relatively simple: a massive reference library, a growing database, multiple rope samples, digital cameras, mechanical and digital devices for measuring forces and dimensions, a small dissecting microscope essential for examining knots tied in thin cords and strings, drawing materials, and computers with multiple large monitors for examining evidence photos in detail. In addition, cumulative experience and constant diligence are essential. Each case usually presents something unique. Some investigations require the acquisition of unconventional tying materials to test strength and security—like bed sheets, for example. Unusual testing procedures are sometimes needed. In one case, it was necessary to assess the elongation of nylon stockings over long periods of time while loaded down with weight.

Since that time, I have analyzed more than 200 domestic and international cases involving knots. Several accidents involving rope and knots have required analysis for civil proceedings. My research has produced peer-reviewed papers published in multiple journals. In 2000, I wrote *The Forensic Analysis of Knots and Ligatures*, which was published in the US. Although much of its content is still relevant and goes beyond Geoffrey Budworth's *Knots and Crime* (1985), it is out of date. I have amassed enough data and new information to extend well beyond the scope of that manual.

My motivation is multifaceted. I enjoy research and believe I am contributing something unique to the field of forensics—no one else appears to be doing any research in this area, and it is a unique and unusual field of study. Within forensic science, knot analysis is not mainstream. It is often overlooked in terms of rigour and detail. My hope is that I can inspire future forensic scientists to further this work and build on the foundation that I and others have established. The avenues for inquiry are open-ended.

QUESTIONS TO PONDER

1. What are the main differences between a correlational study and an experimental design?
2. Define mixed-methods research.
3. What are the seven stages of research design?
4. Why is research design so complicated?
5. Why is experimental design with repetitions considered the most robust approach by most scientists?

GLOSSARY

continuous: a variable value obtained by measurement (Statistics How To, 2018).

discrete: a variable value obtained by counting (Statistics How To, 2018).

grounded theory: an inductive methodology that does not use hypothesis testing (Bryant, 2017).

law of uniqueness: a rule that is used in several forensic disciplines; the most common is friction ridge analysis: "Each individual possesses a unique arrangement of friction ridge skin. Specifically, the ridge arrangements, the robust arrangements of the minutiae within the ridge patterns, and the shapes and structures of the ridges all combine to form a unique arrangement of friction ridge skin in the hands and feet of each individual" (NIJ, 2011).

moving averages: the calculation of a series of averages of different subsets (Oxford English Dictionary, 2018).

nominal: a variable that has two or more categories with no order. Also called a categoric variable (Statistics How To, 2018).

observational design: an uncontrolled study where researchers watch a group of people (Walliman, 2017).

ordinal: a variable that is categoric; that is, the values are ordered (Statistics How To, 2018).

spatial splines: spline methods are used for spatial interpolation of gentle surfaces (Eberhardt & Thomas, 1991).

transdisciplinary: a research strategy that crosses branches of knowledge of two or more disciplines (Aboelela et al., 2007).

triangulation: the use of multiple methods or data sources in a research study to help validate the conclusions (Carter et al., 2014).

FURTHER READINGS

Associated Press. (2017). Las Vegas Shooter's Brain to Undergo Microscopic Study. *Guardian*, October 29. Retrieved from https://www.theguardian .com/us-news/2017/oct/29/las-vegas-shooter-stephen-paddock-brain-study?CMP=Share_iOSApp_Other

Baechler, S. (2019). Do We Need to Know Each Other? Bridging the Gap between the University and the Professional Field. *Policing: A Journal of Policy and Practice*, *13*(1), 102–114. doi:10.1093/police/pax091

Bell, S., Sah, S., Albright, T. D., Gates, S. J., Jr., Denton, M. B., & Casadevall, A. (2018). A Call for More Science in Forensic Science. Proceedings of the National Academy of Sciences of the United States of America. doi:10.1073/pnas.1712161115

Bono, J. P. (2011). Commentary on the Need for a Research Culture in the Forensic Sciences. *UCLA Law Review*, *58*, 781–787.

Cave, R., & Molina, D. K. (2014). Evidence-Based Evidence: A Practical Method for Bayesian Analysis of Forensic Evidence. *Law, Probability and Risk*, *14*(2), 135–145. doi:10.1093/lpr/mgu019

Champod, C. (2014). Research Focused Mainly on Bias Will Paralyse Forensic Science. *Science and Justice*, *54*(2), 107–109.

Gertner, N. (2011). Commentary on the Need for a Research Culture in the Forensic Sciences. *UCLA Law Review*, *58*, 789–793.

Hilborn, R. A. Y., & Mangel, M. (1997). Alternative Views of the Scientific Method and of Modeling. In R. A. Y. Hilborn & M. Mangel (Eds.), *The Ecological Detective* (pp. 12–38). Princeton: Princeton University Press.

Kelty, S. F., & Julian, R. (2011). Success in Forensic Science Research and Other Collaborative Projects: Meeting Your Partners' Expectations. *Forensic Science Policy and Management: An International Journal*, *2*(3), 141–147. doi:10.1080/19409044.2012.674086

Langenburg, G. (2011). Scientific Research Supporting the Foundations of Friction Ridge Examinations. In *The Fingerprint Sourcebook* (pp. 1–27). Washington: National Institute of Justice. Retrieved from http://www.nij.gov/pubs-sum/225320.htm

Linacre, A. (2013). Towards a Research Culture in the Forensic Sciences. *Australian Journal of Forensic Sciences, 45*(4), 381–388. doi:10.1080/00450 618.2012.738246

Margot, P. (2011). Commentary on the Need for a Research Culture in the Forensic Sciences. *UCLA Law Review, 58*, 795–801.

McCartney, C., Cassella, J., & Chin, P. (2011). *Lowering the Drawbridges: Legal & Forensic Science Education for the 21st Century.*

Mnookin, J. L., Cole, S. A., Dror, I. E., Fisher, B. A. J., Houck, M. M., Inman, K., ... Stoney, D. A. (2011). The Need for a Research Culture in the Forensic Sciences. *UCLA Law Review, 58*(3), 725–779.

Platt, J. R. (1964). Strong Inference. *Science, 146*(3642), 347–353.

Public Safety Canada. (2017). Research Summary: Civilianization of Police in Canada. Ottawa: Government of Canada. Retrieved from https://www.publicsafety.gc.ca/cnt/rsrcs/pblctns/2015-s042/index-en.aspx

REFERENCES

Aboelela, S. W., Larson, E., Bakken, S., Carrasquillo, O., Formicola, A., Glied, S. A., ... Gebbie, K. M. (2007). Defining Interdisciplinary Research: Conclusions from a Critical Review of the Literature. *Health Services Research, 42*(1 Part 1), 329–346.

Baber, C., Smith, P., Cross, J., Hunter, J. E., & McMaster, R. (2006). Crime Scene Investigation as Distributed Cognition. *Pragmatics & Cognition, 14*(2), 357–385. doi:10.1075/pc.14.2.14bab

Bordens, K. S., & Abbott, B. B. (2011). *Research Design and Methods: A Process Approach.* New York: McGraw-Hill.

Bruce, C. D., Flynn, T., & Stagg-Peterson, S. (2011). Examining What We Mean by *Collaboration* in Collaborative Action Research: A Cross-Case Analysis. *Educational Action Research, 19*(4), 433–452. doi:10.1080/09650 792.2011.625667

Bryant, A. (2017). *Grounded Theory and Grounded Theorizing: Pragmatism in Research Practice*. New York: Oxford University Press.

Cappelle, D., Neels, H., De Keukeleire, S., Fransen, E., Dom, G., Vermassen, A., ... van Nuijs, A. L. N. (2017). Ethyl Glucuronide in Keratinous Matrices as Biomarker of Alcohol Use: A Correlation Study Between Hair and Nails. *Forensic Science International, 279*, 187–191. doi:10.1016/j.forsciint.2017.08.022

Capsambelis, C. R. (2002). So Your Student Wants to Be a Crime Scene Technician? *Journal of Criminal Justice Education, 13*(1), 113–127.

Cardoso, R., Alves, H., Richter, J., & Botelho, M. C. (2017). Parasites in Forensic Science: A Historic Perspective. *Annals of Parasitology, 63*(4), 235–241. doi:10.17420/ap6304.110

Carter, N., Bryant-Lukosius, D., DiCenso, A., Blythe, J., & Neville, A. J. (2014). The Use of Triangulation in Qualitative Research. *Oncology Nursing Forum, 41*(5), 545–547.

Conlan, X. A., Harvey, M. L., Gunning, T. K., & Durdle, A. (2019). Forensic Undergraduate Cohort; Job Readiness Curricula. *Australian Journal of Forensic Sciences, 51*(sup1), S243–S246. doi:10.1080/00450618.2019.1568550

Creswell, J. W. (2014). *Research Design: Qualitative, Quantitative, and Mixed Methods Approaches, Fourth Edition*. Washington: Sage.

Creswell, J. W., & Creswell, J. D. (2017). *Research Design: Qualitative, Quantitative, and Mixed Methods Approaches, Fifth Edition*. Thousand Oaks: Sage.

Crispino, F. (2008). Nature and Place of Crime Scene Management within Forensic Sciences. *Science and Justice, 48*(1), 24–28. doi:10.1016/j.scijus.2007.09.009

Crispino, F., Ribaux, O., Houck, M., & Margot, P. (2011). Forensic Science—A True Science? *Australian Journal of Forensic Sciences, 43*(2–3), 157–176. doi:10.1080/00450618.2011.555416

de Leeuwe, R. (2017). The Hiatus in Crime Scene Documentation: Visualisation of the Location of Evidence. *Journal of Forensic Radiology and Imaging, 8*, 13–16.

De Moor, S., Vandeviver, C., & Vander Beken, T. (2018). Are DNA Data a Valid Source to Study the Spatial Behavior of Unknown Offenders? *Science & Justice, 58*(5), 315–322. doi:10.1016/j.scijus.2018.04.003

Department of Justice. (2004). *Education and Training in Forensic Science: A Guide for Forensic Science Laboratories, Educational Institutions, and Students.* Washington: National Institute of Justice.

Devane, D., & Healy, P. (2011). Methodological Considerations in Cohort Study Designs. *Nurse Researcher, 18*(3), 32–36.

Eberhardt, L., & Thomas, J. (1991). Designing Environmental Field Studies. *Ecological Monographs, 61*(1), 53–73.

Fink, A. (2005). *Conducting Research Literature Reviews: From the Internet to Paper.* Thousand Oaks: Sage.

Garstang, J., Ellis, C., Griffiths, F., & Sidebotham, P. (2016). Unintentional Asphyxia, SIDS, and Medically Explained Deaths: A Descriptive Study of Outcomes of Child Death Review (CDR) Investigations Following Sudden Unexpected Death in Infancy. *Forensic Science, Medicine, and Pathology, 12*(4), 407–415. doi:10.1007/s12024-016-9802-0

Glenn, N. D. (2005). *Cohort Analysis.* Thousand Oaks: Sage.

Granér, R., & Kronkvist, O. (2015). *The Past, the Present and the Future of Police Research: Proceedings from the Fifth Nordic Police Research Seminar.* Retrieved from http://www.diva-portal.org/smash/get/diva2:798355/FULLTEXT01.pdf

Griffiths, C. T. (2014). *Economics of Policing: Baseline for Policing Research in Canada.* Ottawa: Public Safety Canada.

Hanson, S. T. (2016). *The Assessment of Scientific Reasoning Skills of High School Science Students: A Standardized Assessment Instrument.* Normal: Illinois State University.

Harrison, K. (2006). Is Crime Scene Examination Science, and Does It Matter Anyway? *Science and Justice, 46*(2), 65–68. doi.org/10.1016/S1355-0306(06)71576-3

Hilborn, R. A. Y., & Mangel, M. (1997). Alternative Views of the Scientific Method and of Modeling. In R. A. Y. Hilborn & M. Mangel (Eds.), *The Ecological Detective* (pp. 12–38). Princeton: Princeton University Press.

Horner, R. H., Carr, E. G., Halle, J., McGee, G., Odom, S., & Wolery, M. (2005). The Use of Single-Subject Research to Identify Evidence-Based Practice in Special Education. *Exceptional Children, 71*(2), 165–179.

Horswell, J., & Edwards, M. (1997). Development of Quality Systems Accreditation for Crime Scene Investigators in Australia. *Science and Justice, 37*(1), 3–8. doi:10.1016/s1355-0306(97)72134-8

IAI. (2016). Welcome to the International Society for Identification. Retrieved from https://www.theiai.org/index.php

Illes, M., & Wilson, P. (2020). Forensic Epistemology: Exploring Case-Specific Research in Forensic Science. *Canadian Society of Forensic Science Journal, 53*(1), 26–40. doi:10.1080/00085030.2020.1736811

Illes, M., Wilson, P., & Bruce, C. (2019). Forensic Epistemology: Testing the Reasoning Skills of Crime Scene Experts. *Canadian Society of Forensic Science Journal, 52*(4), 151–173. doi:10.1080/00085030.2019.1664260

Jamieson, A. (2004). A Rational Approach to the Principles and Practice of Crime Scene Investigation: I. Principles. *Science and Justice, 44*(1), 3–7. doi:10.1016/s1355-0306(04)71678-0

Julian, R., Kelty, S., & Robertson, J. (2012). "Get It Right the First Time": Critical Issues at the Crime Scene. *Current Issues in Criminal Justice, 24*(1), 25–37.

Kelty, S. F. (2011). Professionalism in Crime Scene Examination: Recruitment Strategies Using the Seven Key Attributes of Top Crime Scene Examiners. *Forensic Science Policy and Management: An International Journal, 2*(4), 198–204. doi:10.1080/19409044.2012.706689

Kelty, S. F., & Gordon, H. (2012). Professionalism in Crime Scene Examination: Recruitment Strategies, Part 2: Using a Psychometric Profile of Top Crime Scene Examiners in Selection Decision Making. *Forensic Science Policy and Management: An International Journal, 3*(4), 189–199. doi:10.1080/19409044.2013.858799

Kelty, S. F., & Julian, R. (2011). Success in Forensic Science Research and Other Collaborative Projects: Meeting Your Partners' Expectations. *Forensic Science Policy and Management: An International Journal, 2*(3), 141–147. doi:10.1080/19409044.2012.674086

Kelty, S. F., Julian, R., & Robertson, J. (2011). Professionalism in Crime Scene Examination: The Seven Key Attributes of Top Crime Scene Examiners. *Forensic Science Policy and Management: An International Journal, 2*(4), 175–186. doi:10.1080/19409044.2012.693572

Kelty, S. F., Robertson, J., & Julian, R. (2017). Beyond Technical Training to Professionalism in Crime Scene Examination: Enhancing Cognitive, Leadership, and Social Abilities in Career Development Programs. *Forensic Science Policy and Management: An International Journal, 8*(3–4), 65–78. doi:10.1080/19409044.2017.1370039

Kirk, P. L. (1963). The Ontogeny of Criminalistics. *Journal of Criminal Law, Criminology and Police Sciences, 54*, 235.

Kueffer, C. (2006). Integrative Ecological Research: Case-Specific Validation of Ecological Knowledge for Environmental Problem Solving. *GAIA— Ecological Perspectives for Science and Society, 15*(2), 115–120.

Lanier, M., & Briggs, L. T. (2014). *Research Methods in Criminal Justice and Criminology: A Mixed Methods Approach.* New York: Oxford University Press.

Lawson, A. E. (1978). The Development and Validation of a Classroom Test of Formal Reasoning. *Journal of Research in Science Teaching, 15*(1), 11–24.

Lawson, A. E. (2004). The Nature and Development of Scientific Reasoning: A Synthetic View. *International Journal of Science and Mathematics Education, 2*(3), 307–338. doi:10.1007/s10763-004-3224-2

Lawson, A. E. (2005). What Is the Role of Induction and Deduction in Reasoning and Scientific Inquiry? *Journal of Research in Science Teaching, 42*(6), 716–740. doi:10.1002/tea.20067

Lawson, A. E., Alkhoury, S., Benford, R., Clark, B. R., & Falconer, K. A. (2000). What Kinds of Scientific Concepts Exist? Concept Construction and Intellectual Development in College Biology. *Journal of Research in Science Teaching, 37*(9), 996–1018. doi:10.1002/1098-2736(200011)37:93.0.co;2-j

Lawson, A. E., McElrath, C. B., Burton, M. S., James, B. D., Doyle, R. P., Woodward, S. L., … Snyder, J. D. (1991). Hypothetico-Deductive Reasoning Skill and Concept Acquisition: Testing a Constructivist Hypothesis. *Journal of Research in Science Teaching, 28*(10), 953–970. doi:10.1002/tea.3660281006

Linacre, A. (2013). Towards a Research Culture in the Forensic Sciences. *Australian Journal of Forensic Sciences, 45*(4), 381–388. doi:10.1080/00450 618.2012.738246

Ludwig, A., Fraser, J., & Williams, R. (2012). Crime Scene Examiners and Volume Crime Investigations: An Empirical Study of Perception and Practice. *Forensic Science Policy and Management: An International Journal, 3*(2), 53–61. doi:10.1080/19409044.2012.728680

Maclean, B., Powley, K., & Dahlstrom, D. (2001). A Case Study Illustrating Another Logical Explanation for High Velocity Impact Spatter. *Canadian Society of Forensic Science Journal, 34*(4), 191–195. doi: 10.1080/00085030.2001.10757528

Magalhães, A. F. A., & Caldas, E. D. (2018). Underreporting of Fatal Poisonings in Brazil - A Descriptive Study Using Data from Four Information Systems. *Forensic Science International, 287*, 136–141. doi:10.1016/j.forsciint.2018.03.040

Makin, D. A. (2012). Symbolic Evidence Collection or "If All Else Fails, Throw Some Dust Around." *Forensic Science Policy and Management: An International Journal, 3*(3), 126–138. doi:10.1080/19409044.2013.780834

McKim, C. A. (2017). The Value of Mixed Methods Research. *Journal of Mixed Methods Research, 11*(2), 202–222. doi:10.1177/1558689815607096

Milliet, Q., Delémont, O., & Margot, P. (2014). A Forensic Science Perspective on the Role of Images in Crime Investigation and Reconstruction. *Science and Justice, 54*(6), 470–480. doi:10.1016/j.scijus.2014.07.001

Molina, C. M., Pringle, J. K., Saumett, M., & Hernández, O. (2015). Preliminary Results of Sequential Monitoring of Simulated Clandestine Graves in Colombia, South America, Using Ground Penetrating Radar and Botany. *Forensic Science International, 248*, 61–70. doi:10.1016/j.forsciint.2014.12.011

Mottershead, T., Khalifa, N., & Völlm, B. (2020). A Mixed-Methods Examination of Patient Feedback Within Forensic and Non-Forensic Mental Healthcare Services. *The Journal of Forensic Psychiatry & Psychology, 31*(1), 106–122. doi:10.1080/14789949.2019.1680726

NAS. (2009). *Strengthening Forensic Science in the United States: A Path Forward* (T. N. A. Press Ed.). Washington: National Academy of Sciences.

NIJ. (2011). *The Fingerprint Sourcebook*. Washington: National Institute of Justice. Retrieved from http://www.nij.gov/pubs-sum/225320.htm

NVivo. (2018). Product Page. Retrieved from http://www.qsrinternational.com/nvivo/nvivo-products

Onghena, P., Maes, B., & Heyvaert, M. (2018). Mixed Methods Single Case Research: State of the Art and Future Directions. *Journal of Mixed Methods Research, 13*(4), 461–480. doi:10.1177/1558689818789530

Oxford English Dictionary. (2018). Moving Averages. Retrieved from https://en.oxforddictionaries.com/

PCAST. (2016). *Report to the President Forensic Science in Criminal Courts: Ensuring Scientific Validity of Feature–Comparison Methods* (Executive Summary). Washington: President's Council of Advisors on Science and Technology.

Perepechina, I. (2017). Crime Stain as a Forensic Object: Some Essential Aspects of Examination. *Forensic Science International: Genetics Supplement Series, 6*, 531–533.

Pivetti, M., Caggiano, A., Cieri, F., Di Battista, S., & Berti, C. (2017). Support for the Forensic DNA Database and Public Safety Concerns: An Exploratory Study. *The Open Psychology Journal, 10*(1), 104–117. doi:10.2174/1874350101710010104

Platt, J. R. (1964). Strong Inference. *Science, 146*(3642), 347–353.

Public Safety Canada. (2017). Research Summary: Civilianization of Police in Canada. Ottawa: Government of Canada. Retrieved from https://www.publicsafety.gc.ca/cnt/rsrcs/pblctns/2015-s042/index-en.aspx

R Foundation. (2018). R: A Language and Environment for Statistical Computing. R Foundation for Statistical Computing. Retrieved from https://www.r-project.org/

Reiff, R., Harwood, W. S., & Phillipson, T. (2002). *A Scientific Method Based Upon Research Scientists' Conceptions of Scientific Inquiry.* Proceedings of the Annual International Conference of the Association for the Education of Teachers in Science (Charlotte, NC), January 10–13.

Rojek, J., Alpert, G., & Smith, H. (2012). The Utilization of Research by the Police. *Police Practice and Research, 13*(4), 329–341. doi:10.1080/1561426 3.2012.671599

Rossi, C., Herold, L. D., Bevel, T., McCauley, L., & Guadarrama, S. (2017). Cranial Backspatter Pattern Production Utilizing Human Cadavers. *Journal of Forensic Sciences, 63*(5), 1526–1532. doi:10.1111/1556-4029.13713

Saldivar, A. (2017). Minimum Education Requirements for Crime Scene Investigators. *Themis: Research Journal of Justice Studies and Forensic Science, 5*(1), 10.

Shaler, R. C. (2012). *Crime Scene Forensics: A Scientific Method Approach.* Boca Raton: CRC Press.

Shaw, A. (2019). The Role of the Gunshot Residue Expert in Case Review - A Case Study. *Forensic Science International, 300*, 28–31. doi:10.1016/j.forsciint.2019.04.024

Statistics How To. (2018). Home Page. Retrieved from https://www.statisticshowto.datasciencecentral.com/

Steinheider, B., Wuestewald, T., Boyatzis, R. E., & Kroutter, P. (2012). In Search of a Methodology of Collaboration: Understanding Researcher–Practitioner Philosophical Differences in Policing. *Police Practice and Research, 13*(4), 357–374. doi:10.1080/15614263.2012.671620

Talman, K., Hupli, M., Puukka, P., Leino-Kilpi, H., & Haavisto, E. (2018). The Predictive Value of Two On-Site Selection Methods of Undergraduate Nursing Students: A Cohort Study. *Journal of Nursing Education and Practice, 8*(7), 12.

University of Southern California. (2019). Organizing Your Social Sciences Research Paper: Types of Research Designs. Retrieved from http://libguides.usc.edu/writingguide/researchdesigns

Vakhitova, Z., Webster, J., Alston-Knox, C., Reynald, D., & Townsley, M. (2018). Offender–Victim Relationship and Offender Motivation in the Context of Indirect Cyber Abuse: A Mixed-Method Exploratory Analysis. *International Review of Victimology, 24*(3), 347–366. doi:10.1177/0269758017743073

Walliman, N. (2017). *Research Methods: The Basics*. London: Routledge.

Wells, J., & LaMotte, L. (2017). The Role of a PMI-Prediction Model in Evaluating Forensic Entomology Experimental Design, the Importance of Covariates, and the Utility of Response Variables for Estimating Time Since Death. *Insects, 8*(2), 47. doi:10.3390/insects8020047

CHAPTER 8

The Importance of Ethics and Impartiality in Forensic Science

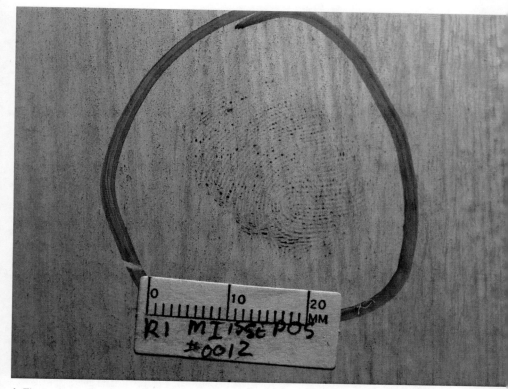

A Fingerprint Dusted with Black Powder

Photo credit: Mike Illes

In short, there exists in the field of criminalistics a serious deficiency in basic theory and principles, as contrasted with the large assortment of effective technical procedures.

—*Paul L. Kirk (1963)*

Based on the current literature on **cognitive bias** as it relates to forensic science in Canada, this chapter defines *bias*, discusses current research and Canadian court decisions on bias, and provides possible solutions, as suggested by experts. In what follows, we support the roles of the scientific method and evidence-based analysis in helping to reduce or control bias.

We also discuss ethics. Forensic science has an array of professional ethics guidelines from a wide array of sources, like the Canadian Society of Forensic Science and the Canadian Identification Society. This chapter aims to provide you with a basic understanding of ethics in Canadian forensic science. You will also learn about the university research ethics board system and the Canadian Tri-Council Policy Statement on Ethical Conduct for Research Involving Humans.

WHY IS BEING AWARE OF BIAS IMPORTANT TO A CANADIAN FORENSIC SCIENCE EXPERT?

Cognitive bias can be defined as an error in thinking when processing information and can come in a number of forms. In forensic science, cognitive bias must be understood by the stakeholders (practitioners, lawyers, judges, and society), as it can impact final conclusions in a case. Some commonly found forms of cognitive bias in forensic science are confirmation bias, where the person only uses the information that confirms their belief in something; contextual bias, where the expert's decision is influenced by extraneous information or factors; and **selection bias**, which is introduced when selecting specific individuals in or for an investigation (Found, 2014; Kukucka et al., 2017; Quigley-McBride & Wells, 2018). These three forms of bias will be demonstrated in the example court cases to follow.

There are two core reasons for the reader to understand and mitigate the risk of bias. The first is to do good science. Our biases infiltrate everything we do—our everyday decision making, our crime scene analyses, our case benchwork, and our research. Therefore, as practitioners, bias can influence the outcome of our analysis and testimony in court. The second reason is that the Supreme Court of Canada has

provided direction to the courts on the duty of an expert witness that
includes "absence of bias." This ruling, the *White Burgess* ruling, indicates that a judge should also assess the independence and impartiality
of an expert witness. These three issues are relevant to the fourth part
(d) of the Mohan test (criteria are listed below: *R. v. Mohan*, 1994),
which determines if an expert is properly qualified and the factors balance the overall costs and benefits of admitting the expert evidence
(*R. v. Livingston*, 2017; *White Burgess Langille Inman v. Abbott and
Haliburton Co.*, 2015).

Instructional Pop Out

See the *R. v. Mohan* (1994) ruling: www.canlii.org/en/ca/scc/doc/1994/
1994canlii80/1994canlii80.html
However, as stated in the ruling, "admission of expert evidence depends on the application of the following criteria:

(a) relevance;
(b) necessity in assisting the trier of fact;
(c) the absence of any exclusionary rule;
(d) a properly qualified expert." (*R. v. Mohan*, 1994)

THE SUPREME COURT'S DECISION

The *White Burgess* ruling on expert-opinion evidence in Canada came
from the Supreme Court and stated three duties of an expert witness:
impartiality, independence, and absence of bias. Judge J. Cromwell
(*White Burgess Langille Inman v. Abbott and Haliburton Co.*, 2015) provides the following description in the criteria:

> Expert witnesses have a duty to the court to give fair, objective and
> non-partisan opinion evidence. They must be aware of this duty and
> able and willing to carry it out. The expert's opinion must be impartial

in the sense that it reflects an objective assessment of the questions at hand. It must be independent in the sense that it is the product of the expert's independent judgment, uninfluenced by who has retained him or her or the outcome of the litigation. It must be unbiased in the sense that it does not unfairly favour one party's position over another. The acid test is whether the expert's opinion would not change regardless of which party retained him or her. These concepts, of course, must be applied to the realities of adversary litigation.

This ruling referenced the Kaufman and Goudge reports (see chapter 1) and how flawed forensic science opinions in these cases played a prominent role in miscarriages of justice. Justice Cromwell also references David Paciocco's (2009) assessment of the topic, *Taking a "Goudge" out of Bluster and Blarney: An "Evidence-Based Approach" to Expert Testimony.* Professor Paciocco skilfully summarizes an evidence-based approach, how that may work within the Mohan test, and the lessons learned from the Goudge report. This article supports the need for all forensic experts (not just pathologists) to confine opinion to their expertise, to use an evidence-based approach, and to understand that science is a dynamic process and that the court needs to be the gatekeeper of testimony. One of the predicates for an evidence-based approach is that the expert must not be biased. These noted documents have been well referenced in case judgments after the *White Burgess* ruling, where expert-witness evidence was ruled inadmissible in the trial because of bias. We will review three of these recent cases.

R. v. Millard

This was a high-profile murder trial in the Ontario courts, where the accused was being tried for the murder of his father, Wayne Millard. Although this is an Ontario Superior Court decision, it has not been appealed and therefore not challenged in a higher court such as the Ontario Court of Appeal. The original 2012 investigation into the death concluded that Wayne Millard had committed suicide by a single gunshot to the face. After the accused had been charged with two other

murders (*R. v. Millard*, 2018), the suicide case was reopened and sufficient evidence gathered to lay a first-degree murder charge on April 10,
2014. The trial commenced on May 31, 2018, and part of this new evidence was the expert opinion of a police officer who had a background
in shooting-scene reconstruction. The officer's opinion on the orientation, position, and location of the gun when discharged and the likelihood that Wayne Millard discharged the shot was ruled inadmissible
by the judge, Maureen Dorothy Forestell (*R. v. Millard*, 2018).

As part of the proceedings, Justice Forestell provided the following:
"that [the officer] understood the concept of bias and that he understood the duty of an expert witness which he described as an obligation
to deliver impartial, honest, full, frank and fair evidence. He testified
that he understood that his evidence was to be as unbiased as possible.
He testified that to the best of his ability he removed any bias from his
experimentation, report and testimony" (*R. v. Millard*, 2018). Due to
the *White Burgess* ruling, this type of questioning will become commonplace in expert witness examination in the Canadian court system.

The witness provided evidence that in his examination he had used
scene and post-mortem photographs and the autopsy report. He had
also experimentally reconstructed the event by test firing the gun into
Styrofoam human heads. The defence questioned the witness regarding
the evidence, and the witness indicated that he relied on the assumption
that the scene had not been contaminated. The defence produced testi-
monial evidence that a blanket with blood on it had been moved prior
to the taking of the scene photographs (*R. v. Millard*, 2018).

In this ruling, the challenge by the defence was that the evidence
was not relevant to the proceedings and that the expert was biased.
Regarding this assertion, the judge concluded that the expert "was
aware of the photograph showing a blanket that must have been moved
from the area of the head of the deceased." The expert had indicated
that there was no intermediary surface at the scene that could have altered the deposit of gunshot residue at the scene. However, this blanket
could have been an intermediary surface and the expert "failed entirely
to disclose the evidence of the blanket or his reasoning process in relation to it, in his notes, report or testimony-in-chief. The photograph

was a significant piece of evidence that could impact adversely on the conclusions he reached" (*R. v. Millard*, 2018).

Justice Forestell wrote:

> The failure of a proposed expert to disclose information that would undermine his opinion goes beyond confirmation bias. A similar situation was considered in the Report of The Commission on Proceedings Involving Guy Paul Morin (the Kaufman Commission). Commissioner Kaufman commenting on a Crown expert's failure to disclose that a search for particular fibres had been conducted, said that the expert witness's "failure to disclose demonstrates a misapprehension of his role as an independent, neutral scientist. A scientist is not entitled to discount a potential defence position (or indeed a Crown position) and then fail to disclose evidence which might bear upon that position." (*R. v. Millard*, 2018)

The expert was not allowed to testify because the judge ruled that he "was unable or unwilling to comply with the duty of an expert to provide independent, impartial and unbiased evidence with respect to the re-creation, observation and interpretation of **GSR [gunshot residue]** deposition at the scene of Wayne Millard's death and the position, location and orientation of the firearm at the time that it was discharged and killed Wayne Millard. The Crown has failed to rebut this concern on a balance of probabilities" (*R. v. Millard*, 2018).

The witness's opinion was ruled inadmissible based on confirmation bias. We recommend that you read the full court ruling (see Instructional Pop Out) as the judge addresses other important issues that provide support for the logic within this book. Beyond the issue of bias, Judge Forestell pointed out her concerns that two five-day courses on shooting reconstruction may be inadequate for providing an opinion on the interpretation of GSR deposits. She also indicated that the re-creation of the scene was not a proper scientific experiment, citing the lack of replication, quantitative data, and hypotheses development. The witness also failed to falsify hypotheses and control variables, and rejected evidence that did not support his opinion. There was also concern about whether the methodology could be attributed to inadequate training or failure to apply the training; however, the inadequacy of training was not resolved in the ruling.

R. v. France

We reviewed this court case within chapter 5, as it linked to the requirement of conducting a complete literature review as an expert witness before the courts. This court ruling also provides an example of expert witness bias and the offering of an opinion outside the expert's area of expertise. In this case, the pathologist provided an opinion on abdominal trauma that was outside of his expertise. He failed to consult all the research literature on assaults and falls causing abdominal trauma in children but provided categoric evidence that the injury was from an assault and not a fall. In this approach he was predisposed to seeing the case as an assault and failed to consider other explanations. This was a biased approach.

A second type of bias was displayed in this case. The defence approached the witness with research literature evidence on child falls that caused abdominal trauma and asked the pathologist to consider other explanations. According to Justice Molloy, the pathologist failed to be objective, indicating, "now grudgingly prepared to say that an accidental fall cannot be ruled out completely as the cause of the injury, he stands by his characterization of it as 'an unprecedented accident' while adding that it is 'improbable.' I find this to be an illustration of professional credibility bias" (*R. v. France*, 2017).

R. v. Livingston

The third court case provides an example of an individual developing contextual bias by being too close to the investigative team. Although this is an Ontario Superior Court decision, it has not been appealed and therefore has not been challenged in a higher court such as Ontario's Court of Appeal. In 2012, a retired police officer was hired back by his police service to complete computer forensic analysis on Project Hampden, the police service's name for the criminal investigation that led to the charges within the court proceedings. The witness was hired to examine 24 computer hard drives seized from the Ontario provincial government's cyber-security branch. His role expanded quickly, and he began to participate in team activities such as conference calls and team meetings. At one point in the investigation, the witness was noted to be recommending specific additional Criminal Code charges and was involved in the execution of search warrants.

The defence submitted that the witness should not be allowed to testify because he "has impermissibly conflated his role as an investigator with that of his role as an expert" (*R. v. Livingston*, 2017). The Crown relied on the *White Burgess* ruling, indicating that the threshold requirement for an expert witness is not onerous. The judge ruled that the expert witness did not maintain "his distance and independence from the day-to-day activities of the Project Hampden team.... He participated in numerous project meetings by either conference call or in person.... The most concerning example of partisanship occurred on February 22, 2015" (*R. v. Livingston*, 2017). The witness sent an email to the lead investigators recommending that the defendants in this case be charged with mischief to data, contrary to section 430 (1.1) of the Criminal Code. "And he went even further, providing a summary of the investigation to show that 'the facts' of the case would 'meet the test' for the charge" (*R. v. Livingston*, 2017). The judge commented that this behaviour, "made two months before he offered his final forensic report," demonstrated a lack of independence and impartiality, effectively nullifying the witness's opinion and evidence (*R. v. Livingston*, 2017).

Instructional Pop Out

View the full rulings for each of the reviewed court cases (*R. v. Millard*, 2018 ONSC 4410; *R. v. France*, 2017 ONSC 2040; *R. v. Livingston*, 2017 ONCJ 645): https://www.canlii.org/en/on/

SOURCES OF BIAS

I think there's responsibility both at the federal and provincial levels for education in a grander sense—and that is to provide recognition

financially to people who are educators, to help provide access to on-the-spot learning, so kids are not biased against science. Especially when people are younger, their curiosity needs never to be beaten down. It has to go someplace. And you can only do that if you have people who love the subject they're teaching, and who provide the student with the ability to do it in the field.
    —*Roberta Bondar (Buck, 2015)*

Dr. Itiel E. Dror is a research psychologist at University College, London, UK, who studies human cognition and can be credited as one of the first scientists to study cognitive bias in forensic science. In 2017, Dr. Dror published a paper entitled "Human Expert Performance in Forensic Decision Making: Seven Different Sources of Bias." In this article, he advises that forensic practitioners must understand the different stages/sources of bias before they can recognize bias and find ways to mitigate it. In table 8.1, we show Dr. Dror's list of different sources of bias that may influence observations and forensic conclusions. The original sources come from Francis Bacon's doctrine of idols but have been expanded for forensic science work. The table lists the dependent factor, in which the stage of bias can be influenced; for example, just being part of the human species can influence cognitive architecture and the brain,

Table 8.1. Different Sources of Bias That May Influence Forensic Observations and Conclusions

Stage of Bias	Dependency
Cognitive architecture and the brain	Human nature
Training and motivation	Human nature
Organizational factors	Environment, culture, and experience
Base rate expectations	Environment, culture, and experience
Irrelevant case information	Case-specific
Reference materials	Case-specific
Case evidence	Case-specific

Source: Zapf & Dror, 2017

or organizational factors can be influenced by the social groups with which we are connected (Zapf & Dror, 2017).

RESEARCH ON BIAS IN FORENSIC SCIENCE

Many forensic practitioners work in unpredictable environments that are rich in contextual case information, and they use subjective methodologies (Zajac et al., 2015). If humans are involved in forensic case analysis, the elimination of bias is impossible; however, it can be mitigated (Zapf & Dror, 2017). Relevant factors when discussing bias within forensic science include: human perception, memory of events or a person's knowledge; contextual information from an investigation that may not be required in forensic analysis; expertise or experience in certain areas; decision making on what should or should not be included in a forensic analysis; communication; verification or peer review of conclusions; confidence; organizational/workplace culture; and feedback from others (Edmond et al., 2017). Therefore, a forensic research culture that embraces the aid of cognition-focused scientists will improve the value and utility of forensic science (Edmond et al., 2017). The following sections summarize current research studies in forensic science for your consideration when thinking about bias. First, we will review articles that support the need for forensic practitioners to recognize bias and examine current studies that have explored bias in different forensic disciplines. Second, we will investigate the research on suggested solutions to mitigate bias in casework.

Recognizing That Bias Does Exist

The first step in recognizing bias is to acknowledge that it exists. Most of the literature summarized in this section will be from the past few years. However, there is one article that was written in 2006, at the infancy of cognitive bias research in forensic science, that we think you should be aware of. The article, "Contextual Information Renders Experts Vulnerable to Making Erroneous Identifications," written by Dror and colleagues (2006), was on fingerprint comparisons and the introduction of contextual information. The researchers took earlier fingerprint cases in which the fingerprint expert individualized a crime scene fingerprint to a suspect and had the experts re-examine the prints. However, in the second examination the researchers introduced information that the fingerprints were not a match. When the experts completed a second analysis (five years after the first analysis), it was found that the examiners came up with different conclusions that contradicted their previous individualization. In four out of the five cases the experts had changed their conclusion. This was an influential study that caused forensic examiners to think about bias in their work.

Dr. Bryan Found (2014) provided an opinion article in the *Australian Journal of Forensic Sciences* on the progress of cognitive research in forensic science. He specifically discussed the change in basic assumptions within the identification disciplines and how the examination of cognition has increased in these disciplines. Found listed the most common types of bias that require research in the sciences, including the following:

- **contextual bias**: when contextual information from a case or scene has influenced an analysis or opinion
- confirmation bias: when a person uses information that only confirms their opinion or belief
- **motivational bias**: a conscious inconsistency that is influenced by a person's situation *personal situation*
- **expectation bias**: usually relates to researchers who only present what they believe is expected

As you read further, try to recognize the type of bias exhibited or researched in the articles.

Cognitive bias in non-metric anthropological assessments was studied by Nakhaeizadeh and colleagues (2014). The researchers divided experts into three groups and provided skeletal remains for them to conduct non-metric analyses for age, sex, and ancestry. Two of the groups were given "extraneous contextual information" about the skeletal remains that included DNA results indicating gender, the origin of the skeleton, and age at death estimation. A third group was provided no information other than the skeletal remains. The researchers found that there was a significant bias effect when the extraneous contextual information was present, suggesting that research is required to develop an evidence-based approach for skeletal assessments that could help control bias.

A study conducted by Smalarz and colleagues (2016) looked at how criminal stereotypes can bias forensic evidence analysis. In this study, the researchers provided university students with two different mock police incident reports, one of a stereotypical crime and one of a non-stereotypical crime. The students were asked to judge whether the suspect's fingerprint matched the fingerprint recovered at the crime scene. The participants were given personal information about the suspect type such as race and sex. The researchers found that the students most often believed the fingerprints to match when the suspect fit the stereotype, even when the prints did not match. Therefore, knowing the suspect's information when conducting examinations has been shown to be a source of bias in forensic science.

Kukucka and colleagues (2017) studied how exposure to case contextual information can lead to confirmation bias in forensic science. The researchers surveyed 403 forensic practitioners from 21 countries. They found that these practitioners had a limited appreciation of the concept of cognitive bias. In fact, many believed that they were immune to bias and could reduce it by willpower. The practitioners also exhibited **bias blind spots**, indicating that they thought there may be bias in other disciplines and for other scientists but not for them. This research supported the idea that forensic practitioners may be unaware of bias and that procedural reform is required (Kukucka et al., 2017). We will discuss ideas on reform and how to help mitigate bias in forensic analyses in the next section of this chapter.

Contextual information can bias how individuals, whether experts in law enforcement or civilian university students, evaluate physical evidence. In 2017, Charman and colleagues (2017) conducted a study where police officers and undergraduate students were provided a fictitious criminal case and received incriminating, exonerating, and neutral evidence.

The participants were asked to provide their belief of the suspect's guilt within the case. They were then given more pieces of ambiguous evidence and had their belief in the suspect's guilt re-evaluated. It was found that the initial belief in guilt significantly biased the evaluation of the ambiguous evidence. This indicated that there was a snowball effect on the belief of guilt with the addition of new evidence. This study helps us understand that bias is part of human nature, and as forensic science students and practitioners we need to know that it can creep into any situation. In this study it was shown that the sequence (and control) of information release is important in combatting a biased approach.

Instructional Pop Out

The following video links may be helpful for further study on this subject:

PI Now, "Applying Fundamental Attribution Error to the Investigation": www.pinow.com/articles/1402/applying-the-fundamental-attribution-error-into-the-investigation

YouTube, "Dr. Itiel Dror on Forensic Decision Making, Bias, and Fingerprint Identification": www.youtube.com/watch?v=uo_AtXdSFfE

Mitigating Bias

Numerous articles have suggested ways to mitigate bias in forensic analysis and reporting, covering disciplines including friction ridge analysis, DNA, and bloodstain pattern analysis, plus some generalizations for forensic science. In table 8.2, we have summarized these suggested remedies and explained the application as intended by the researchers.

As you reviewed the previous list of remedies, you may have noticed a pattern forming—the articles suggest the same methods of control. Many of these solutions are derived from science and methods of scientific research, such as controlling variables and peer review. Therefore, as suggested in this book, the understanding and use of the scientific method, hypothetico-deductive reasoning, and an evidence-based approach can help control bias in your forensic science work and research.

Table 8.2. Research on Solutions to Mitigate Bias in Forensic Science Casework

Research Article	Solution Type	Application
Fillers Can Help Control for Contextual Bias in Forensic Comparison Tasks (Quigley-McBride & Wells, 2018)	• Filler-control procedure	The filler-control procedure can be used in a discipline like fingerprint analysis. Instead of supplying one fingerprint to compare, the analyst would receive many samples. Therefore, the examiner cannot relate contextual knowledge to any one print/case.
Understanding and Mitigating Bias in Forensic Evaluation: Lessons from Forensic Science (Zapf & Dror, 2017)	• Scientific method/ testing • Hypotheses • Evaluator characteristics • Methods used • Training	The researchers suggest that the use of alternative hypotheses testing, knowing the evaluators' abilities, the methodologies used, and standardized training with certification of experts can help mitigate bias.
A Biased Opinion: Demonstration of Cognitive Bias on a Fingerprint Matching Task through Knowledge of DNA Test Results (Stevenage & Bennett, 2017)	• Blind analysis and verification • Sequential unmasking • Evidence pack (filler-control) • Case management	This research is related to bias in fingerprint analysis; however, the solutions could be applicable to multiple disciplines. The researchers suggest keeping contextual information blind to the examiner, controlling information and unmasking as needed, using filler control, and having managerial oversight.
Diagnosing Crime and Diagnosing Disease: Bias Reduction Strategies in the Forensic and Clinical Sciences (Lockhart & Satya-Murti, 2017)	• Error rates • Knowing sources of bias in a discipline	This study suggests going beyond blinding and masking by developing statistical data that can show error rates and specific biases.

Research Article	Solution Type	Application
Strengthening Forensic DNA Decision Making through a Better Understanding of the Influence of Cognitive Bias (Jeanguenat, Budowle, & Dror, 2017)	• Training and education • Quality control • Review process • Analysis and interpretation process • Controlling information	The listed solution types have been suggested for DNA analysis but could be used in any laboratory environment.
Implementing Context Information Management in Forensic Casework: Minimizing Contextual Bias in Firearms Examination (Mattijssen et al., 2016)	• Context information management (CIM)	CIM is used to control the information flow to the forensic examiner. A case manager would decrease task-irrelevant case information and increase task-relevant information.
Contextual Bias: What Bloodstain Pattern Analysts Need to Know (Zajac et al., 2015)	• Awareness • Training • Objective methods • Information control • Multiple hypothesis testing • Technical and peer review • Research	This list of solutions is suggested for bloodstain pattern analysis; however, these strategies are common among the other articles that have been reviewed.
Practical Solutions to Cognitive and Human Factor Challenges in Forensic Science (Dror, 2013)	• Blind verification • Dummy cases • Randomized lists, e.g., Automated Fingerprint Identification System (AFIS) • Training • Remove irrelevant information • Triage approach • Context management • Domain-specific cognitive profiles for recruitment	Blind verification and dummy case submission can help with controlling base rate irregularities. The other solutions have been suggested and discussed above.

Sources: In table

ETHICS IN FORENSIC SCIENCE

Cognitive bias is not an ethical issue; however, ethics play a complex role in forensic science. Ethics can be defined as the "moral principles that govern a person's behaviour or the conducting of an activity" (Oxford English Dictionary, 2018). This description integrates scientific concepts with the application of law. To make this even more complicated, though, in this book we introduce the application of research to forensic science. It is important to note that ethical issues can be controlled in forensic science by following codes of ethics (Dror, 2013; Houck, 2015). Therefore, in this section we will review two areas of ethics. The first pertains to the ethical considerations for forensic practitioners as provided by the Canadian Society of Forensic Science (CSFS); the second relates to conducting research. Although the different forensic and research disciplines have specific codes of ethics, we present these two leading Canadian examples for your consideration.

The CSFS provides ethical guidelines for their membership. Gold (2003) has suggested that there are 11 different things that an expert witness can do to improve their legitimacy in the Canadian court system, and one of the listed items is to be part of a professional society or association.

The CSFS's website and policy manual (Canadian Society of Forensic Science, 2018) offer the following 17 rules of professional conduct for their members:

> Members of the Canadian Society of Forensic Science,
> *with respect to their responsibilities to the CSFS, shall:*

> 1. comply with the By-laws of the Society;
> 2. report to the Board any violation of these "Rules of Professional Conduct" by another member of the Society;
> 3. accept that their membership in the Society demonstrates an active interest in forensic science; however, this membership does not by itself mean that they have the necessary qualifications to

practice in their forensic science discipline nor does it mean that they are competent in their forensic science discipline;

with respect to their responsibilities to their client, employer or to the court, shall:

4. treat all information from an agency or client with the appropriate confidentiality;

5. make all reasonable efforts to treat items of potential evidential value with the care and control necessary to ensure their integrity;

6. take reasonable steps to ensure that all items in a case receive appropriate technical analysis;

7. a. utilise methods, techniques, standards and controls, provided that they exist, that they are generally accepted and that they are current; and

   b. utilise methods and techniques with standards and controls to conduct examinations and analysis such that they could be reproduced by another qualified and competent person;

8. make full and complete disclosure as required by law of the findings to the submitting agency or client;

9. make and keep work notes on all items received, the examinations done, the results obtained and the findings and conclusions made in a timely fashion;

10. render opinions and conclusions strictly in accordance with the results and findings in the case and only to the extent justified by those results and findings;

11. make all efforts to testify in a clear, straightforward manner and refuse to extend themselves beyond their field of expertise or level of competence;

12. not exaggerate, embellish or otherwise misrepresent qualifications when testifying;

13. be impartial and independent in their analysis, reporting and testimony;

with respect to their responsibilities to the profession of forensic science, shall:

14. carry out their duties in a professional manner and strive to be worthy of the confidence of the public;

15. regard and respect their peers with the same standards that they hold for themselves;

16. a. set a reasonable fee for services if it is appropriate to do so, taking care not to set unreasonably high fees for services, not to charge fees for services not done or services that are unnecessary, while being able to reduce or waive fees;

    b. not, under any circumstances, render services on a contingency basis; and

17. strive to maintain and improve their skills and knowledge and to keep current with advances and standards in their discipline.

Finally, we would like to briefly discuss researcher ethics. Most tertiary research institutions will have a research ethics board (REB). A university REB is a group of appointed academics who review ethics applications from researchers and students when ethical considerations are required in a research project, in order to maintain a high ethical standard and ensure that research participants are protected. REB submissions and approvals deal with three major areas: the use of human subjects, the use of animals, and the use of biohazardous materials. This is a risk-management benefit for those who are part of a university or college environment; however, research conducted outside of these institutions may not be as monitored.

Instructional Pop Out

We recommend for anyone conducting research in Canada to be familiar with the Canadian Interagency Advisory Panel on Research Ethics and to complete the online Tri-Council Policy Statement (TCPS) tutorial. This course on research ethics is an introduction to the second edition of the Tri-Council Policy Statement: Ethical Conduct for Research Involving Humans (TCPS 2). It can be found at: https://tcps2core.ca/welcome

SUMMARY

You should now be aware that researcher bias exists and the different types of bias that may be associated with your science. This is important so that we can conduct credible scientific research and provide fair, objective, and non-partisan expert opinions and evidence. We have reviewed how bias can creep into court evidence by an expert straying outside of their expertise, not controlling contextual information or confirmation bias, not recognizing their own biases, and making categoric statements that may force professional credibility bias. We reviewed sources of bias and solutions, with many of the research articles suggesting the same solutions and how important the scientific method is in mitigating bias in casework.

We know bias is not related to ethics; however, professional and research ethics play a central role in forensic science. Thus, we studied the CSFS conduct code for forensic professionals along with the university REB system and the TCPS.

Frank Crispino

Personal Profile

Graduate of the French Air Force Academy (École de l'Air, Salon-de-Provence, France), bachelor of law from Paris XI University, and holder of a dental identification degree from the University of Nancy and MPhil and PhD degrees in forensic science from the École des sciences criminelles, Lausanne (Switzerland), Colonel Frank Crispino joined the academics in 2012 after 27 years in the French Gendarmerie (IRCGN).

As a European Union (EU) forensic adviser, he built from scratch counterterrorist

Continued

forensic capacities in Gaza and Ramallah from 1999 to 2002 under the umbrella of the EU Special Adviser's Office on Counterterrorism in the West Bank and the Gaza Strip, which were destroyed by the Israeli Defense Force during the Second Intifada in 2001 and 2002. During that mission, he established the infrastructure for a terrorism-dedicated forensic laboratory and its attached crime scene unit as well as designing and implementing a curriculum for Palestinian experts in document forgery, firearms identification, and explosives analysis after he became educated in biological traces preservation and physical traces identification.

After graduating in 2004 from the French War College, he spent five years commanding two criminal investigation departments (Section de recherche—SR) in the regions of Bourges (2002–2003) and Bordeaux (2007–2011). His operational career at the IRCGN and in the SRs allowed him to oversee various scientific investigations on serious crimes, such as plane crashes, mass murder, organized crimes, and terrorism.

From 2004 to 2007, he was appointed deputy head of the Antiterrorist Bureau at the general headquarters of the French Gendarmerie in Paris. During this mandate, he was a member of the G8 Lyon-Roma counterterrorist group, French representative at the EU II (defence) and III (police) pillars' meetings in Brussels (Belgium), French government representative for the 2006 legislation on antiterrorist law, an OSCE (Organization for Security and Co-operation in Europe) hate-crime expert, and involved in many bilateral initiatives in Europe and abroad. He ended his military career as representative of the general division in charge of the Pôle judiciaire de la Gendarmerie nationale (PJGN), the forensic and intelligence hub of the French Gendarmerie, merging the forensic laboratory of the Gendarmerie with its criminal intelligence centre (Service central de renseignement criminel, SCRC) to launch a new forensic academic curriculum at l'Université du Québec à Trois-Rivières (UQTR).

A fellow of the International Association for Identification since 1998, the Asia-Pacific Center for Security Studies since 2004, the Association Québécoise de criminalistique since 2012, the Canadian Society of Forensic Science since 2013, the Association international des criminologues de langue française since 2018, and former fellow of various other societies (International Association for Craniofacial Identification, Finger-print Society, the UK-based Chartered Society of Forensic Sciences, etc.), Professor Crispino is author or co-author of two books, 10 book chapters, more than 40 peer-reviewed articles, and more than 50 presentations worldwide. He is a researcher in the forensic research group at the UQTR (Laboratoire de recherche en criminalistique, for which he was the first director, see www.uqtr.ca/LRC) and at the International Centre for Comparative Criminology in Montreal (www.cicc.umontreal.ca/en).

Knight of the Légion d'Honneur (2006), recipient of the Ordre National du Mérite (2002), and holder of the French Gendarmerie Medal with bronze badge and citation at the Gendarmerie level (2002), Crispino is married, father to three adult kids, and still loves watching (after having played) rugby.

Frank's Path to Forensic Science

In 1993, answering a call for joining the Gendarmerie laboratory, he became the first officer recruited to launch the Forensic Anthropology Department at the IRCGN and took part in the creation of the disaster victims identification unit (Cellule d'identification des victimes de catastrophe—CIVC) in the present French national unit. He became head of the fingermarks and shoemarks department once he returned from his postgraduate education in Lausanne in 1997.

Frank's Role as a Forensic Scientist

As a general forensic scientist, Frank Crispino's interests today aim to address the ontological nature of trace evidence (be it physical, chemical, biological, or digital) and the sound transmission of its probative value for decision makers (be they investigators, security managers, jurists, or juries). Besides being in charge of conceptualizing the long-term forensic curriculum at the UQTR (at the BSc, MSc, and PhD levels) with various academic and practitioner partners, he teaches or develops courses on general forensic science and the history and philosophy of science, crime scene management, forensic intelligence, and interpretation within

Continued

a theoretical decision-making perspective. His present research projects are as follows:

- the understanding of forensic science by laypeople and stake-holders to better address education on and the communication of forensic results
- the interpretation of trace transfer at the activity level, leading to the creation of a database that will be open to academics, practitioners, and stakeholders
- an interdisciplinary approach to death—associating the experimental sciences, humanities, and art; to support body donation for forensic purposes, as the UQTR is settling the first Canadian human decomposition facility to support UQTR professor Shari Forbes's Canada 150 Research Chair on forensic thanatology.

The Kind of Equipment That Frank Uses

As his former work involved scientific photography, microscopy, and using various physical and chemical devices to develop traces on site or in laboratories (using organic and inorganic chemistry, chambers, etc.), on which he can still provide relevant advice, his current typical equipment includes image and data software (R, FileMaker Pro, ImageJ, Adobe Photoshop, Hugin, Genie, Analyst's Notebook, etc.) to manage crime scene data collection and analysis.

QUESTIONS TO PONDER

1. How does using the scientific method help with controlling bias?
2. What are the common types of bias that should be considered in forensic science casework?
3. What are the main suggested solutions to help mitigate bias in forensic science?

4. Should forensic scientists engage the expertise of cognitive science researchers?
5. Why is ethics such a complex issue for forensic science?

GLOSSARY

bias blind spots: to recognize biases in others while denying the existence of those same biases in themselves (Kukucka et al., 2017).

cognitive bias: an error in thinking when processing information, it can take various forms (Found, 2014).

contextual bias: occurs when contextual information from a case or scene has influenced an analysis or opinion (Quigley-McBride & Wells, 2018).

expectation bias: bias usually relating to researchers who only present what they believe is expected (Found, 2014).

gunshot residue (GSR): the traces produced from the discharge of a firearm. A GSR kit is used in the field at firearm scenes to collect samples of gunshot residue (Maitre et al., 2017).

motivational bias: a conscious inconsistency that is influenced by a person's situation (Found, 2014).

selection bias: introduced when selecting specific individuals in an investigation (Found, 2014).

FURTHER READINGS

Canter, D., Hammond, L., & Youngs, D. (2013). Cognitive Bias in Line-Up Identifications: The Impact of Administrator Knowledge. *Science and Justice, 53*(2), 83–88.

Champod, C. (2014). Research Focused Mainly on Bias Will Paralyse Forensic Science. *Science and Justice, 54*(2), 107–109.

Cole, S. A. (2013). Implementing Counter-Measures against Confirmation Bias in Forensic Science. *Journal of Applied Research in Memory and Cognition, 2*(1), 61–62.

Dror, I. E., & Hampikian, G. (2011). Subjectivity and Bias in Forensic DNA Mixture Interpretation. *Science and Justice, 51*(4), 204–208.

Dror, I. E., McCormack, B. M., & Epstein, J. (2015). Cognitive Bias and Its Impact on Expert Witnesses and the Court. *The Judges' Journal, 54*, 8.

Dror, I. E., Morgan, R. M., Rando, C., & Nakhaeizadeh, S. (2017). Letter to the Editor—The Bias Snowball and the Bias Cascade Effects: Two Distinct Biases That May Impact Forensic Decision Making. *Journal of Forensic Sciences, 62*(3), 832–833.

Jeanguenat, A. M., Budowle, B., & Dror, I. E. (2017). Strengthening Forensic DNA Decision Making through a Better Understanding of the Influence of Cognitive Bias. *Science and Justice, 57*(6), 415–420. doi:10.1016/j.scijus.2017.07.005

Kassin, S. M., Dror, I. E., & Kukucka, J. (2013). The Forensic Confirmation Bias: Problems, Perspectives, and Proposed Solutions. *Journal of Applied Research in Memory and Cognition, 2*(1), 42–52.

Kerstholt, J., Eikelboom, A., Dijkman, T., Stoel, R., Hermsen, R., & van Leuven, B. (2010). Does Suggestive Information Cause a Confirmation Bias in Bullet Comparisons? *Forensic Science International, 198*(1–3), 138–142.

Koehler, J. J. (2018). How Trial Judges Should Think about Forensic Science Evidence. *Judicature, 102*, 28–38.

Neal, T. M. (2016). Are Forensic Experts Already Biased before Adversarial Legal Parties Hire Them? *PLoS One, 11*(4), e0154434.

Oliver, W. R. (2018). Comment on Kukucka, Kassin, Zapf, and Dror (2017), "Cognitive Bias and Blindness: A Global Survey of Forensic Science Examiners." *Journal of Applied Research in Memory and Cognition, 7*(1), 161.

Paciocco, D. (2009). Taking a "Goudge" Out of Bluster and Blarney: An "Evidence-Based Approach" to Expert Testimony. *Canadian Criminal Law Review, 13*(2), 135.

Page, M., Taylor, J., & Blenkin, M. (2012). Context Effects and Observer Bias—Implications for Forensic Odontology. *Journal of Forensic Sciences, 57*(1), 108–112.

Stevenage, S. V., & Bennett, A. (2017). A Biased Opinion: Demonstration of Cognitive Bias on a Fingerprint Matching Task through Knowledge of DNA Test Results. *Forensic Science International, 276*, 93–106. doi:10.1016/j.forsciint.2017.04.009

Whitman, G., & Koppl, R. (2010). Rational Bias in Forensic Science. *Law, Probability and Risk, 9*(1), 69–90.

REFERENCES

Buck, G. (2015). Question and Astronaut: Roberta Bondar. *MacLean's,* August 24.

Canadian Society of Forensic Science. (2018). Home Page. Retrieved from https://www.csfs.ca/

Charman, S. D., Kavetski, M., & Mueller, D. H. (2017). Cognitive Bias in the Legal System: Police Officers Evaluate Ambiguous Evidence in a Belief-Consistent Manner. *Journal of Applied Research in Memory and Cognition, 6*(2), 193–202. doi:10.1016/j.jarmac.2017.02.001

Dror, I. E. (2013). Practical Solutions to Cognitive and Human Factor Challenges in Forensic Science. *Forensic Science Policy and Management: An International Journal, 4*(3–4), 105–113.

Dror, I. E. (2017). Human Expert Performance in Forensic Decision Making: Seven Different Sources of Bias. *Australian Journal of Forensic Sciences, 49*(5), 541–547. doi:10.1080/00450618.2017.1281348

Dror, I. E., Charlton, D., & Péron, A. E. (2006). Contextual Information Renders Experts Vulnerable to Making Erroneous Identifications. *Forensic Science International, 156*(1), 74–78.

Edmond, G., Towler, A., Growns, B., Ribeiro, G., Found, B., White, D., ... Martire, K. (2017). Thinking Forensics: Cognitive Science for Forensic Practitioners. *Science and Justice, 57*(2), 144–154. doi:10.1016/j.scijus.2016.11.005

Found, B. (2014). Deciphering the Human Condition: The Rise of Cognitive Forensics. *Australian Journal of Forensic Sciences, 47*(4), 386–401. doi:10.1080/00450618.2014.965204

Gold, A. D. (2003). *Expert Evidence in Criminal Law: The Scientific Approach.* Toronto: Irwin Law.

Houck, M. (2015). *Professional Issues in Forensic Science.* San Diego: Elsevier.

Jeanguenat, A. M., Budowle, B., & Dror, I. E. (2017). Strengthening Forensic DNA Decision Making through a Better Understanding of the Influence of Cognitive Bias. *Science and Justice, 57*(6), 415–420. doi:10.1016/j.scijus.2017.07.005

Kirk, P. L. (1963). The Ontogeny of Criminalistics. *Journal of Criminal Law, Criminology and Police Science, 54,* 235.

Kukucka, J., Kassin, S. M., Zapf, P. A., & Dror, I. E. (2017). Cognitive Bias and Blindness: A Global Survey of Forensic Science Examiners. *Journal of Applied Research in Memory and Cognition, 6*(4), 452–459. doi:10.1016/j .jarmac.2017.09.001

Lockhart, J. J., & Satya-Murti, S. (2017). Diagnosing Crime and Diagnosing Disease: Bias Reduction Strategies in the Forensic and Clinical Sciences. *Journal of Forensic Science, 62*(6), 1534–1541.

Maitre, M., Kirkbride, K. P., Horder, M., Roux, C., & Beavis, A. (2017). Current Perspectives in the Interpretation of Gunshot Residues in Forensic Science: A Review. *Forensic Science International, 270,* 1–11. doi: https://doi.org/10.1016/j.forsciint.2016.09.003

Mattijssen, E. J., Kerkhoff, W., Berger, C. E., Dror, I. E., & Stoel, R. D. (2016). Implementing Context Information Management in Forensic Casework: Minimizing Contextual Bias in Firearms Examination. *Science & Justice, 56*(2), 113–122.

Nakhaeizadeh, S., Dror, I. E., & Morgan, R. M. (2014). Cognitive Bias in Forensic Anthropology: Visual Assessment of Skeletal Remains is Susceptible to Confirmation Bias. *Science and Justice, 54*(3), 208–214. doi:10.1016/j.scijus.2013.11.003

Oxford English Dictionary. (2018). Ethics. Retrieved from https:// en.oxforddictionaries.com/

Paciocco, D. (2009). Taking a "Goudge" out of Bluster and Blarney: An "Evidence-Based Approach" to Expert Testimony. *Canadian Criminal Law Review, 13*(2), 135.

Quigley-McBride, A., & Wells, G. L. (2018). Fillers Can Help Control for Contextual Bias in Forensic Comparison Tasks. *Law and Human Behavior, 42*(4), 295–305. doi:10.1037/lhb0000295

R. v. France. (2017). *Her Majesty the Queen v. Joel France.* ONSC 2040, CR-17-10000034-0000.

R. v. Livingston. (2017). *Her Majesty the Queen v. David Livingston and Laura Miller.* ONCJ 645.

R. v. Millard. (2018). *Regina versus Dellen Millard.* ONSC 4410, CR-16-50000176-0000.

R. v. Mohan. (1994). *Her Majesty the Queen versus Chikmaglur Mohan.* 2 SCR 9, No. 23063.

Smalarz, L., Madon, S., Yang, Y., Guyll, M., & Buck, S. (2016). The Perfect Match: Do Criminal Stereotypes Bias Forensic Evidence Analysis? *Law and Human Behavior, 40*(4), 420–429. doi:10.1037/lhb0000190

Stevenage, S. V., & Bennett, A. (2017). A Biased Opinion: Demonstration of Cognitive Bias on a Fingerprint Matching Task through Knowledge of DNA Test Results. *Forensic Science International, 276*, 93–106. doi:10.1016/j.forsciint.2017.04.009

White Burgess Langille Inman v. Abbott and Haliburton Co. (2015). SCC 23, 35492.

Zajac, R., Osborne, N. K. P., Singley, L., & Taylor, M. C. (2015). Contextual Bias: What Bloodstain Pattern Analysts Need to Know. *Journal of Bloodstain Pattern Analysts, 31*(2), 7–16.

Zapf, P. A., & Dror, I. E. (2017). Understanding and Mitigating Bias in Forensic Evaluation: Lessons from Forensic Science. *International Journal of Forensic Mental Health, 16*(3), 227–238. doi:10.1080/14999013.2017.1317302

CHAPTER 9
The Key to Effective Communication in Forensic Science

Forensic Science Teaching Laboratory Displaying Metal Detectors

Photo credit: Mike Illes

The art of communication is the language of leadership.
—*James Humes (Paymar, 2012)*

This chapter will synthesize the information in all the other chapters, which have created a path of scientific research to support evidence-based reporting and presentation. Readers will see the development of a report-writing and presentation style that has been reinforced from the beginning of the book. This style aligns with the scientific method and the format used in academic journal articles, theses, and dissertations (Found & Edmond, 2012). This chapter will also emphasize writing and oral structure, advocating for the truth, owning your expertise, and the importance of peer review in report writing.

EVIDENCE-BASED REPORTING: THE FORENSIC REPORT

The methods that have been explored in this book provide a natural progression to writing the forensic science report. In the end, all of your scene work, laboratory benchwork, literature review, control of bias, case notes, statistics used, logic employed, and use of the scientific method is the evidence that will support your conclusions in a report. The report and subsequent court testimony are the final and most critical pieces of a forensic practitioner's work, because what is said and how the case analysis is presented directs the court's conclusion. We have read several cases (*R. v. France*, 2017; *R. v. Livingston*, 2017; and *R. v. Millard*, 2018) in the previous chapters where experts were not allowed to submit their findings or opinions due to flawed procedures. This may have altered the verdict in those cases. An effective forensic submission provides a witness with a scientifically robust, linear path of reporting an opinion in court as well as the confidence that the best scientific analysis available to date was done (Ng & Friedman, 2015).

The types of reporting used in forensic science are as diverse as the disciplines within it (Biedermann et al., 2015; DeMier & Otto, 2017; Hecker & Scoular, 2004; Howes, Kirkbride, et al., 2014; Siegel et al., 2014; Sjerps & Berger, 2012; Young, 2016). In this chapter, though, we suggest standardizing the forensic reporting system by relying on an old but well-recognized method. The publishing of scientific research began in 1665, when the Royal Society first featured peer-reviewed articles in its *Philosophical Transactions* (Royal Society, 2018). Through this process, and the work of scientific philosophers in establishing the scientific method, a system of reporting evidence-based information has become well established over the past 350-plus years.

We recommend that forensic report writing follow a method like that used for academic manuscript writing. A number of scientists have supported this approach (Biedermann et al., 2015; Melson, 2014; Siegel et al., 2014). Found and Edmond (2012) argue that the forensic comparison disciplines were established outside of academia and traditional scientific report-writing norms. These researchers suggest that these forensic disciplines should follow the well-established writing style used by academics.

General Guide to Forensic Reporting

A forensic report should:

- state the forensic question clearly
- be organized coherently
- eliminate jargon
- include only the data relevant to forensic opinion
- separate observations from inferences
- consider multiple sources of data
- use scientific tests appropriately
- consider alternate hypotheses
- support opinions with data
- clearly connect data and opinions (Karson & Nadkarni, 2013; Witt, 2010)

Forensic reports carry a significant weight and cost of error. A well-written report will advocate for the truth and not contain emotional opinions or statements. It should answer one question without opening new questions that could cause unnecessary inquiry in court. The expert should choose evidence that will stand up in court, and because the report is an expert opinion it should be written in a way that indicates ownership of one's expertise using a style that enhances credibility (Karson & Nadkarni, 2013).

The writer should avoid colloquial language and use scientifically informed speech while attempting to avoid unnecessary jargon. A report that looks sloppy and has spelling, grammatical, and/or factual errors will weaken an expert's credibility. Avoid authoritative assertions or conclusions made without supporting scientific evidence (**Ipse Dixits**). The report can also be undermined by citing computerized interpretations without fully explaining or interpreting the results. Therefore, evidence should be linked to its source when presented in a report—the more sources cited, the stronger the conclusion (Karson & Nadkarni, 2013).

Anchoring is a term used within cognitive psychology to describe how the ordering of information affects how people think. We recommend the following reporting order, with a clear writing style to avoid confusing the reader. In complex reports, you may cite the document and page spans of each reference used to help readers locate the information (Karson & Nadkarni, 2013). The use of a cite-as-you-write software can assist in this task.

Instructional Pop Out

Cite-as-you-write software can be used to help with organizing your essays, reports, theses, and so on. View the training videos, manuals, and other resources for EndNote creation:

www.endnote.com/training

Software packages such as Mendeley are open access:

www.mendeley.com/?interaction_required=true

Report Structure

1. Title Page

The title page may include a report title, agency, file number, and author's name.

2. Abstract or Executive Summary

The abstract introduces the context of the report, briefly explains the report's approach to the problem and its main conclusions. The abstract does not contain data and generally cannot be trusted as it is a brief interpretation of the research.

3. Introduction

The introduction provides background information like a literature search, the reasons that the author performed the study, and where it fits in the grand scheme of the topic, and clearly states the hypotheses and their testability. The introduction of a report should contain

a. a list of exhibits that were examined
b. a statement as to the origin of exhibits
c. chain of custody
d. examination(s) requested
e. information provided to the examiner(s)
f. qualifications and experience

Other things to consider: at the beginning of each report, the author should state the objective(s) and content of the report in an effort to overcome the reader's confirmation bias and manage their **frame of mind** (Karson & Nadkarni, 2013; Neumann et al., 2016). The reader's frame of mind is an emotional or mental disposition— thus, if an idea is clearly identified within the introduction, the reader will have a strong understanding of the report's purpose. In a framing example provided by Karson and Nadkarni (2013), "physicians are more likely to recommend surgery if the 1-month survival rate is 90% than if the 1-month mortality rate is 10%. These are statistically identical but emotionally different ways of describing the situation." In this example, if a doctor was told that the surgery had a 1-month mortality rate of 10%, they may elect not to do a procedure that actually has a high survival rate.

A similar example of juror perception was presented by Lincoln and colleagues (2014) where mock jurors (200 university students) were asked to interpret the presentation of DNA evidence. The evidence was framed in five scenarios, and results indicated that participants were more likely to convict when the evidence was presented as a probability focusing on the defendant rather than a frequency that focused on a reference group. This is a good example that displays how the presentation of forensic evidence can change the outcome of a trial and the responsibility of the expert witness to report the true meaning.

4. Method and Materials
This section should contain a detailed description of the methods used. It will allow the reader to replicate the study and assess if the methods are appropriate for testing the hypotheses. Issues to consider here include whether the analyses are appropriate for the data and hypotheses and if the data were collected in a way that was unbiased.

5. Results
The results should not contain any interpretation (e.g., whether or not the hypotheses are rejected). This section contains the empirical data that was used to test the hypotheses.

6. Conclusion including Limitations
This is the interpretation of the data and an opinion based on scientific evidence. The conclusion will provide a final statement of opinion on the evidence that may be tendered to the courts, if effective. This book has stressed an evidence-based approach, from crime scene to report, and this theme should continue in any conclusion and analysis. If the foundational stages of the investigation have been completed using evidence-based thinking, then the conclusion should be apparent and supported by the evidence. The wording of the conclusion will be critical. Therefore, significant time and thought should be given to writing these statements.

This is particularly important in the Canadian criminal court system, where specific offences (e.g., murder) can be tried by a jury. The jury system has been set up for an accused to have the option of being tried by a set of peers (12 jurors) who are citizens of the province. Many times, jurors are unaccustomed to and unaware of the criminal justice system. Reporting in a clear, concise manner is very important in conveying the evidence.

The conclusion of a scientific report usually answers the following questions:

- What was the report about/what did you do?
- What were your objectives—hypotheses?
- What did you find—results, numbers, and observations?
- What is the concluding statement, based on the above list?

A good concluding statement should be scientifically robust, unbiased, and transparent. The conclusion should be supported by your prior work (methods, observations, analysis, results) and the published literature on the topic (see Lobban & Schefter, 1992). To assist with your writing, Lobban and Schefter (1992) have provided the following questions to consider:

- What is your interpretation of the results, in light of your analysis (hypotheses) and published literature?
- What are the significant sources of error?
- How reliable are the results?
- Do the results support your analysis (hypotheses)?
- Are there additional experiments/analyses required?

It is also important for the forensic expert witness to assist the court and laypeople of the jury in understanding the expert's findings. This communication strategy has not been well researched; however, studies conducted by Howes and colleagues (Howes et al., 2013; Howes, Julian, et al., 2014; Howes, Kirkbride, et al., 2014) have suggested that there are aspects of conclusions that pose difficulties for non-scientific persons. We recommend that conclusions be written for general readability while maintaining scientific integrity. As Howes and colleagues (2013) further suggest:

> Readability refers to the ease with which something can be read and understood due to the style of writing and is a prerequisite to comprehensibility. Strong predictors of reading difficulty include sentence length and word frequency.

These reports recommend that the writer use active rather than passive voice, which will show more personal responsibility to the reader (Karson & Nadkarni, 2013). Passive voice leads to ambiguity and confusion and should be avoided within the report. To help you with sentence structure and readability, Microsoft Word, for example, has a built-in feature that automatically evaluates for passive sentence structure while advising on the **Flesch Reading Ease and Flesch-Kincaid Grade Level**—see figure 9.1.

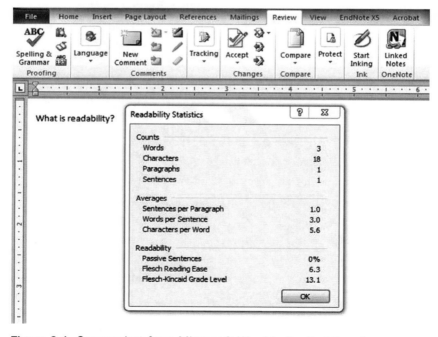

Figure 9.1. Screenshot from Microsoft Word Indicating Passive Sentence, Flesch Reading Ease, and Grade Level Scores

Source: Microsoft Word

7. References

Include all references used in the report. These references will provide support for evidence-based conclusions.

CASE EXAMPLE FROM COURT TESTIMONY

R. v. Guthrie (2018) is an Ontario Superior Court ruling providing an example of how good forensic science reporting and expert knowledge can lead to scientifically robust testimony in court. The voir dire in this ruling determined whether the expert witness could give evidence on fingerprint analysis and whether the methods used were scientifically valid. The fingerprint expert, Sgt. Scarlett, worked for the RCMP and was a certified fingerprint examiner, conducting fingerprint comparisons since 2008. The expert described the method used as

> the ACE-V method to analyze and compare fingerprints. The process consists of the following:
>
> > A—analysis of the unknown friction ridge
> >
> > C—comparison of the unknown friction ridge print to the known control inked friction ridge
> >
> > E—evaluation as to the sufficiency of detail present to establish individualization
> >
> > V—verification occurs when another qualified examiner verifies the process used, inspects the observations made and validates the conclusions reached (*R. v. Guthrie*, 2018)

The defence argued that fingerprint analysis is not a science and that "there is no scientific evidence that fingerprints are unique to one human being. The defence relies heavily on the Report to the President in arguing that the ACE-V method is not a proper method to conduct these examinations. Since the verification process is not a blind test it is susceptible to confirmation bias. Further, since there are no fixed standards for the ACE-V method the opinion is purely subjective. In summary, the defence submits that fingerprint analysis and comparison is in fact 'junk science'" (*R. v. Guthrie*, 2018).

The crown attorney indicated that "the Mohan threshold for admissibility of expert opinion has been met. The forensic identification of fingerprints is an area of specialized knowledge that has long been accepted by the courts" and that the expert was qualified to provide an opinion due to his training, certification, and experience (*R. v. Guthrie*, 2018). The judge concluded that the expert was qualified in fingerprint analysis. The judge also indicated "that the threshold requirements of admissibility set out in *R. v. Mohan* [1994] 2 SCR 9, namely, relevance, necessity, absence of an exclusionary rule and a properly qualified expert, have been met. I am also satisfied that in my duties as a gatekeeper the expert evidence is sufficiently beneficial to the trial process to warrant its admission." When the judge considered the defence argument "that the Report to the President establishes that the ACE-V method is so flawed it cannot be relied on, it is important to note that this Report is not evidence. In *R. v. Bornyk*, 2015 BCCA 28, the BC Court of Appeal commented on the fact that a judge may only rely on evidence" (*R. v. Guthrie*, 2018).

Instructional Pop Out

We suggest reading the full Ontario Superior Court of Justice judgment: www.canlii.org/en/on/onsc/doc/2018/2018onsc795/2018onsc795 .html?resultIndex=1

JOURNAL ARTICLES

We extensively reviewed the journal article and peer-review process in chapter 4, How to Critically Review a Published Journal Article. Our suggested report structure follows the format and process for a scientific journal manuscript and its review. Therefore, in this chapter, we suggest standardizing the forensic reporting system by relying on an old but well-recognized reporting method. We also recommend this style because it provides the opportunity for a forensic practitioner to use the scientific method on a continual basis. If a practitioner is providing analytical reports, they must apply formal reasoning skills in all phases of the process, from crime scene to court. We also contend that a peer-review process like that used in academic writing should likewise be integral to the forensic report process. The same processes and skills used for writing essays, manuscripts, and laboratory reports within post-secondary educational environments are naturally transferable to writing forensic reports.

THESIS OR DISSERTATION

The Oxford English Dictionary defines a thesis as "a long essay or dissertation involving personal research, written by a candidate for a university degree, 'a doctoral thesis'" and a dissertation as "a long essay on a particular subject, especially one written for a university degree or diploma" (2018). This suggests that the names are interchangeable; however, in the university environment, a thesis is usually completed at the end of a fourth-year research project or at the end of a master's degree. The thesis may not be original research but should be a "logical and intelligent approach to the elected problem and the language of the written submission should be clear and precise; the work should demonstrate the development and support of a sustained argument or originality in the application of knowledge" (Office of the Registrar, 2018).

A dissertation is usually associated with a doctorate in philosophy (PhD) and should show that the student has advanced scholarship or produced novel research. A dissertation should satisfy peer review and merit publication (Office of the Registrar, 2018). Both the thesis and dissertation can be written in a traditional or manuscript style.

Instructional Pop Out

View traditional and manuscript style forensic research theses: http://digitalcollections.trentu.ca/islandora/search/forensic%20science?type=dismax

PRESENTATIONS: SIMPLE APPROACHES

Communication skills are essential for a good forensic expert. If an expert cannot articulate their science/discipline in a clear and understandable way in court, their work leading to this event becomes of significantly less value (Wechsler et al., 2015). Providing presentations is a common event in forensic science (Ng & Friedman, 2015). A forensic practitioner can be called upon to present on their trade to community groups, schools, their supervisors, and in court.

In the Canadian court system, the advent of technology has placed a requirement on the practitioner to be more demonstrative when providing expert-witness evidence (Tung et al., 2015). It has become a norm in the courts for judges, crown attorneys, and defence lawyers to use charts, posters, and slideshow presentations to display evidence. Slideshow-type presentations can aid in conveying complex scene or analytical evidence to a lay jury. Therefore, it is important to follow a few simple rules when developing presentations. Whether you are preparing a poster presentation for a conference, a workshop, or a slideshow for a large audience, the following recommendations apply:

- use a large font
- use a readable font
- use readable contrasting colours and enhancing background colours
- don't clutter the presentation space
- keep it simple
- limit animation in presentations
- use high-quality graphics, but remember that you do not require large file sizes in a slideshow-type presentation
- have a theme, keep it consistent with a continual story
- limit bullet points
- show, don't tell (Reynolds, 2018)

SUMMARY

Our hope is that each chapter of this book has built a pathway to understanding how to apply the scientific method in forensic science and the necessity of evidence-based collection, analysis, and reporting. This chapter focused on how to organize and process the material discussed in the book into a scientific report structure and how to do presentations. We have supplied evidence for the need to standardize report writing in forensic science and recommended using a well-established scientific process. You now know the importance of framing the reader's mind and how anchoring can change the reader's perspective on the message conveyed in a report. These skills can also be used in academia, as discussed in the section on journal articles, theses, and dissertations.

This chapter's court document provides a real-world example of how good reporting and expert knowledge can lead to scientifically robust testimony in court. The introduction of the voir dire placed weight on the need for proper court preparation, as the expert witness was being challenged on his credentials and whether the methods he used were scientifically valid. This is something that is becoming commonplace in the Canadian court system.

Gail S. Anderson

Personal Profile

I am a professor in the School of Criminology, an associate director of the School, and co-director of the Centre for Forensic Research at Simon Fraser University (SFU). I hold a Burnaby Mountain Endowed Professorship at SFU. I am a forensic entomology consultant to the police and Coroners Service as well as for the SPCA and wildlife enforcement. I have been analyzing forensic entomology cases since 1988 and have testified as an expert witness in court many times. My work has been featured in numerous television programs. I have been honoured with Canada's Top 40 Under 40 Award, a YWCA Women of Distinction Award for science and

Continued

technology, and the SFU Alumni Association Outstanding Alumni Award. I was listed in *TIME* magazine as one of this century's top five Global Innovators in the world, in the field of criminal justice, in 2001 (the only Canadian listed), and as one of the Leaders for the 21st Century by *TIME* in 1999. I received the Derome Award in 2001—the most prestigious award the CSFS bestows, for "outstanding contributions to the field of forensic science." I am a past president of the CSFS, the North American Forensic Entomology Association, and BC's Entomological Society as well as a past chair of the American Board of Forensic Entomology and am presently first vice president of the Entomological Society of Canada. I was listed as one of the 100 most influential women in British Columbia by the *Vancouver Sun* in 2010, received a Dean's Medal for Academic Excellence in 2014, and in 2015 was listed as one of the six most influential scientists in BC by the *Vancouver Sun*. In 2017, I was awarded the American Academy of Forensic Sciences' pathology biology section Award for Achievement in the Life Sciences.

Q. How Did You Get Into Forensic Science?

I am an entomologist and always wanted to do something useful with my science. Dr. John Borden was one of my senior supervisors for my PhD. He was, and still is, a great networker and had encouraged our insectary supervisor to take forensic entomology cases, but he had not enjoyed it and so had quit. By this time, the police were used to using a forensic entomologist in homicide cases and they did not want to lose the service. So, John looked around for someone else, and there was me, a young and fairly new PhD student. As I was passing his office, John asked me if I would like to be a forensic entomologist. I said, "Sure! What is that?!" He explained it to me and I said, "Okay, I will give it a year." That was back in 1988. And the rest is history.

Q. What Is Your Role as a Forensic Scientist?

I study the insects associated with a dead body, human or animal, and calculate how long insects have been colonizing the body and so infer the minimum elapsed time since death. For example, if the body is supporting seven-day-old insects, then the person has been dead for at least seven days. Insects on a body can also be used to determine whether a body has been moved or disturbed after death, the presence and position of wounds, whether the person used drugs or was poisoned, and whether the person or animal had been abused or neglected.

Insects colonize a body very rapidly after death, assuming conditions such as season, temperature, time of day, geography, and accessibility are appropriate. The first insects to colonize are usually the Calliphoridae or blow flies. These flies lay their eggs on the body, usually at a wound if present, or at natural orifices, both of which provide liquid protein. These eggs eclose into larvae, which feed on the body and develop through their life stages at a predictable rate, based primarily on temperature and species. By estimating the age of the oldest insects, I can estimate the minimum elapsed time since death.

Insects also colonize remains in a predictable sequence, with blow flies usually first, then a sequence of insects continue to colonize over time until there are no nutrients left in the body. This sequence, while predictable, does vary with geography, season, and habitat. If databases have been developed for a specific area and season, they can be used to estimate the elapsed time since death based on the presence and past remains of insects that have colonized the body.

As many insects are habitat-specific, they can be used to suggest whether a body has been moved, if insects found on the remains do not fit the scenario. Also, if a body is concealed and then disturbed, there may be several colonization times, which can be analyzed to estimate times of disturbance. Decomposition often obscures wounds, but as blow flies are attracted to a wound first, if older insects are found in a certain area, this may suggest there was a wound at this site. Larvae also bioaccumulate, so they can be used as toxicological specimens when more usual specimens such as liver or blood are too decomposed to use. Some blow fly species will also colonize necrotic tissue in live people, resulting in cutaneous myiasis. Aging the maggots in a wound can indicate the length of time that the wound has been present and so indicate time of abuse

Continued

or length of neglect; this is often used in child, senior, or animal abuse or cruelty cases.

Q. What Kind of Equipment Do You Use?

My equipment is very simple. I use basic insect collecting equipment such as vials, alcohol, forceps, small paint brushes at the crime scene and morgue to collect and preserve insects, and microscopes and dichotomous keys to identify the insects. I use normal entomological techniques to raise a sample of insects to adulthood. I use dataloggers at the scene to compare with weather station data. On rare occasions, I may need DNA analysis to identify damaged specimens. I do, however, need a very secure laboratory, as the insects I handle are evidence in homicides and so must be carefully maintained for continuity. There are, therefore, three levels of security to enter my laboratory and a further level to enter my high-security sections of the lab.

QUESTIONS TO PONDER

1. What is the recommended way of standardizing forensic reports?
2. What does a good forensic report provide a witness?
3. Is there a difference between a thesis and a dissertation?
4. Why is a conclusion so important?
5. Is critical thinking required when authoring a forensic report?
6. What does "framing the reader's mind" mean? disposition
7. Explain the concept of anchoring as it relates to report writing. order of SP.

GLOSSARY

anchoring: a term used in cognitive psychology describing how the order of information can affect how people think (Karson & Nadkarni, 2013).

Flesch Reading Ease and Flesch-Kincaid Grade Level: readability tests that tell the writer the approximate grade level that is required for the reader. There are different grading systems (Flesch, 1948; Williamson & Martin, 2010).

frame of mind: an emotional or mental disposition of a reader (Karson & Nadkarni, 2013; Neumann et al., 2016).

Ipse Dixits: statements without proof (Oxford English Dictionary, 2018).

FURTHER READINGS

Biedermann, A., Vuille, J., Taroni, F., & Champod, C. (2015). The Need for Reporting Standards in Forensic Science. *Law, Probability and Risk*, *14*(2), 169–173. doi:10.1093/lpr/mgv003

Carter, K. (2015). Evidence-Based Medicine. *Townsend Letter*, 379–380.

Cooper, S. L., & Scanlon, P. (2017). Juror Assessment of Certainty about Firearms Identification Evidence. *University of Arkansas Little Rock Law Review*, *40*, 95.

Greenhalgh, T. (2014). *How to Read a Paper: The Basics of Evidence-Based Medicine*. Hoboken: John Wiley & Sons.

Makar, S., Malanowski, A., & Rapp, K. (2016). Visualizing Forensic Publication Impacts and Collaborations: Presenting at a Scientific Venue Leads to Increased Collaborations between Researchers and Information Professionals. *Science and Technology Libraries*, *35*(2), 109–118. doi:10.1080/0194262X.2016.1184116

Melson, K. E. (2014). Review of: Principles of Forensic Report Writing. *Journal of Forensic Sciences*, *59*(2), 576–577. doi:10.1111/1556-4029.12395

Ng, L. L., & Friedman, S. H. (2015). Testifying in a Mock Court: The Experiences of Forensic Advanced Trainees. *Australasian Psychiatry*, *23*(2), 177–180. doi:10.1177/1039856214568222

Otto, R. K., DeMier, R., Boccaccini, M. T., & Boccaccini, M. (2014). *Forensic Reports and Testimony: A Guide to Effective Communication for Psychologists and Psychiatrists*. Hoboken: John Wiley & Sons.

Young, G. (2016). Psychiatric/Psychological Forensic Report Writing. *International Journal of Law and Psychiatry*, *49*, 214–220. doi:https://doi.org/10.1016/j.ijlp.2016.10.008

REFERENCES

Biedermann, A., Vuille, J., Taroni, F., & Champod, C. (2015). The Need for Reporting Standards in Forensic Science. *Law, Probability and Risk*, *14*(2), 169–173.

DeMier, R. L., & Otto, R. K. (2017). Forensic Report Writing. In R. Roesch & A. N. Cook (Eds.), *Handbook of Forensic Mental Health Services* (pp. 216–235). London: Taylor & Francis.

Flesch, R. (1948). A New Readability Yardstick. *Journal of Applied Psychology*, *32*(3), 221.

Found, B., & Edmond, G. (2012). Reporting on the Comparison and Interpretation of Pattern Evidence: Recommendations for Forensic Specialists. *Australian Journal of Forensic Sciences*, *44*(2), 193–196.

Hecker, J. E., & Scoular, R. J. (2004). Forensic Report Writing. In W. T. O'Donohue and E. R. Levensky (Eds.), *Handbook of Forensic Psychology* (pp. 63–81). San Diego: Academic Press.

Howes, L. M., Julian, R., Kelty, S. F., Kemp, N., & Kirkbride, K. P. (2014). The Readability of Expert Reports for Non-Scientist Report-Users: Reports of DNA Analysis. *Forensic Science International*, *237*, 7–18.

Howes, L. M., Kirkbride, K. P., Kelty, S. F., Julian, R., & Kemp, N. (2013). Forensic Scientists' Conclusions: How Readable Are They for Non-Scientist Report-Users? *Forensic Science International*, *231*(1–3), 102–112.

Howes, L. M., Kirkbride, K. P., Kelty, S. F., Julian, R., & Kemp, N. (2014). The Readability of Expert Reports for Non-Scientist Report-Users: Reports of Forensic Comparison of Glass. *Forensic Science International*, *236*, 54–66.

Karson, M., & Nadkarni, L. (2013). *Principles of Forensic Report Writing*. Washington: American Psychological Association.

Lincoln, R., Southerland, A., & Jarrett-Luck, M. (2014). The Persuasive Powers of DNA: An Experimental Study in Perceptions of Expert Evidence. *GSTF Journal of Law and Social Sciences (JLSS)*, *3*(2), 20–27.

Lobban, C. S., & Schefter, M. L. (1992). *Successful Lab Reports: A Manual for Science Students*. Cambridge: Cambridge University Press.

Melson, K. E. (2014). Review of: Principles of Forensic Report Writing. *Journal of Forensic Sciences, 59*(2), 576–577.

Neumann, C., Kaye, D., Jackson, G., Reyna V., & Ranadive, A. (2016). Presenting Quantitative and Qualitative Information on Forensic Science Evidence in the Courtroom. *Chance, 29*(1), 37–43.

Ng, L. L., & Friedman, S. H. (2015). Testifying in a Mock Court: The Experiences of Forensic Advanced Trainees. *Australasian Psychiatry, 23*(2), 177–180.

Office of the Registrar. (2018). Graduate Academic Calendar. Peterborough: Trent University.

Oxford English Dictionary. (2018). Dissertation / Ipse Dixits / Thesis. Retrieved from https://en.oxforddictionaries.com/

Paymar, J. (2012). Speak Like a Leader. *Forbes*, February 2. Retrieved from https://www.forbes.com/sites/jimpaymar/2012/02/02/speak-like-a-leader/#282ff2007144

Reynolds, G. (2018). Top Ten Slide Tips. *Garr Reynolds*. Retrieved from http://www.garrreynolds.com/preso-tips/design/

Royal Society. (2018). The Royal Society—History of the Royal Society. Retrieved from https://royalsociety.org/about-us/history/

R. v. France. (2017). *Her Majesty the Queen v. Joel France.* ONSC 2040, CR-17-10000034-0000.

R. v. Guthrie. (2018). *Her Majesty the Queen versus Greg Guthrie and Delon Griffith.* ONSC 795, CRIM J(F) 1876/16.

R. v. Livingston. (2017). *Her Majesty the Queen v. David Livingston and Laura Miller.* ONCJ 645.

R. v. Millard. (2018). *Regina versus Dellen Millard.* ONSC 4410, CR-16-50000176-0000.

Siegel, J. A., King, M., & Reed, W. (2014). The Laboratory Report Project. *Forensic Science Policy and Management: An International Journal, 4*(3–4), 68–78.

Sjerps, M. J., & Berger, C. E. H. (2012). How Clear Is Transparent? Reporting Expert Reasoning in Legal Cases. *Law, Probability and Risk, 11*(4), 317–329.

Tung, N. D., Barr, J., Sheppard, D. J., Elliot, D. A., Tottey, L. S., & Walsh, K. A. (2015). Spherical Photography and Virtual Tours for Presenting

Crime Scenes and Forensic Evidence in New Zealand Courtrooms. *Journal of Forensic Sciences*, *60*(3), 753–758.

Wechsler, H. J., Kehn, A., Wise, R. A., & Cramer, R. J. (2015). Attorney Beliefs Concerning Scientific Evidence and Expert Witness Credibility. *International Journal of Law and Psychiatry*, *41*, 58–66.

Williamson, J. M. L., & Martin, A. (2010). Analysis of Patient Information Leaflets Provided by a District General Hospital by the Flesch and Flesch–Kincaid Method. *International Journal of Clinical Practice*, *64*(13), 1824–1831.

Witt, P. H. (2010). Forensic Report Checklist. *Journal of Forensic Psychology*, *2*, 233–240.

Young, G. (2016). Psychiatric/Psychological Forensic Report Writing. *International Journal of Law and Psychiatry*, *49*, 214–220.

APPENDIX
Exercise Answers

ANSWERS TO EXERCISE 3.2

Question 1: Define the problem(s) in this case.

Answer 1: The silos are creating an inefficiency and risk within the organization.

Question 2: How would you solve the problem(s)?

Answer 2: The specialty team leaders should have cross-pollinating team meetings, even though the teams may be in different physical locations.

There should be a broadening of team members' focus, as they are very much concentrated on only their area of expertise—they don't see the big picture.

The members should receive team dynamics training.

Question 3: What are the possible solutions that could help with the problem(s)?

Answer 3: Provide opportunity for cross pollination—meeting, cross-command experience.

Work with the team leaders to come up with a plan of action.
The leader should become more involved and set an example.

Change of the physical location; if this is not viable, create a work-around by:

- setting up visiting days for the technical members to see and appreciate what the other teams are doing
- providing some social time
- providing team training courses and practicums involving members from each unit

ANSWERS TO EXERCISE 5.2

1. Campbell, A. (2011). *The Fingerprint Inquiry Report*. Edinburgh: APS Group.
   A: secondary source; not peer reviewed
2. Eldridge, H. (2011). Meeting the Fingerprint Admissibility Challenge in a Post-NAS Environment. *Journal of Forensic Identification*, *61*(5), 430–446.
   A: primary source; peer reviewed
3. Langenburg, G. et al. (2012). Informing the Judgments of Fingerprint Analysts Using Quality Metric and Statistical Assessment Tools. *Forensic Science International*, *219*(1–3), 183–198.
   A: primary source; peer reviewed, this is an example of a double-blind process
4. Mnookin, J. L. (2010). The Courts, the NAS, and the Future. *Brooklyn Law Review*, *75*(4), 1–67.
   A: secondary source; not peer reviewed
5. Egli, N., Moret, S., Bécue, A., & Champod, C. (2013). 17th Interpol International Forensic Science Managers Symposium: Review Papers; Fingermarks and Other Impressions. Lyon: Interpol.
   A: secondary source
6. Laber, T. L. et al. (2014). *Reliability Assessment of Current Methods in Bloodstain Pattern Analysis*. Washington: National Institute of Justice.
   A: secondary/primary source—it is peer reviewed but not in a journal. These reports are peer reviewed
7. Brunetto, Y. et al. (2012). Emotional Intelligence, Job Satisfaction, Well-Being and Engagement: Explaining Organisational Commitment and Turnover Intentions in Policing. *Human Resource Management Journal*, *22*(4), 428–441.
   A: primary source; peer reviewed
8. McDonald, S. P. (2013). Promoting Critical Thought. *Military Review*, *93*(3), 79–82.
   A: secondary source—commentary

9. McDermott, P. J., & Hulse-Killacky, D. (2012). Strengthening Police Organizations through Interpersonal Leadership. *FBI Law Enforcement Bulletin, 81*(10), 19–23.
A: secondary source
10. Mnookin, J. L. et al. (2011). The Need for a Research Culture in the Forensic Sciences. *UCLA Law Review, 58*(3), 725–779.
A: secondary source

ANSWERS TO EXERCISE 5.3

1. Krishan, K. et al. (2016). A Review of Sex Estimation Techniques During Examination of Skeletal Remains in Forensic Anthropology Casework. *Forensic Science International, 261,* 165.e1–165.e8.
A: critical review
2. Maitre, M. et al. (2017). Current Perspectives in the Interpretation of Gunshot Residues in Forensic Science: A Review. *Forensic Science International, 270,* 1–11.
A: systematic search and review
3. Lynøe, N. et al. (2017). Insufficient Evidence for "Shaken Baby Syndrome"—A Systematic Review. *Acta Paediatrica, 106*(7), 1021–1027.
A: systematic review
4. Langer, S., & Illes. M. (2015). Confounding Factors of Fly Artefacts in Bloodstain Pattern Analysis. *Canadian Society of Forensic Science Journal, 48*(4), 215–224.
A: systematic search and review
5. Abrami, P. C. et al. (2015). Strategies for Teaching Students to Think Critically: A Meta-Analysis. *Review of Educational Research, 85*(2), 275–314.
A: meta-analysis + integrated
6. Pollitt, M. M. (2007). An Ad Hoc Review of Digital Forensic Models. Systematic Approaches to Digital Forensic Engineering (SADFE), Second International Workshop.
A: rapid review

7. Swann, L. M., Forbes, S. L., & Lewis, S. W. (2010). Analytical Separations of Mammalian Decomposition Products for Forensic Science: A Review. *Analytica Chimica Acta*, *682*(1–2), 9–22.
   A: state-of-the-art review
8. Lupariello, F. et al. (2018). Staged Crime Scene Determination by Handling Physical and Digital Evidence: Reports and Review of the Literature. *Forensic Science International*, *288*, 236–241.
   A: qualitative systematic review/qualitative evidence synthesis

INDEX